GUN VIOLENCE and GUN CONTROL

Critical Engagements

Edited by
Annette Bailey, Thomas S. Harrison,
Rebecca Jaremko Bromwich

DEMETER

Gun Violence and Gun Control Critical Engagements

Edited by Annette Bailey, Thomas S. Harrison, Rebecca Jaremko Bromwich

Demeter Press
PO Box 197
Coe Hill, Ontario
Canada
K0L 1P0
Tel: 289-383-0134
Email: info@demeterpress.org
Website: www.demeterpress.org

Demeter Press logo based on the sculpture "Demeter" by Maria-Luise Bodirsky www.keramik-atelier.bodirsky.de

Printed and Bound in Canada

Cover design and typesetting: Michelle Pirovich
Proof reading: Jena Woodhouse

Library and Archives Canada Cataloguing in Publication
Title: Gun violence and gun control : critical engagements / edited by Annette Bailey, Thomas S. Harrison, and Rebecca Jaremko Bromwich.
Names: Bailey, Annette, editor. | Harrison, Thomas, editor. | Bromwich, Rebecca, editor.
Description: Includes bibliographical references and index.
Identifiers: Canadiana 20210364890 | ISBN 9781772583779 (softcover)
Subjects: LCSH: Gun control. | LCSH: Firearms and crime. | LCSH: Violent crimes.
Classification: LCC HV7435 .G86 2022 | DDC 364.2—dc23

Acknowledgments

The publication of this book was made possible by a publication grant from the Faculty of Community Services, Ryerson University. Special thanks to Ashley Lyew and Germayne Flores for their support with formatting the manuscript.

Contents

And the Phone Rang Under the Yellow Blanket

Renee Bailey and Annette Bailey

I couldn't believe it really happened. Was I not paying attention? Is this fate? His first look of the world was of brightness and life. Now I wonder was his last look of the world empty, lonely, and dark?

As I entered my apartment, I wanted to fall robustly on my couch and leave the anxieties, problems, and disappointments of the day behind. But I couldn't. My elderly mother was waiting for a cooked meal. Slowly pacing myself, barely able to lift my feet, I walked hesitantly to the kitchen, all the time murmuring under the exhaustion. Finally, the meal was ready and packed for my son Isiah to deliver to his grandmother.

With Isiah on his way, I thought the hardest part of the day had passed. I placed my naked feet on the coffee table, and with my meal in one hand, I search the television stations for something peaceful and enticing. About to skip over CTV news, I saw the report of a fatal shooting. I kissed my teeth and slapped my hand across the wind. "Crazy shootings," I thought. But my eyes defied my request to divert to another channel. The familiarity of the area where the shooting occurred held my attention. It was close to the building where my elderly mother lived, where my son was delivering the meal.

A cold shiver of fear raced across my abdomen. "It is certainly not Isiah. He is a good student, a respectful son, and a future neurosurgeon. He told me he would be the next Ben Carson," I said, attempting to reassure myself. But, this time, it did not make me smile. I called Isiah's cell phone many times, no answer. No worries, I thought. He usually turns off his phone when he meets with grandma. This shooting was in my neighbourhood, so I felt obligated to find out who was shot. I slipped on my shoes and hurried out the door.

I curiously came off the bus. Just outside of the building where my mother lived, I saw a crowd huddled over a body covered with a yellow, depressing-looking blanket. I headed towards the elevator, but then I thought, *Maybe Isiah is in the crowd.* I took out my phone and dialed his number again: 416-667-4598. I could hear a phone ringing close by, but no answer. I went closer to the crowd. Again, I carefully dialed his phone: 4-1-6-6-6-7-4-5-9-8. *Dear God. Did the phone ring under the yellow blanket?* My heart desperately tried to jump out my chest. I felt a sharp, abrupt puncture in my abdomen. I dialed again. Oh God. The phone rang under that yellow blanket.

Under that yellow blanket laid the hands that once caressed me, eyes that enlightened me, dreams that strengthened me, and the love that connected me. All replaced by the sound of a cold, hopeless ring of a cell phone.

Introduction

Annette Bailey, Thomas S. Harrison,
and Rebecca Jaremko Bromwich

With nearly a quarter million people killed by guns each year worldwide (Geneva Declaration), the issue of gun violence has progressively unfolded into a serious global and public health problem—one that Amnesty International describes as a humanitarian crisis. But the crisis of gun violence does not stop at those killed; it extends to debilitating injuries that require extensive and long-term rehabilitation, as well as prolonged psychological trauma impacts on families and communities. Globally, upwards of two million people are living with firearm injuries. In 2017 alone, close to 134,000 people were shot and injured in the United States (US) (Amnesty International, *Gun Violence*). Just in Ontario, Canada, from 2002 to 2016, there were 6,483 firearm-related injuries, with an approximate annualized injury rate of 3.58 per 100,000 population (Gomez). The global consequence from gun violence death, injuries, and trauma is immense. The Geneva Declaration on Armed Violence and Development estimates that nearly two trillion US dollars of the world's economy could be saved if we are able to significantly reduce gun violence consequences (Naghavi).

Gun violence has remained a long-lasting, prominent, and ubiquitous phenomenon. Although it has fluctuated, there are little signs that the substantial challenge of gun violence is decreasing. Its longevity is facilitated by the pervasive use of guns as the weapon of choice in interpersonal violence, suicides, and mass shootings across international contexts (Steelesmith), as well as by local and global factors relevant to socioeconomic vulnerabilities and mental health issues. Indeed, gun violence is caused by intersecting cultural, political, and economic factors. Although these causes and consequences are contextualized distinctively, and in different degrees across regions and borders, they are no less devastating to the social and economic functioning of any country community, and/or family. Nor are the geopolitical processes that underpin these consequences any less pervasive and consequential across contexts. This book brings together collective voices across diverse disciplines to engage in critical and political discussion of the various issues and intersections inherent in gun violence—race, rap culture, gender, mental health, and poverty—using diverse theoretical frameworks. Conversations aimed at deconstructing the complexities and intersections in gun violence and reframing discourse relevant to gun violence prevention and control are pivotal points of analysis.

Recent gun violence catastrophes in the US, Canada, and other parts of the world remind us that more nuanced and intervention-driven perspectives of factors involved in the persistence and proliferation of gun violence are needed. Such factors as racism, poverty, trauma, and other mental health challenges are not new to the discussion of gun violence, but the intricacies of their individual and intersecting influence in gun violence prevention and gun control have never before been handled in a manner done by this anthology. Scholars and advocates from diverse disciplines discuss the political nuances surrounding these factors in gun violence while speaking to unique approaches to remedy their involvement, especially from the domains of government, public health, community, and the judicial system. Attention is given to the politics of justice and access to justice. These discussions are situated in the context of mental health, gun control, public policy, securitization, and conflicting legal and social trends. This knowledge will continue to be relevant to the work of advocates, stakeholders, and researchers regardless of context and the degree to which progress has been made in gun violence prevention and control across jurisdictions.

Gun violence solutions are too often located at the remedial and reactive level, focusing largely on increased police surveillance in communities and criminalization. Yet gun violence and gun control are constructed and complicated by a multifaceted, integrated system of inequity, power, and politics. This book is an eclectic mix of chapters that situate the issue of gun violence in a social context, and provides readers a more connected understanding of the multifaceted socio-political and psychological issues that inform gun violence. This holistic understanding of gun violence is needed to challenge and counteract the effects of such violence, which extend far beyond individuals directly involved. Some chapters discuss the disproportional risk of gun violence among Black youth, with an emphasis on reframing how this disproportionality is represented in mainstream discourse and media. These chapters raise questions, provide insights, and shed a critical light on social structures of vulnerability surrounding Black youth's increased risk and victimization with gun violence, particularly within the North American context.

The evolving nature of gun violence in the Canadian context, as in other contexts, has been socially and politically shaped and contextualized. Wedged into discourse and decisions of gun violence is the politics of race and the politics of access to guns. Gun politics are antagonistic to race and complicated by gun distribution and access. Discussions about Black youth and gun violence incite criminalization and hinder social justice solutions, whereas demands from primarily white male civilians for the right to own and carry guns hinder gun control measures. Moreover, the manufacturing and distribution of guns, both of which are driven by profit, make it difficult to make headway in reducing access to guns. In *Policing the Second Amendment: Guns, Law Enforcement, and the Politics of Race*, Jennifer Carlson refers to this political entanglement as the paradox of guns. With these entangled and diametrically opposing motivations in a capitalist society, social justice efforts to confront gun violence continue to be dominated by political and economic agendas. Specific to race, a number of chapters in this book work to demystify the complex intersections between race, systemic oppression, and racialized youth's involvement in gun violence. A social justice approach to address these intersections is an important thread in this discussion. In essence, this book represents a call to social action.

The objectives of every effort and decision regarding gun violence should be to keep communities safe, reduce its traumatic effects on families and communities, and create safe and vibrant cities. Keeping the conversations of gun violence alive and active is necessary to these objectives. Gun violence affects everyone, though differently, and its effects converge in various systems of society, such as healthcare, justice, education, social services, and immigration. We recognize that no one book can completely remedy this complex issue of gun violence. This book serves as an important resource for policy makers/decision-makers and community advocates who are developing solutions to the issue of gun violence and gun control. Readers of different professions, interests, and expertise can benefit from the knowledge presented in this book—whether that pertains to shifting social norms, improving service models, reshaping narratives about gun violence, or clarifying ideas. The book begins with a short story of a real-life experience of a mother who lost her son to gun violence (pseudonyms used). Written by Renee Bailey and Annette Bailey, this short story is meant to support an emotional understanding of the lived experience of survivors and a humanistic representation of the impact of gun violence.

In chapter one, Tanya Sharpe, Kendra Van de Water, and Jheanelle Anderson explore the role of structural inequities in gun homicide. The authors also address the role of structural inequities in the prevalence of homicide among Black people and in shaping their experience with homicide trauma and access to victims' services. Key recommendations focus on culturally responsive approaches to understanding and addressing the invisibility and legacy of structural inequities in Black homicide.

In chapter two, social work educators Paul Banahene Adjei, Delores E. Mullings, and Sulaimon Giwa powerfully challenge popular discourse suggesting that violence is endemic to the physicality, culture, and the DNA of Black families. While employing critical race and anticolonial theories, they critique this racist discourse, arguing that youth violence in Toronto is not the result of aberrant behaviour of pathologized, racialized families but rather is a symptom of a racist and classist society. They contend that increased policing and harsher penalties for perpetrators of violent crimes do not address the systemic and institutional racism that create a sense of hopelessness, leading Black youth to violence. The authors suggest a collaborative approach among stakeholders and decisionmakers to address the problem.

In chapter three, Santana Stallberg provides an engaging and timely examination of popular media and "gangsta rap" on gun violence in the context of youth gangs. Her analysis builds on social learning theory to examine how songs influence perceptions of conflict management and gun use among young people. Her thesis persuasively argues that although some rap lyrics provide a catalyst to gun and gang-related violence, they actually reflect the underlying social and economic causes of gun violence in the inner city, which first need to be addressed before gun violence can be reduced.

In chapter four, Akwatu Khenti explores the grim reality of Black youth and gun violence in Toronto. He discusses a range of factors that complicate this reality and make solutions challenging. Although he admits that the scope of the problem is huge, he recognizes that a public health approach is important to any meaningful and sustainable change. Given Canada's long history in yielding competencies in health promotion, Khenti believes that a public health response to address the issue of racialized risks in gun violence may yield positive results.

In chapter five, Annette Bailey, Renee Bailey, Divine Velasco, and Michelle Jubin discuss the overwhelming burden of gun violence death, injury, and survivorship on Black youth. They contend that the framing of these youths' experiences from the perspectives of criminality and race-based flaws limits opportunities for public health solutions that are based on violence-prevention perspectives and are informed by an understanding of how the intersection of race, social deprivation, and trauma play out in their experiences.

In chapter six, Thomas S. Harrison employs a social-legal perspective to examine the ways in which gun violence discourses have been portrayed. He suggests that much of the conversation is rooted in conflicting perceptions, which may depend on social situations, and which may result from sometimes inaccurate media portrayals. Harrison explores why gun violence is perceived as it is, which must be considered alongside empirical measures in decreasing gun crimes in Canada.

In chapter seven, Rebecca Jaremko Bromwich presents a discourse analysis of mainstream media articles published about the 2014 Ottawa shootings on Parliament Hill. She looks critically at how the majority of media reports and political discourse constructed the shooter, Michael Zehaf-Bibeau, as a terrorist, which supported a particular agenda that erased mental health and gun control concerns from the public conversation. Bromwich examines other possible discourses that could have been used to discuss him—ones that could have supported political activism towards gun control.

In chapter eight, Alisha Chohan uses the case of *R. v. Day, 2006* to interrogate the complications inherent in Canadian case law relative to dealing with gun ownership and the forfeiture of firearms among individuals with mental health issues. Chohan's contribution looks critically at how gun control measures are, in many instances, rendered ineffective by their uneven or incomplete enforcement. The analysis demonstrates that the intersection of mental health and gun violence prevention is more complicated than how courtrooms would make it seem. There is no clearcut legal formula used federally or provincially when an individual's mental capacity is scrutinized as a gun owner.

In chapter nine, Lynn M. Eckert and Joanne Myers use an ethnographic approach to masterfully explore the political, legal, and philosophical debates around gun ownership in the US. The chapter presents a case study of an attempt to establish a gun range in New York state to effectively tease out the practical implications of broader issues related to rights and questions about public safety, racism, gender, class, and economic development. The work is a microcosm of deep country-wide divisions and illustrates how attitudes about guns are linked to politics and are often strongly shaped by demographics and individual identity factors.

In chapter ten, Sky Starr narrates the story of two grieving mothers who established the OK tournament—a communal legacy initiative created to honour their sons lost to gun violence. Starr discusses how the ongoing involvement of these mothers in this communal event has promoted their incremental healing. Community-based grief and trauma support work in tandem with mothers' involvement and community mobilization to promote a process of healing and resilience for both grieving mothers and the community.

We end this anthology with the inclusion of the news article "The Devil in the Details. Why Trudeau's Ban on Assault Weapons Might Not Be Effective to Reduce Gun Crime after Canada's Largest Mass Shooting in Nova Scotia." In this news article, Thomas S. Harrison discusses the 2020 shooting of twenty-two people in Nova Scotia. This event led to new Federal Government efforts to control assault weapons. However, Harrison argues that even though many Canadians are united in the cause to remedy the national devastation of gun violence, this ongoing challenge has yet to prove amenable to efforts of gun control. Widespread frustration with continued gun violence may mean that a majority of Canadians are willing to support attempts to regulate firearms; however, discussions about gun violence solutions are still situated within diverse experiences and perspectives, without resolutive consensus. Given the complexity of gun violence and diversity of viewpoints, an effective government policy likely requires a holistic approach—one that addresses many of the social and other complexities deeply embedded in this issue. The 2020 gun violence attack in Nova Scotia suggests that discussions about gun violence prevention and control must be unremitting. Solutions must be considered within a complex social context, which is a premise strongly supported by this anthology.

Endnotes

1. The 2015 edition of the *Global Burden of Armed Violence* estimates that 508,000 people die violently every year. Firearms are used in close to half of all homicides committed. Findings from this research shows that close to two trillion USD in global violence-related economic losses could have been saved.

Works Cited

Amnesty International. "Gun Violence—Key Facts." *Amnesty International, 2016,* www.amnesty.org/en/what-we-do/arms-control/gun-violence/. Accessed 22 Mar. 2022.

Geneva Declaration. *Global Burden of Armed Violence. Geneva Declaration,* 2015, www.genevadeclaration.org/measurability/global-burden-of-armed-violence/global-burden-of-armed-violence-2015.html. Accessed 22 Mar. 2022.

Gomez, David, et al. "Firearm-Related Injuries and Deaths in Ontario, Canada, 2002-2016: A Population-Based study." *CMAJ*, vol. 192, no. 42, 2020, pp. E1253-E1263.

Naghavi, Mohsen, et al. "Global Mortality from Firearms, 1990-2016." *JAMA*, vol, 320, no. 8, 2018, pp. 792-814.

Steelesmith, Danielle L., et al. "Contextual Factors Associated with County-Level Suicide Rates in the United States, 1999 to 2016." *JAMA Network Organ*, vol. 2, no. 9, 2019, e1910936-e1910936.

Chapter 1

The Transactional Relationship between Structural Inequities and Homicide

Tanya L. Sharpe, Kendra Van de Water, and Jheanelle Anderson

In 2017, the United Nations Office on Drugs and Crime (UNODC) reported that there were 6.1 homicide victims per 100,000 population worldwide, resulting in 464,000 people killed. The Americas had the highest rate of homicide victims at 17.2 victims per 100,000 population and 173,000 victims for 2017 (UNODC). Africa was the only other region with a homicide rate exceeding the global average, with 13 victims per 100,000 population, or 163,000 victims (UNODC). Descendants of the African diaspora (hereafter referred to as Black people) suffer disproportionately from homicide. For example, the UNODC reported that between 2013 and 2018, Jamaica averaged 54 homicides per 100,000 persons, an estimated 1,540 homicide victims annually. In South Africa, the murder rate (42 per 100,000 persons) resulted in 18,571 homicide victims annually (UNODC). In the United States (US), Black people comprise approximately 13 per cent of the population, yet account for 51 per cent of all homicide victims annually (Langley and Sugarmann).

The disproportionate and devastating impact of homicide on Black people throughout the global community is a direct result of structural inequities that have created a complicit cycle of poverty, unequal access to education, disparate employment opportunities, and a lack of access to affordable, stable, and suitable housing (Natl. Academies of Sciences, Engineering, and Medicine; Noonan, Velasco-Mondragion, and Wagner). According to the 2018 US Census, 20.8 per cent of Black Americans fell below the poverty line compared to 8.1 per cent of white Americans, despite Black people making up approximately 13 per cent of the population (Semega et al.). Although Black people are 3.4 per cent of the population in Canada, 23.9 per cent live in poverty (Colour of Poverty–Colour of Change). This socioeconomic stratification is evident in other contexts as well. In Jamaica, 91.6 per cent of the population identify as Black or mixed race, and they are more likely to be among the poorest (Kelly). In South Africa, due to apartheid, nearly 80 per cent of Black people are more likely to live in poverty, almost half below the poverty line (Lehola).

These inequities are further amplified by actions of anti-Black racism, the legacy of settler colonization, and, importantly, the transatlantic slave trade, which continues to pathologize, criminalize, subordinate, and traumatize Black bodies throughout the global community (Fanon; Maynard). The transatlantic slave trade was responsible for the enslaving and trafficking of twelve to fifteen million people from Africa to the Western Hemisphere and for the violent victimization, physical brutality, and mass murder of Black people (Galtung; Martin and Harrod; Klaus; Martin and Osterholtz). Already inherently violent, social inequities continue to perpetuate higher rates of interpersonal homicide and state-sanctioned police violence and death among Black people.

In this chapter we explore the role of structural inequities in the prevalence of homicide death among Black people and in shaping their experience with homicide trauma and access to victims' services. Although we draw knowledge primarily from the US context, the posthomicide experiences of Black survivors in other contexts are similar due to the common legacy of structural inequities across borders. We end this chapter with suggestions for addressing the invisibility and pervasiveness of structural inequities in Black survivors' experiences with homicide.

Homicide and Structural Violence

Johan Galtung, a sociologist and founder of the discipline peace and conflict studies, coined the term "structural violence" to describe social systems (e.g., economic, political, legal, religious, and cultural) that prevent people from thriving. According to Galtung, violence deprives people of accessing necessities of living. He links structural violence to social injustice and oppression, which are built into the foundation of society and dictate the allocation and access of psychological resources, political power, education, healthcare, and legal rights inequitably for marginalized and disenfranchised people of colour (Galtung; Maynard; Winter and Leighton). These societal ways of creating barriers for Black people are not often referred to as structural violence because they appear commonplace in the dominant culture's way of understanding the world—making these purposeful forms of injustice appear "almost invisible" (Winter and Leighton 99). The World Health Organization defines violence as "the intentional use of physical force or power, threatened or actual, against oneself, another person, or a group or a community, that results in, or has a high likelihood of resulting in injury, death, or psychological harm." Galtung's definition of structural violence further helps to enhance our understanding of structural inequities as structural violence. The insidious nature of structural violence, embedded in the very fabric of society and institutions, not only works to disadvantage people through political, criminal justice, and economic structures but also perpetuates experiences of homicide, trauma, and repeat victimization (Winter and Leighton).

Structural violence exists globally, and the project of globalization and neocolonialism works to universally increase disparities and exploit Black and Brown bodies. For forty-six years (1948 to 1994), apartheid used structural violence to implement racial segregation policies designed to dictate where Black South Africans could live, work, and eat, what type of education they could receive, and whether they could vote (Mayne). The strategic dismantling of Black South African humanity resulted in socioeconomic stratification and psychosocial deprivation, which have left a legacy of anguish in its wake. In the US and Canada, structural violence manifests in ways that can result in overpolicing and mass incarceration, inequitable access to medical care, surveilling of Black women by the welfare state, and the overdisciplining, suspensions, and expulsion of Black youth in schools (Maynard). Perhaps the most explicit and direct form of structural violence today is the surveillance and dehumanizing use of the police force on Black and Brown bodies. Scholars point out that this dispossession by law enforcement serves to maintain the status quo of racial, social, and economic stratification in resource distribution (Maynard; Winter and Leighton).

Police Homicide of Black Bodies

Recent social media coverage of the murders of George Floyd, Breonna Taylor, Dominique Fells, and Ahmaud Arbery has made visible the continued brutality of Black bodies by police and the deep-rooted racism underlying responses to this brutality. Occurring in the span of less than two months, these murders were witnessed over two billion times on social media through videos shared on Instagram, Facebook, YouTube, and Twitter (Blake). These murders have not stopped at Black men; recent killings of Black women by police have also come to light. For example, Breonna Taylor a 26-year-old Black woman, was shot eight times and killed on March 13, 2020, by Louisville Metro Police, after officers forced their way into her home with a "no-knock warrant," which was based on erroneous information that people were using her home to receive packages of drugs (Oppel Jr., Taylor, and Bogel-Burroughs). Shortly after her death, her family's requests for the coroner's records and for an independent investigation were denied until the murder of George Floyd by police on May 25, 2020. As another example, Dominique Fells, a Black transgender woman, was murdered on June 8, 2020 (McDonald). Not only does her murder remain unsolved, but she joins many Black transgender women whose homicides have received little attention. The Human Rights Campaign reported that in 2019 there were approximately 27 murders of transgender or gender nonconforming people in the US, with the majority of victims being Black transgender women (Human Rights Campaign Foundation). The visible murders of Black men and women have ignited protests and civil uprisings that have brought together a global community of Black survivors of homicide victims and their allies from all over the world in an effort to address the anti-Black racism behind these murders. We have seen similar movements in the

1960s, when Black protestors organized demonstrations and marches to advocate for the civil rights and liberties of Black people (Mowatt; Richardson). Their expression of fury and rage was a response to racial discrimination, social injustice, and structural oppression. However, four decades later, these systemic issues remain, since all forms of injustice, including modern-day policing of Black bodies, are firmly rooted in history.

Modern police organizations in the South emerged from the legacy of slave patrols (Potter; Platt). The first formal slave patrol was created in the Carolina colonies in 1704 with three functions: apprehending runaway slaves, deterring slave revolts, and disciplining slave workers who violated plantation rules (Potter; Reichel). The history of law enforcement illustrates the problematic correlation between systems designed to perpetuate acts of enforced structural violence while simultaneously tasked with providing services and safety to people for whom they were trained to treat as property. Cellphone footage has captured the repeated and frequent violent brutality that Black people experience, often at the hands of police. This history would otherwise remain hidden to the public without the emergence of social media. However, it is recognized that while social media serves as a place where survivors of police brutality seek support, and gather to mobilize for social change, it has also been a place where Black survivors are repeatedly exposed to acts of homicide via graphic videos and images depicting the brutal murders of Black bodies. A consequence of bringing wide visibility to the excessive number of Black homicides to a larger platform is the risk of retraumatizing Black people who are exposed to these traumatic and violent deaths (Ramsden). Moreover, Black people may experience an added layer of fear, anxiety, and distrust after seeing people who look similar to them or a loved one being killed by police.

Therefore, even though mass-media-produced images can be praised as a pedagogical tool for counter-messaging resistance work, bell hooks notes that images "maintain oppression, exploitation, and overall domination of black people" (hooks 2; Mowatt 786). Essentially, the sharing of Black death across social media platforms has made it possible for detractors to criminalize Black bodies and justify Black death. Despite these complexities, there is something different about the shift in the current global response to Black homicides. Social media has exposed the frequency with which Black people experience structural violence and homicide while demonstrating the direct and indirect impacts of homicide that connect a global community of survivors of homicide victims. For many Black viewers and activists, the recorded images of the murdering of Black bodies serve as a rallying symbol for solidarity.

Black-on-Black Homicide

While examining the disproportionate rates of homicide among Black people globally, it is also important to examine the structural factors inherent in Black-on-Black homicide. According to the Bureau of Justice, homicide victimization occurring against Black people in the US was more likely to occur in densely populated areas (Braga and Brunson; Harrell). This can be traced back to the historical exclusion of Black people from economic and social mobility opportunities, which accounts for Black people primarily living in densely populated low-income urban areas (Braga and Brunson; Bruce, Roscigno, and McCall; Harrell; Lo, Howell, and Cheng; Muhammad; Ulmer, Harris, and Steffensmeier). The literature indicates that homicide is more likely to occur interracially—that is, within racial groups—which explains why Black people are often victimized or murdered by other Black people. In 2020, the Bureau of Justice Statistics reported that 70 per cent of violent crimes committed by Black people were against other Black people (Morgan and Truman). In addition, 62 per cent of violent crimes committed by white people were against other white people, and 45 per cent of violent incidents committed against Latinx people were by other Latinx people (Morgan and Truman). Although these statistics speak to the reality of intergroup violence being a common phenomenon for all races, the data on violent crime are often misused and misrepresented to paint a false narrative that violent crimes are disproportionately committed by Black people (Muhammad).

The "Black-on-Black crime" trope reduces the issue of disproportionate homicide rates among Black people to a so-called Black problem while erasing the insidious structural inequities that contribute to this issue. This "Black problem" is then seen as unworthy for responsive interventions, as Blackness becomes criminalized and stereotyped as inherently a characteristic of Black people

(Muhammad). The media contributes to the proliferation of Black-on-Black crime in how the reporting of crime in predominantly Black neighbourhoods is distorted and decontextualized from the realities of inequalities faced by Black people (Braga and Brunson; Muhammad). Black-on-Black crime has been a greatly politicized cliché and is used to dismiss concerns over the disproportionate violent experiences of Black people's encounters with police (Muhammad). It has inspired "tough on crime" rhetoric from both Republican and Democratic politicians across the US—a rhetoric ushered in during the Nixon and Regan era of brutalization, surveillance, and mass incarceration of Black bodies (Maynard; Muhammad). This platitude frequently gets used as a dog whistle in addition to rampant labelling of Black offenders as "super predators," "thugs," and "sewer rats" (Maynard; Muhammad).

Homicide Victims, Grief, and Trauma

According to the American Medical Association's Global Mortality from Firearms 1990 to 2016 study, an estimated 251,000 people died by guns in 2016 compared to 209,000 deaths in 1990 (The Global Burden of Disease 2016 Injury Collaborators). The researchers called the results "a major public health problem for humanity" (793). However, no mention was made about the overrepresentation of Black homicide victims and the impact of these violent deaths on family members and friends faced with the challenge of learning how to survive the murder of their loved ones. These covictims are often referred to as indirect victims or survivors of homicide victims (Connolly and Gordon). They are individuals who have familial connections with the murdered victim and are victimized by the murder of their loved one as well as by the posthomicide experience (e.g., engagement with the medical examiner, criminal justice system, and media) (Miranda, Molina, and MacVane). Lula M. Redmond estimates that each homicide victim leaves behind between and ten family members, friends, coworkers, and neighbours struggling to make sense out of what is senseless ("Surviving"). When we contextualize Black families, whose members often include chosen persons not related by blood, the number of Black family members faced with surviving the murder of their loved ones may be far greater than what is predicted (Sharpe, "Understanding the

Sociocultural Context of Coping").

Posthomicide research indicates that when a homicide occurs, family members and friends are faced with managing their own grief and the grief of other family members. Due to the unexpected and violent nature of homicide, surviving family members of homicide victims are often at greater risk for experiencing post-traumatic stress (Baliko and Tuck; Rheingold et al.) than survivors of other forms of violence (e.g., physical assault, robbery, burglary, and sexual assault) (Zinzow et al., "Examining Posttraumatic Stress Symptoms"). Homicide increases the risk of long-term trauma reactions, which can obscure and magnify the grieving process (Armour; Parkes; Rando; Rynearson and McCreery). Researcher Karen Onderko refers to trauma as a "response to deeply distressing or disturbing events that overwhelm an individual's ability to cope, cause feelings of helplessness, and diminish their sense of self and ability to feel the full range of emotions and experiences" (para. 1). The experience of historical trauma and existing systemic oppression makes grieving for Black survivors a pervasive and prolonged predicament. Jason Holland et al. refer to this prolonged grieving process as complicated grief. In a study examining complicated grief among Black Americans who experienced the sudden or unanticipated death of a loved one, Benjamin Goldsmith et al. found that Black Americans are 2.5 times more likely to experience symptoms of complicated grief than their white bereaved counterparts. Kenneth Doka ("Disenfranchised Grief"), Lula Redmond ("Sudden Violent Death") and Deborah Spungen opine that social stigma, blame, and shame for the way the victim lived and died often coincide with the grieving process.

The increased risk of complicated grief and PTSD for survivors of homicide victims may be due to the violence and suddenness of homicide (Amick-McMullan et al.); the extensive involvement with the criminal justice system and media (Allen; Asaro; Doka, "Living with Grief After Sudden Loss," "Disenfranchised Grief"; Rando; Spungen; Zinzow et al., "Prevalence and Mental Health"); the upheaval brought about by emotions of anger; and the management of injured relationships with friends and family members suspected of being involved in the crime (Asaro). Moreover, the murders of Black people often carry stigma based on the assumption that illegal activity (e.g., drug trafficking and gang activity) was the cause of the violent death. This stigmatization may lead to surviving family members feeling that shame has been brought upon their family. Additionally, surviving family members often blame themselves for their inability to protect their loved one from harm. According to a sample of Black American survivors of homicide victims, such stigmatization further perpetuates the stereotype that Black Americans are prone to criminal activity (Sharpe, "Sources of Support"; Sharpe and Boyas).

Tanya Sharpe's model of coping for African American survivors of homicide victims (MCAASHV) elucidates the complexity of interaction between structural violence and homicide ("Understanding the Sociocultural Context of Coping"). The MCAASHV suggests that before a homicide occurs, the traumatic impact of cultural trauma (e.g., historical and contemporary experiences with racism and oppression) shapes how Black people experience and view the world. When a homicide occurs, Black people enter into a culture of homicide in which feelings of shame, blame, stigmatization, and a sense of injustice are paramount. The interaction between cultural trauma and the culture of homicide helps to explain how Black Americans racially appraise the traumatic experiences of structural violence and homicide and identify coping resources and strategies to manage the traumas (McGuffey; Sharpe "Understanding the Sociocultural Context of Coping").

Coping with Homicide

Research on coping strategies suggests that communities of colour rely on communal and collectivistic approaches to cope with stress (Sharpe "Understanding the Sociocultural Context"; Wong, Wong, and Lonner). They place great value on relational coping strategies such as help-seeking and support from family and friends, rather than acquiring support from therapeutic counseling services (Moore and Constantine). These values and strengths are derived from cultural aspects and the belief in communal spiritual traditions and holistic forms of healing such as prayer and other faith-based practices (Boyd-Franklin; Taylor, Chatters and Jackson). Understanding the identification and utilization of coping strategies from this cultural lens helps to inform the coping strategies of Black survivors of homicide victims. Tanya Sharpe and Javier suggest that the Black American experience of coping with the homicide of a loved one entails a psychosocial, cultural, and structural process of adaptation to survive the traumatic experience. Their experiences are shaped by inequitable social structures that impact the perception, utilization, and allocation of psychosocial resources. The transactional relationship between structural violence and homicide helps to elucidate Black survivors' reliance on informal coping strategies to manage the psychological trauma experienced from homicide. These shared experiences of collective trauma have contributed to a reliance on informal communal supports to cope with the lasting effects of both structural violence and homicide (Billingsley; Boyd-Franklin; McAdoo; Sharpe "Understanding the Sociocultural Context of Coping"; Wong, Wong, and Lonner.). These informal communal supports have expanded to include social media platforms, which make clear that the connection between Black survivors of homicide victims—regardless of class, status, and geographical location—is significant to coping in the aftermath of a homicide. Delivering the necessary training and education to service providers, such as the MCAASHV, can enhance the provision of culturally responsive services and is vital to the individual and collective healing of Black survivors of homicide victims.

Homicide Survivors and Victim Services

After a homicide, survivors are quickly forced into navigating complex systems, often with limited support and limited understanding of what to expect. No one can prepare for how intricate, isolating, and debilitating it may feel to pick up the pieces of one's life after a loved one is murdered. In the aftermath of a murder, survivors of homicide victims must repeatedly interact with detectives, lawyers, funeral homes, coroners, victim advocates, reporters, prothonotaries, family members, neighbours, and friends (Spungen; Armour). In 1985, the United Nations (UN) adopted the "Declaration of Basic Principles of Justice for Victims of Crime and Abuse of Power," highlighting that victims should have access to justice, restitution, compensation and assistance (Spalek). This charter encourages governments to incorporate initiatives addressing the needs of victims of crime while minimizing "secondary victimization" (Spalek). Australia, Canada, Hong Kong, Ireland, Jamaica, Japan, and South Africa have charters outlining public institutions' responsibilities to provide victim services. Since the 1990s, South Africa's victim support centres have been housed within local police services, established as the result of a national crime prevention strategy to address rising crime levels (Spalek). These volunteer-operated centres offer emotional and practical support to victims of crime (Spalek). Jamaica's Victim Support Unit (VSU) was established by the Ministry of Justice in 1998, providing advocacy, advice, and counselling to crime victims (UN Women; Gov't of Jamaica). Britain and Australia provide specialized homicide support services. For example, in partnership with the Victim Support Homicide Service, in 2011, Britain developed ASSIST Trauma Care to provide therapeutic support service for survivors of homicide victims (Spalek). Although there is limited research on the sociocultural context of survivors of homicide victims in the global context, services available to survivors may include therapy (cost or no cost), emotional support through court proceedings, support groups, advocacy, relocation assistance, and financial reimbursement for funeral services or loss of wages. Although these services for survivors of homicide victims are vital, many barriers—such as eligibility criteria, wait times, and grief—can deter survivors from following through with processes to obtain the support they need (Office of Victim Advocate).

Victim Compensation—The Undeserving

The historical evolution of victim services must be understood, particularly as it pertains to the establishment of services for victims through law enforcement, and the barriers that this presents for Black families. Victim service laws and organizations generally do not account for the sociocultural context in which Black family members and friends of homicide victims must learn to bereave and grieve the murder of loved ones. Additionally, the provision of victim services through law enforcement structures has only subjugated Black survivors who require these services, and further perpetuates structural violence. Historically, these laws were created to serve people who were victims of a crime (including survivors of homicide victims) by reimbursing certain surviving family members for some out-of-pocket costs (e.g., medical and funeral expenses) (Victim Compensation Assistance Program) and by connecting survivors to services such as therapy, court accompaniment, or support groups. However, these laws continue to focus on a service model for victims or survivors who are considered deserving. So-called deserving survivors are those deemed worthy of victim services, according to the laws based on race, class, criminal, and economic status. Black victims of homicide who have lived in poverty and may have had a criminal record are generally considered undeserving and are thus discriminated against, leaving their surviving family members ineligible to receive services. In many cases, surviving family would not be eligible for victim compensation or monetary reimbursement if it was believed that the homicide victim was complicit in the cause of their own death (Office of Victim Advocate). For example, if a homicide detective reports that marijuana was found at a crime scene, family members would become ineligible for any and all state monetary reimbursement or support. Furthermore, if the homicide detective reports to the state government that the surviving family is not cooperating with the investigation or believes they are withholding information, the family becomes ineligible for any and all reimbursement services pertaining to the murder of their loved one (Office of Victim Advocate).

The denial of access to victim services to the undeserving can be seen in the provision of finances to pay for crime scene cleanup. For example, if someone is murdered in a home, the surviving family is solely responsible for the cost of cleaning the crime scene. The cost for a professional company to properly disinfect and clean can range from two thousand dollars to more than forty thousand. Whereas state reimbursement will cover this cost to a maximum of five hundred dollars per crime scene, the full cost may only be covered through a homeowner's insurance policy. A 2015 study in Philadelphia found that 38.7 per cent of Black people owned their homes (Dent). To date, no data have been collected on the percentage of homeowners who have homeowner's insurance.

Surviving families who cannot afford to cover the cost of crime scene cleanup may ultimately end up cleaning and disinfecting the crime scenes on their own. This is an example of victim service policy that does not account for structural inequities that contribute to prolonged grief and retraumatization. Although crime scene cleanup is one example of a victim service compensation policy, it is a critical need that should be fully covered by the state. Moreover, homicide victims' funerals should be paid for by the state regardless of why they were murdered. The examination of victim services policies can offer insight into how services for victims of crime were developed and implemented to reflect systemic and structural violence instead of being created to meet the needs of diverse groups of people. Given Black people's persistent and cumulative experience with inequality, if the needs of Black survivors of homicide remain unmet, their experiences with trauma will remain an ongoing burden for communities and societies. If service policies are not changed to reflect the needs of survivors of homicide victims, then services are complicit in the perpetuation of trauma and complicated grief for survivors and their families most in need.

A Pathway Forwards

Homicide and its disproportionate impact on Black communities are a scourge, which in the absence of systemic race-based data collection will continue to contribute to the invisibility of the murder of Black bodies as well as structural inequities that permeate the fabric of society. To best serve Black survivors of homicide victims, it is imperative to understand the legacy of collective trauma and the insidious nature in which both structural violence and homicide are systemically yoked to chronically impact Black people.

Race-Based Data Collection

To our knowledge, race-based homicide and victimization data are not systematically collected across countries, nor are they readily available and publicly accessible. Despite providing an accurate comparison of homicide between countries over time, the assessment of death rates does not allow us to ascertain the racial makeup of the victim or survivor, nor do the data provide information on the type of homicide (e.g., state-sanctioned, intrafamilial, mass violence, and interpersonal). The absence of race-based homicide data speaks to a larger systemic issue of the continued erasure of Black people. It is the authors' opinion that if "Black people aren't counted, then they don't count." Although homicide rates vary across countries, the lack of race-based homicide data limits our ability to fully understand the magnitude and impact of homicide on Black people throughout our global community. This lack of data ultimately impedes our understanding of collective trauma experienced by Black people and our understanding of when, where, and how to prevent homicide and respond to the needs of Black communities in a culturally responsive manner. Race-based data on homicide and victimization should be collected systematically, capturing the typology and context of homicide.

Addressing Structural Violence

Paul Farmer et al. and Johan Galtung suggest that structural inequalities are embedded in societal structures, ultimately affecting resources and the physiological needs of homicide survivors. The insidious nature through which Black people are deprived of access to needed coping resources is structurally violent, causing them to disproportionately experience trauma even before experiencing a homicide. Therefore, approaches to supporting Black survivors of homicide victims must begin with a fundamental understanding of their historical and contemporary experiences with structural violence and the subsequent intergenerational complexity of trauma they experienced. Moreover, it is important to recognize that the deprivation of basic human rights is a form of structural violence that often directly contributes to homicide and victimization. To ignore the deep-rooted connection between structural violence and homicide perpetuates the continued demise of Black people.

Culturally Relevant Responses

The disproportionate representation of Black survivors of homicide victims throughout the global community suggests that it is crucial to focus on implementing culturally responsive research, policies, and practices to support and engage survivors of homicide victims. Further, it is imperative to reimagine systems of care and what they can do to lead to the betterment of our communities, rather than perpetuate systemic injustice that fosters the chronic traumatization of Black survivors of homicide victims (Sharpe, "Understanding the Sociocultural Context of Coping"). In a symposium on governmental compensation for victims of violence, an associate justice of the Supreme Court, Arthur J. Goldberg, stated that "one who suffers the impact of criminal violence is also the victim of society's long inattention to poverty and social injustice" (Sharpe, "Understanding the Sociocultural Context of Coping" 2). These injustices are particularly pronounced for Black people. Transformative systemic change requires that a system of care for survivors of homicide victims be developed through policies that address the social injustices caused by inherently violent structural inequities. There are several considerations for how service providers (e.g. police, clinicians, physicians, faith-based communities, and victim advocates) should interact with survivors of homicide victims. A large part of this work requires that we 1) hire individuals to fill the aforementioned positions from communities disproportionately affected by homicide and 2) educate and train service providers to understand the intersection and impact of racism, structural violence, and homicide on Black people and their traditional ways of coping.

Recruitment and retainment of service providers who work with homicide victims requires: 1) a formal process of outreach to individuals from neighbourhoods impacted by homicide; 2) retention strategies that include equitable pay for their knowledge and skills; 3) opportunities to advance within the organization; 4) opportunities to further their education at a reduced cost; and 5) training and clinical services designed to unpack and support intergenerational and complex trauma they experience from chronic exposure to violence in their own communities. As violence continues to disproportionately impact Black people, we must earnestly examine and address its root causes. Understanding the intersection of structural violence and homicide on Black people means understanding that the root causes of such violence are a direct result of historical and contemporary experiences with racism and structural inequities.

The 2020 global social justice movements in response to anti-Black racism—which manifests in the form of structural inequities and the repeated denial of justice for Black homicide victims and those who are surviving their murders—make it clear that the denial of authentic discourse that translates into actionable policy reform, culturally responsive research and services can no longer be the status quo. If we are to create authentic structural systemic change, a pathway forwards must not only include creating victim services for and with Black survivors of homicide victims but also address the structural inequities that disproportionately perpetuate violence among and against Black people.

Works Cited

Allen, Irving M. "PTSD Among African Americans." *Ethnocultural Aspects of Posttraumatic Stress Disorder: Issues, Research, and Clinical Applications*, edited by Anthony J. Marsella et al. American Psychological Association, 1996, pp. 209-38.

Amick-McMullan, Angelynne et al. "Family Survivors of Homicide Victims: Theoretical Perspectives and an Exploratory Study." *Journal of Traumatic Stress*, vol. 2, no. 1, 1989, pp. 21-35.

Armour, Marilyn. "Meaning Making in the Aftermath of Homicide." *Death Studies*, vol. 27, no. 6, 2003, pp. 519-40.

Asaro, M. Regina. "Working with Adult Homicide Survivors, Part I: Impact and Sequelae of Murder." *Perspectives in Psychiatric Care*, vol. 37, no. 3, 2001, pp. 95-101.

Baliko, Beverly, and Inez Tuck. "Perceptions of Survivors of Loss by Homicide Opportunities for Nursing Practice." *Journal of Psychosocial Nursing and Mental Health Services*, vol. 46, no. 5, 2008, pp. 26-34.

Billingsley, Andrew. *Climbing Jacob's Ladder: The Enduring Legacy of African-American Families*. Simon & Schuster, 1993.

Blake, Sam. "Why The George Floyd Protests Feel Different — Lots and Lots of Mobile Video." *Dot.LA*, Jun. 2020, dot.la/twitter-protest-video-2646171594.html. Accessed 23 Mar. 2022.

Block, Sheila, and Grace-Edward Galabuzi. *Canada's Colour Coded Labour Market*. Wellesley Institute, March 2011.

Borda, Jennifer L., and Bailey Marshall. "Creating a Space to #SayHerName: Rhetorical Stratification in the Networked Sphere." *Quarterly Journal of Speech*, vol. 106, no. 2, 2020, pp. 133-38.

Boyd-Franklin, Nancy. *Black Families in Therapy: A Multisystems Approach*. The Guilford Press, 1989.

Braga, Anthony A., and Rod K. Brunson. "The Police and Public Discourse on 'Black-on-Black' Violence." *National Criminal Justice Reference Service*. U.S. Department of Justice, National Institute of Justice, May 2015.

Bruce, Marino A., V.J. Roscigno, and McCall. "Structure, Context, and Agency in the Reproduction of Black-on-Black Violence." *Theoretical Criminology*, vol. 2, no. 1, 1998, pp. 29-55.

Colour of Poverty–Colour of Change. *Understanding the Racializiation of Poverty in Ontario, Canada*. 2019, colourofpoverty.ca/wp-content/uploads/2020/04/cop-coc-fact-sheet-cover-page-2.pdf. Accessed Apr. 7 2022.

Commission on Social Determinants of Health. *Closing the Gap in a Generation: Health Equity Through Action on the Social Determinants of Health*. World Health Organization, 2008, www.who.int/social_determinants/final_report/csdh_finalreport_2008.pdf. Accessed Apr. 7 2022.

Connolly, Jennifer, and Ronit Gordon. "Co-Victims of Homicide: A Systematic Review of the Literature." *Trauma, Violence, & Abuse*, vol. 16, no. 4 S, 2014, pp. 494-505.

"Crime Victims' Rights." *Office of Victim Advocate. www.ova.pa.gov*, www.ova.pa.gov:443/AboutOVA/CrimeVictimsRights/Pages/default.aspx. Accessed 17 July 2020.

Crime Victims' Rights in America: A Historical Overview. https://www.ncjrs.gov/ovc_archives/ncvrw/2005/pg4b.html. Accessed 18 July 2020.

Dent, Mark. "Philly Homeowner Stats: Fewer People of Color Own Homes Now Than They Did in 1980." *Billy Penn*, Aug. 2017. *billypenn.com*, billypenn.com/2017/08/23/philly-homeowner-stats-fewer-people-of-color-own-homes-now-than-they-did-in-1980/. Accessed 7 Apr. 2022.

Doka, Kenneth. *Disenfranchised Grief: New Directions, Challenges, and Strategies for Practice*. Research Press, 2002.

Doka, Kenneth, ed. *Living with Grief After Sudden Loss: Suicide, Homicide, Accident, Heart Attack, Stroke*. Taylor & Francis, 1996.

Fanon, Frantz. *Black Skin, White Masks*. Pluto Press, 2008. eBook Collection (EBSCOhost), *EBSCOhost*, search.ebscohost.com/login.aspx?direct=true&db=nlebk&AN=247433&site=ehost-live.

Farmer, Paul E., et al. "Structural Violence and Clinical Medicine." *PLOS Medicine*, vol. 3, no. 10, 2006, pp. 1686-91.

Galtung, Johan. "Violence, Peace, and Peace Research." *Journal of Peace Research*, vol. 6, no. 3, 1969, pp. 167-91.

Goldberg, Arthur J. "Symposium: Governmental Compensation for Victims of Violence: Preface." *Southern California Law Review*, vol. 3, no. 1, 1970, pp. 1-3.

Goldsmith, B., et al. "Elevated Rates of Prolonged Grief Disorder in African Americans." *Death Studies*, vol. 32, no. 4, 2008, pp. 352-65.

Government of Jamaica, Ministry of Justice. *Victim Support*. moj.gov.jm/programmes/victim-support. Accessed Apr. 7 2022.

Harrell, Erika. *Black Victims of Violent Crime*. NCJ 214258, US Department of Justice. Bureau of Justice Statistics, 2007, p. 12. *Zotero*, www.bjs.gov/content/pub/pdf/bvvc.pdf. Accessed 7 Apr. 2022.

Harrell, Erika, et al. *Household Poverty and Nonfatal Violent Victimization, 2008–2012*. NCJ 248384, US Department of Justice. Bureau of Justice Statistics, 2014, p. 18. *Zotero*, www.bjs.gov/content/pub/pdf/hpnvv0812.pdf. Accessed 7 Apr. 2022.

Holland, Jason M., et al. "The Underlying Structure of Grief: A Taxometric Investigation of Prolonged and Normal Reactions to Loss." *Journal of Psychopathology and Behavioral Assessment*, vol. 31, no. 3, 2009, pp. 190-201.

hooks, bell. *Black Looks: Race and Representation*. Routledge, 2014.

Hull, Akasha G., Patricia Bell-Scott, and Barbara Smith, eds. *All the Women Are White, All the Blacks Are Men, but Some of Us Are Brave: Black Women's Studies*. Feminist Press, 1982.

Human Rights Campaign Foundation. "Violence Against the Transgender Community in 2020." *Human Rights Campaign. www.hrc.org*, www.hrc.org/resources/violence-against-the-trans-and-gender-non-conforming-community-in-2020/. Accessed 18 July 2020.

Kelly, Monique D. A. "Examining Race in Jamaica: How Racial Category and Skin Color Structure Social Inequality." *Race and Social Problems*, vol. 12, no. 4, 2020, pp. 300-12.

Kelly, Monique D. A., and Stanley R. Bailey. "Racial Inequality and the Recognition of Racial Discrimination in Jamaica." *Social Identities*, vol. 24, no. 6, 2018, pp. 688–706.

Klaus, Haagen D. "The Bioarchaeology of Structural Violence: A Theoretical Model and Case Study." *The Bioarchaeology of Violence*, edited by Debra L. Martin, Ryan Harrod, and Ventura R. Perez, University Press of Florida, 2012, pp. 29-62.

Langley, Marty, and Josh Sugarmann. *Black Homicide Victimization in the United States: An Analysis of 2018 Homicide Data*. Violence Policy

Center, 2021, vpc.org/studies/blackhomicide21.pdf. Accessed 7 Apr. 2022.

Lehohla, Pali. *Poverty Trends in South Africa: An Examination of Absolute Poverty Between 2006 and 2015.* 03-10–06, Statistics South Africa, 2017, www.statssa.gov.za/publications/Report-03-10-06/Report-03-10-062015.pdf. Accessed Apr. 7 2022.

Lo, Celia C., Rebecca J. Howell, and Tyrone C. Cheng. "Explaining Black–White Differences in Homicide Victimization." *Aggression and Violent Behavior,* vol. 18, no. 1, 2013, pp. 125-34.

Martin, Debra L., and Anna J. Osterholtz. "Broken Bodies and Broken Bones: Biocultural Approaches to Ancient Slavery and Torture." *New Directions in Biocultural Anthropology,* edited by Molly K. Zuckerman and Debra L. Martin, John Wiley & Sons, 2016, pp. 471–90.

Martin, Debra L., and Ryan P. Harrod. "Bioarchaeological Contributions to the Study of Violence." *American Journal of Physical Anthropology,* vol. 156, no. S59, 2015, pp. 116-45.

Maynard, Robyn. *Policing Black Lives: State Violence in Canada from Slavery to the Present.* Fernwood Publishing, 2017.

Mayne, Alan J. *From Politics Past to Politics Future: An Integrated Analysis of Current and Emergent Paradigms.* Praeger, 1991.

McAdoo, Harriette Pipes, editor. *Black Families. SAGE Publications, 2007.*

McDonald, Natalie Hope. "Death of Transgender Woman Dominique Rem'mie Fells Ruled a Homicide; Gruesome Slaying Shakes Community." *PhillyVoice,* 12 June 2020, www.phillyvoice.com/dominique-remmie-fells-death-black-transgender-woman-homicide-lgbtq-reaction/. Accessed 7 Apr. 2022.

McGuffey, C. Shawn. "Blacks and Racial Appraisals: Gender, Race, and Intraracial Rape." *Black Sexualities: Probing Powers, Passions, Practices and Policies,* edited by Juan Battle and Sandra L. Barnes, Rutgers University Press, 2010, pp. 273-98.

Miranda, Alexis O., Bogusia Molina, Sandi L. MacVane. "Coping With the Murder of a Loved One: Counseling Survivors of Murder Victims in Groups." *The Journal for Specialists in Group Work,* vol. 28, no. 1, 2003, pp. 48-63.

Moore, James L., and Madonna G. Constantine. "Development and Initial Validation of the Collectivistic Coping Styles Measured with African, Asian, and Latin American International Students." *Journal of Mental Health Counseling*, vol. 27, no. 4, 2005, pp. 329-347.

Morgan, Rachel E., and Jennifer L. Truman. *Criminal Victimization, 2019*. NCJ 255113, US Department of Justice. Bureau of Justice Statistics, 2020, p. 53. *Zotero*, www.bjs.gov/content/pub/pdf/cv19.pdf. Accessed 7 Apr. 2022.

Mowatt, Rasul A. "Black Lives as Snuff: The Silent Complicity in Viewing Black Death." *Biography*, vol. 41, no. 4, 2018, pp. 777-806.

Muhammad, Khalil Gibran. *The Condemnation of Blackness: Race, Crime, and the Making of Modern Urban America, With a New Preface*. Harvard University Press, 2010.

National Academies of Sciences, Engineering, and Medicine. "The Root Causes of Health Inequity." *Communities in Action: Pathways to Health Equity*, edited by James N. Weinstein et al., National Academies Press, 2017, pp. 99-184.

Noonan, Allan S., Hector Eduardo Velasco-Mondragon, and Fernando A. Wagner. "Improving the Health of African Americans in the USA: An Overdue Opportunity for Social Justice." *Public Health Review*, vol. 37, no. 12, 2016, p. 12.

Onderko, Karen. "What Is Trauma?–Definition, Symptoms, Responses, Types & Therapy." *Unyte-ILs*, integratedlistening.com/what-is-trauma/. Accessed 17 July 2020.

Oppel Jr., Richard A., and Derrick Bryson Taylor. "Breonna Taylor's Death: What To Know." *The New York Times*, 17 July 2020, www.nytimes.com/article/breonna-taylor-police.html. Accessed 7 Apr. 2022.

Parkes, Colin Murray. "Psychiatric Problems Following Bereavement by Murder or Manslaughter." *British Journal of Psychiatry*, vol. 162, no. 1, 1993, pp. 49-52.

Platt, Tony. "Crime and Punishment in the United States: Immediate and Long-Term Reforms from a Marxist Perspective." *Crime and Social Justice*, vol. 18, 1982, pp. 38-45.

Potter, Gary. "The History of Policing in the United States, Part 1." *Eastern Kentucky University*, June 2013, plsonline.eku.edu/insidelook

/history-policing-united-states-part-1. Accessed 7 Apr. 2022.

Ramsden, Pam. *Vicarious Trauma, PTSD and Social Media: Does Watching Graphic Videos Cause Trauma?* 2017.

Rando, Therese A. "Complications in Mourning Traumatic Death." *Living with Grief After Sudden Loss: Suicide, Homicide, Accident, Heart Attack, Stroke*, edited by Kenneth J. Doka, Taylor & Francis, 1996, pp. 139-59.

Redmond, Lula. M. "Sudden Violent Death." *Living with Grief After Sudden Loss: Suicide, Homicide, Accident, Heart Attack and Stroke*, edited by Kenneth J. Doka, Taylor & Francis, 1996, pp. 53-71.

Redmond, Lula. M. *Surviving: When Someone You Love Was Murdered: A Professional's Guide to Group Grief Therapy for Families and Friends of Murder Victims*. Psychological Consultation and Education Services, 1989.

Reichel, Philip L. "The Misplaced Emphasis on Urbanization in Police Development." *Policing and Society*, vol. 3, no. 1, 1922, pp. 1-12.

Rheingold, Alyssa A., et al. "Prevalence and Mental Health Outcomes of Homicide Survivors in a Representative US Sample of Adolescents: Data from the 2005 National Survey of Adolescents." *Journal of Child Psychology and Psychiatry*, vol. 52, no. 6, 2012, pp. 687-94.

Richardson, Allissa V. *Bearing Witness While Black: African Americans, Smartphones, and the New Protest #Journalism*. Oxford University Press, 2020.

Rynearson, E. K., and Joseph M. McCreery. "Bereavement After Homicide: A Synergism of Trauma and Loss." *American Journal of Psychiatry*, vol. 150, no. 2, 1993, pp. 258-61.

Semega, Jessica, et al. *Income and Poverty in the United States: 2018*. P60-266(RV), U.S. Government Printing Office, 2020, www.census.gov/content/dam/Census/library/publications/2019/demo/p60-266.pdf. Accessed Apr. 7 2022.

Sharpe, Tanya L. "Sources of Support for African-American Family Members of Homicide Victims." *Journal of Ethnic & Cultural Diversity in Social Work*, vol. 17, no. 2, 2008, pp. 197-216.

Sharpe, Tanya L. "Understanding the Sociocultural Context of Coping for African American Family Members of Homicide Victims: A

Conceptual Model." *Trauma, Violence, & Abuse*, vol. 16, no. 1, 2015, pp. 48-59.

Sharpe, Tanya L., and Javier Boyas. "We Fall down: The African American Experience of Coping with the Homicide of a Loved One." *Journal of Black Studies*, vol. 42, no. 6, 2011, pp. 855-73.

Spalek, Basia. *Crime Victims: Theory, Policy and Practice*. Palgrave Macmillan, 2017.

Spitzer, Steven. "The Rationalization of Crime Control in Capitalist Society." *Contemporary Crises*, vol. 3, no. 2, 1979, pp. 197-206.

Spungen, Deborah. *Homicide: The Hidden Victims: A Guide for Professionals*. SAGE Publications, 1998.

Taylor, Robert Joseph, Linda M. Chatters, James S. Jackson. "Religious and Spiritual Involvement Among Older African Americans, Caribbean Blacks, and Non-Hispanic Whites: Findings From the National Survey of American Life." *Journal of Gerontology*, vol. 62, no. B.4, 2007, pp. S238-50.

The Global Burden of Disease 2016 Injury Collaborators. "Global Mortality From Firearms, 1990-2016." *JAMA*, vol. 320, no. 8, 2018, pp. 792-814.

Ulmer, Jeffery T., Casey T. Harris, and Darrell Steffensmeier. "Racial and Ethnic Disparities in Structural Disadvantage and Crime: White, Black, and Hispanic Comparisons." *Social Science Quarterly*, vol. 93, no. 3, 2012, pp. 799-819.

United Nations Office on Drugs and Crime. *Global Study on Homicide 2019*. 2019, www.unodc.org/documents/data-and-analysis/gsh/Booklet1.pdf. Accessed Apr. 7 2022.

United Nations Women. "Victim Support Unit." *Global Database on Violence Against Women*, evaw-global-database.unwomen.org/fr/countries/americas/jamaica/1998/victim-support-unit. Accessed 7 Apr. 2022.

Winter, Deborah DuNann, Dana C. Leighton. "Structural Violence Section Introduction." *Peace, Conflict, and Violence: Peace Psychology for the 21st Century*, edited by Daniel J. Christie, Richard V. Wagner, and Deborah DuNann Winter, Prentice Hall, 2001, pp. 99-101.

Wong, Paul T. P., Lilian C. J. Wong, and W. J. Lonner, editors. *Handbook of Multicultural Perspectives on Stress and Coping*. Springer, 2005.

World Report on Violence and Health: Summary. World Health Organization, 2002. *Gemeinsamer Bibliotheksverbund ISBN*, www.who.int/violence_injury_prevention/violence/world_report/en/summary_en.pdf. Accessed 7 Apr. 2022.

Zinzow, Heidi. M., et al. "Prevalence and Mental Health Correlates of Witnessed Parental and Community Violence in a National Sample of Adolescents." *Journal of Child Psychology and Psychiatry*, vol. 50, no. 4, 2009, pp. 441-50.

Zinzow, Heidi M., et al. "Examining Posttraumatic Stress Symptoms in a National Sample of Homicide Survivors: Prevalence and Comparison to Other Violence Victims." *Journal of Traumatic Stress*, vol. 24, no. 6, 2011, pp. 743-46.

Chapter 2

Using Critical Race and Anticolonial Theories to Reframe the Conversation on Youth Violence

Paul Banahene Adjei, Delores V. Mullings, and Sulaimon Giwa

Reports of Black youth shootings, stabbings, and beatings in Toronto have become a common occurrence in mainstream media crime stories. Today, almost every Black person knows somebody—a friend, neighbour, family member, or community member—who has been affected by violence, and particularly gun violence. In 2019 alone, there were 490 shootings, with forty-four gun-related deaths in Toronto (Cardoso).[1] The year 2018 was dubbed "a deadly year of gun violence in Toronto" (MacLeod). Seventeen victims were killed in gun-related attacks in the first half of 2018 in the City of Toronto alone. By the end of 2018, Toronto recorded over 406 shooting incidents and fifty-one gun-related deaths. Even without race-based statistics, we are aware through media coverage of these deaths that Black youth living in socially vulnerable neighbourhoods constitute a substantial proportion of shooting victims in Toronto.

The death of Black youth to gun violence in Toronto is not a recent issue. In 2007, *CityNews* reported eighty-three incidents of gun-related homicides involving Black youth in Toronto alone. Mr. Bacchus, who works with Black youths, has attended more than fifteen funerals involving gun-related violence against Black youths between 2007 and

2012 (Paperny). Victor Beausoleil, who lives in a predominantly Black neighbourhood, has grieved the loss of at least twenty of his friends who have been gunned down at subway stations, barbershops, and on the streets of Toronto (Paperny). In 2013, the incidence of gun violence among Black youths in Toronto reached epidemic proportions and motivated Josh Matlow, a Toronto city counsellor, to urge the city to implement the 2008 Roy McMurtry Committee's Report on Youth Violence (Dhillon).[2] The Black population in Toronto has remained approximately 7 to 9 per cent of the population over several years (Statistic Canada "Population Estimates Program"). Yet we have seen escalation of gun-related deaths among Black youths, without much abating over the years. This is a crisis of proportion and an important indication of a systemic problem that cannot be stereotyped as merely personal deficiencies.

Oftentimes, the media and public conversations around gun violence in Toronto are framed in a way that vilifies Black families and neighbourhoods that are primarily populated by Black Canadians. For example, Marcus Gee, in an article published in the *Globe and Mail,* described Black youth violence as a disfiguring stain on the success story of Toronto's multiculturalism. Chris Doucette wrote in the *Toronto Sun* that politicians and public officers who hold dialogue with members of Black Lives Matter (Toronto) to hear their concerns about racism are responsible for violence among Black youth in Toronto: "I don't blame Black Lives Matter, I blame the idiots who listened to them" (Doucette, par. 6). The vilification continued when Mayor John Tory and Councillor Giorgio Mammoliti of Toronto equated Black youth to "sewer rats" and "cockroaches" because of their involvement in gun violence (Morgan). The anti-Black racist rhetoric and discriminatory attitudes towards Black people in general reached an obscene level when the Ontario Minister of Community Safety and Corrections Michael Tibollo suggested that he had to wear a bulletproof vest before going to a section of Jane and Finch—a predominantly Black-populated neighbourhood (Merali).

For Michael Tibollo, John Tory, Mammoliti, and other politicians and administrators who think like them, Black Canadians are a homogenous group in which degeneracy—such as gun violence, drugs trafficking and dependency, criminality, and immorality—is a part of their normative history, culture, and identity (Adjei; Walcott et al.).

Consequently, anti-Black racist state policies have been established to ensure that Black people in Toronto are consistently under the gaze of racist law enforcement individuals and decisionmakers, who must necessarily demonstrate through their own violent actions the rhetoric of keeping white Torontonians safe. One such example of anti-Black racist policies is the community contacts policy, also known as "carding"—a supposedly intelligence gathering policy that gives police officers the right to stop and question individuals in public or private places and document the encounter without any particular offence being investigated. Although carding is a policy expected to be implemented across race, class, gender, and other matrices of differences, it eventually became a legalized means of targeting and harassing young Black men and women. In the book *The Skin We're In: A Year of Black Resistance and Power,* Toronto journalist Desmond Cole notes that he has been stopped and interrogated by the police more than fifty times. The *Toronto Star* agrees with Desmond Cole after the paper analyzed police data about the carding system: Black people are seventeen times more likely than white people to be carded by police (Rankin and Winsa). Such was the problem with carding for Black people that in 2016, the United Nations Working Group of Experts on People of African Descent expressed serious concerns about systemic anti-Black racism in the criminal justice system in Canada. The group specifically mentioned the arbitrary use of carding to target Black people disproportionately in Canada (United Nation News). Given the stereotypes and misconceptions about Black people in Toronto, particularly Black youth, what is the relevance of critical race and anticolonial theories in helping to understand the white mainstream discourse of Black youth violence in Toronto?

In this chapter, we employ such theories to frame the conversation about Black youth violence in Toronto. We argue that Black youth violence in Toronto is neither a pathology nor the aberrant behaviour of Black families but rather is a symptom of colonial, racist, and classist society. Throughout the discussion, the term youth and young people are used interchangeably to include individuals who are between the ages of fifteen and twenty-nine years. We recognize that Black youth is not the only group that lives with the consequences of youth gun violence; however, for the purpose of this discussion, Black youth is the focus.

Critical Race and Anticolonial Theoretical Readings of Youth Violence

Several academic theories have offered some explanations for youth violence in general. Biosocial theory attributes youth violence to biological anomalies or physical disabilities (Ellis; Englander; Fishbein). Psychological theories see the root cause of youth violence as how one's mental process interacts with their social environment (Aichorn; Bandura; Kohlberg). For social disorganization theory, youth violence has more to do with neighbourhood dynamics and less to do with biological defects (Bursik; Sampson and Groves). The economic deprivation theory blames capitalism and economic exploitation that push youth to the point where violence becomes the only choice (Bursik and Grasmic; Feather). Social learning theory sees a direct correlation between youth violence and the individual's family and peer network (Akers and Jensen; Winfree Jr. et al.). The perceptions of injustice, crime and violence theory suggests that any perception of unfairness and bias treatments in the justice system based on racial and socio-economic differences can create mistrust that may trigger violence (James, Bunch, and Clay-Warner; MacDonald et al.).

Although these theories are useful to understand some aspects of youth violence in Toronto, they do not adequately demonstrate how youth violence can be a product of historical and contemporary colonial and racist sociopolitical arrangements. We argue in this chapter that youth violence, particularly Black youth violence, cannot be fully understood unless these arrangements are explored within historical and contemporary colonial and racist contexts that affect today's social relations. Frantz Fanon demonstrated in *Black Skin, White Masks* that the deployment of racism persistently portrays racialized and classed people as degenerates devoid of human characteristics and therefore unworthy of respect. Such understanding, as rightly noted in Fanon's writings, informs how Black youth and their violence experiences are analyzed and responded to by state-sponsored institutions. Research demonstrates that Critical Race Theory and Anti-Colonial Theory can be useful frameworks to understand how the regime of Whiteness and White supremacy relies on laws, policies, and practices to maintain the subordination of racialized people in society. In this Chapter, we employ critical race and anticolonial theories to flesh out ways in which

Black youth violence might be understood within the broader context of structural colonial and racist practices in Toronto.

Critical Race Theory

Critical race theory (CRT) emerged in the 1980s from a group of predominantly racialized civil rights activists and legal scholars, including Derrick Bell, Kimberlé Crenshaw, Richard Delgado, and Patricia Williams. Legal scholars felt the enthusiasm that greeted racial reforms in the United States during the Civil Rights Movements was gradually dissipating (Bell, "Serving Two Masters"; "Brown v. Board"; Freeman). They also noted that the old approaches of conducting protests and appealing to the moral sensibilities of American citizens were yielding fewer results (Crenshaw, "Critical Race Theory"; Ladson-Billings, "Just What Is Critical Race Theory"). After the seminal critical legal studies alternative conference on the silence of race in 1977, CRT as an activist movement exploded and such scholars as Richard Delgado, Kimberlé Crenshaw, Angela Harris, Charles Lawrence, Mari Matsuda, Patricia Williams, Neil Gotanda, Eric Yamamoto, Francisco Valdes, and Kelvin Johnson built on the earlier discussion of race and racism in jurisprudence. Today, CRT has expanded to several facets of academic disciplines, including the field of education (Ladson-Billings, "Just What Is Critical Race Theory") and social work (Adjei et al., "The Fragility of Goodness"; Adjei and Minka; Mullings, "Racism in Canadian Social Policy"; Mullings, "The Racial Institution of Whiteness").

CRT's tenets are used as an across-academic discipline guide for academic scholars. Black youth violence, as a phenomenon of historical and current racial oppression, can be viewed, analyzed, and understood from a CRT perspective. First, CRT recognizes that racism is engrained in the fabric and system of Euro-American Canadian society and that racism is normal and a natural order of doing things. Crenshaw argues that racism is the scaffold that structures Euro-American Canadian society to the extent that there cannot be any "perch outside the social dynamics of racial power from which to merely observe and analyze" ("Critical Race Theory" 13). The Canadian nation state was founded on racial laws that sanctioned white people as "exalted subjects" with unlimited access to wealth, status, and power (Thobani). These Canadian racial laws sought to reject the humanities of Black and

Indigenous people, subjecting them to a life structured by poverty, poor housing, crime, poor healthcare (even when it is universal), over-policing, unemployment, and underemployment (Walcott). These structural inequalities have been the subjects of discourse in the exacerbation and persistence of different forms of violence, especially gun violence, among Black youth within the Toronto context and beyond, spanning several decades. In her article "So Seldom for Us, So Often Against Us: Blacks and Law in Canada," Esmeralda Thornhill argues that the laws of Canada, which are supposed to serve and protect Black people, have historically failed them and have often, by acts of omission and commission, colluded with racism to subordinate and inferiorize Blacks. Thornhill argues that Blacks who entered Canada between 1791 and 1860 with the hope of a promise of fulfilled lives soon learned the hard way that the Canadian promise of prosperity and safety did not include Black people. Instead, Blacks were alienated, excluded, segregated, and most often denied opportunities to access public education and services. Blacks who sought redemption from the laws soon learned that the Canadian justice system is "a sword of oppression and not a shield of protection" for Black people (Thornhill, "So Seldom for Us" 324). For example, it was the law of Canada in 1734 that sanctioned the public execution of the Black slave Marie-Joseph Angelique (Cooper). Again, it was Canadian law in 1743 that notarized and authenticated the bill of sale of five "Negroes" by businessperson Charles Rhéaume to Louis Cureux de St-Germain, a resident of Montreal, thus making it normal and legal to buy Black people as chattel property to be used at the whims and caprices of white slave owners (Thornhill, "Focus on Racism"). It was the same Canadian law in 1760, after the French surrendered to the English, that decreed all Black and Indigenous people would remain slaves, the sellable property of the French and Canadian owners (Thornhill, "So Seldom for Us"). The same Canadian laws decreed between 1918 and 1945 that white merchants' right to contract freely with whomever they pleased far outweighed the right to protect and shield Black Canadians from any discriminatory treatments (Thornhill, "So Seldom for Us"). We also know that Canadian law of the 1950s opened the door for white Canadian middle and upper classes to visit the Caribbean and recruit young, healthy, and educated Black women with no dependents to come to Canada to serve as nannies to white Canadian families (Calliste).

To think of these anti-Black racist laws as something rooted in the past, that exist outside of Black youths' experience with violence, is to disregard their structural and systemic effects on contemporary Black experiences. Rinaldo Walcott argues that Black-on-Black crime is the end product of failed initiatives of racial inclusion in a post-civil-rights world as well as the failure of Canadian institutions to effectively incorporate the experience, histories, and identities of Black people into the fabric of Canadian society (Austin). From CRT perspective, therefore, Black youth violence in Toronto, like elsewhere, cannot be understood without examining the racist, social, and cultural arrangements in these contexts that deny and ignore the humanity of Black people.

CRT calls for a race-based intersectional analysis of social issues in order to understand their material consequences on racialized people (Crenshaw, "Critical Race Theory"). Intersectionality centres race in multiple and complex ways in which identity matrices of race, class, gender, sexuality, disability, religion, and ethnicity interact to shape multiple dimensions of people's life. CRT argues that race and racism are so endemic and permanent in our society that they are "central rather than marginal factors in defining and explaining individual experiences of the law" (Russel 762-63). One major challenge in policies and practices designed to bring social change is their failure to engage race in its analysis of social difference. These days, it has become a habit for people to use class-based analysis to dismiss race-based suggestions. We do not deny that race and racism intersect with class and other forms of discrimination to impact negatively on Black people. We, however, agree with Critical race scholars that "class oppression alone cannot account for racial oppression" (Barnes 1868). Thus, we argue that racism intersects with broad and entrenched structural inequalities to impact on Black youths' disproportional involvement with gun violence.

In the article "The Canadian War on Drugs: Structural Violence and Unequal Treatment of Black Canadians," Akwatu Khenti's analysis shows the centrality of race to understanding the Canadian war on drugs. Khenti argues that Black people in Canada have been victims of intensive policing since the inception of the war on drugs in the 1980s. Although the war on drugs was designed to arrest high-level drug dealers considered dangerous to public safety, the war was waged against low-level cannabis users and dealers. Further, the war on drugs was supposed to target every Canadian, yet second only to Indigenous people, Black people have been the most arrested and imprisoned group in Canada (Owusu-Bempah and Wortely). The suggested explanation would be that Black people commit more crimes than other Canadians do. The Canadian law enforcement officials appear to subscribe to the same idea and often hold Black people responsible for the widespread illicit drug use in Canada (Mosher). This is why Black people are overrepresented in federal and provincial prisons. This overrepresentation among mainly young Black men, has implications for lower employment skill sets, higher levels of unemployment, and low access to education that eventually affect their reintegration into communities after imprisonment, and subsequent violence involvement. Scot Wortley and Julian Tanner argue that white people spread illicit drugs equally or more than Black people do. In their survey of 2000 Toronto youth, Wortley and Tanner observed that more white high school students reported greater drug use and trafficking patterns than Black students. Specifically, 45 per cent of White students indicated lifetime cannabis use compared to 39 per cent of Black students. In the same survey, 6 per cent of white students reported lifetime use of cocaine or crack in contrast to 2 per cent of Black students.

Similarly, 17 per cent of white students reported selling illicit drugs during their lifetime compared to 15 per cent of Black students (Owusu-Bempah and Wortley; Wortley and Tanner). Despite the reality that whites are equally, if not more, responsible for spreading illicit drugs as Blacks, the 1995 Report of the Commission on Systemic Racism in the Ontario Criminal Justice System reported an increase of 1164 per cent in the number of Black prison admissions for drug trafficking between 1986 and 1993 compared to an increase of 151 per cent for white admissions in the same period (Gittens, Cole and Commission on Systemic Racism in the Ontario Criminal Justice System). If whites use and sell illicit drugs equally and sometimes more than Blacks do, what explains Black people's overrepresentation in prisons for using or/and selling more illicit drugs than whites? Anti-Black racism stereotypes Black people as criminals and therefore targeted as the enemy in the war on drugs even if whites are equally or more involved in illicit drug use and sale (Alexander; Tanovich; Welch).

The extent of the war on drugs and its impact on the Black communities have been determined to be partly accountable for Black youth violence (Ontario Human Rights Commission, *Paying the Price;* Rankin; Rankin and Winsa). Many young Black people have been traumatized by their constant interactions with militarized police units whose only interest is to arrest, harass, and dehumanize Black people because they are presumed criminals, even before they act (Fitzgerald). From an intersectional point of view, theoretical analysis of Black people's experiences must ground the material existence of living as Black in Canada. This is more reason why Black youth violence cannot be fully understood if it is examined outside the lens of race and racism.

CRT recognizes the power of storytelling. In a white settler society like Canada, where White hegemony continues to determine how systems and structures function and whose story is to be believed and accepted, counter-storying is an effective method of pushing Black people's stories into the centre of knowledge production (Solórzano and Yosso; Stovall). Carmen Montecinos rightly argues that the ideology of racism creates, maintains, and justifies the use of "master narratives" in storytelling. Here, we draw from the earlier work of Richard Valencia and Daniel Solórzano, which demonstrates that the master narratives, or majoritarian stories, tend to pathologize and blame communities of colour for their social problems.

Within Toronto, the majoritarian narratives on Black youth violence blame Black single motherhood and absentee fathers for Black youth violence (Lawson). In the majoritarian narratives, Black youth are called "thugs," "gangsters," "criminals," "brutes," "cockroaches," and "sewer rats." Tamari Kitossa argues that the use of such race-coded words in the majoritarian narratives are not innocent of racist content. Rather, they are intended to trigger deep-seated feelings of revulsion against Black people and to give police officers permission to harass, arrest, and even use violence against them. In fact, those who speak about violent policing in the Black communities are often told that Black-on-Black violence is insidious and deserves more attention than overpolicing in the Black communities (Gee; Paradkar).

Understandingly, Black-on-Black violence is high, but so is white-on-white violence. Yet the gaze is never cast on white-on-white violence because in majoritarian narratives, whites exist only as individuals and Blacks exist as a collective. The privilege of being white is that the majoritarian narratives will never use one's mistakes to judge the rest of white people. Thus, every white Canadian can be assured that the crimes of Hells Angels Motorcycle Club members (Bolan; Edwards) or serial killers—such as Paul Bernardo, Robert Pickton, and Russell Johnson, to name a few—will never be used to judge them. Yet, Black people are not accorded the same treatment. Instead, Black people are treated as a collective group and the crime of one Black person is treated as the crime of all Black people.

The majoritarian narratives about Black youth violence distort and silence the Black experience. They fail to mention anti-Black racism in policing, which through carding and other oppressive methods, harass, intimidate, and racially profile many young Black people. The majoritarian narratives do not include information that the darker one's skin is, the less likely one is made to fit into Canadian society (Reitz et al.). The majoritarian narratives do not include the fact that driving an expensive car as a Black person poses a real threat to the driver being stopped and arrested or being shot by the police (Blatchford). Such majoritarian narratives do not consider the suggestion of Judges Rosenberg, Justice Dennis O'Connor, and Justice Karen Weiler, as well as that of Superior Court Justice David Harris, that young Black people's behaviours must be examined through the lenses of their systemic racist experiences in Canada (Gordon; Makin). In sentencing Jeremy Kandhai—a twenty-five-year-old Black male who had pleaded guilty to possessing a prohibited firearm—the Superior Court Justice David Harris writes, "One's head would have to be in the sand not to acknowledge that Mr. Kandhai's responsibility is affected in some measure by the racism and poverty in the community in which he grew up" (Hasham, para. 6).

The silencing within the majoritarian narratives about how academic streaming and suspensions hinder Black students' academic progress in Canada (Gordon) requires counter-storying of Black experiences in Canada. As Gerald Vizenor puts it, "When the victims talk back, they stop being victims" (85). Counter-storying links the current Black youth violence to the systemic anti-Black racism experiences in Canada and demonstrates that Black youth violence is not aberrant behaviour of criminal individuals but an expected outcome of a racist society. The majoritarian narratives of shaming and blaming victims must give way to counter-storying that identifies the main source of the problem: a racist system. We are talking about a racist system that engages in mass incarceration of young Black people for offenses that if they were White, they would just get away with a warning (Owusu-Bempah and Wortley; Wortley). In counter-storying, we want to talk about a racist system that hesitates to hold police officers accountable when they shoot and kill unarmed Black people (Dunn). By employing counter-storying, we hope to challenge the colour-blind analysis of Black youth violence in Toronto and elsewhere.

Anticolonial Theory

Anticolonial theory allows for effective theorization of social issues emerging from colonial relations. The theory explores the nature and extent of social domination, in particular how relations of power in multiple places work to establish dominant-subordinate relations. History and contexts are important to anticolonial theory. For example, anticolonial theory acknowledges the important roles of European colonialism in constructing dominant images for white people and subordinate images for Black people. One such racist colonial creation is the false representation of Black people as violent and white people as innocent, benevolent, and saviours (Principe). Yet white settlers were the ones who used violence to impose their values, culture, and worldviews on Africans and Indigenous people. As Fanon rightly notes, "Their [White settlers and Indigenous and Black people] first encounter was marked by violence and their existence together—that is to say the exploitation of the native by the settler-was carried on by dint of a great array of bayonets and cannons" ("Grove Press" 36). In Canada, the white settlers committed physical, cultural, and spiritual violence against Indigenous people as well as Black people, who were brought to Canada and treated as slaves (Aiken; Gallant; Henry and Tator; Wigmore). White settlers dehumanized Black people in Canada and subjected them to exploitative and repressive conditions (Aiken; Gallant; Henry and Tator; Wigmore). Black people in Canada are still living with the detrimental effects of colonial racist violence. In many ways, we cannot fully understand and discuss Black youth violence without delving into the violent colonial racist history of Canada. White settlers used random acts of torture as well as physical and psychological violence to achieve their objectives of taking Indigenous people's land and forcing Black people to work for free to develop the land. Black youth have learned through violent colonial experience that physical violence can achieve a lot if used against others. How can we today tell the same people who lost everything—history, identity, values, worldviews, cultures, and possessions—through colonial violence that violence is not good. In a way, the only violence Black people know is the white settlers' violence. As Jean-Paul Sartre wrote in his preface to Fanon's *The Wretched of the Earth*: "You said they [Black people] understand nothing but violence? Of course, first, the only violence is the settler's, but soon they will make it their own; that is to say, the same violence is thrown back upon us [white settlers] as when our reflection comes forward to meet us when we go toward a mirror" (17).

There are three key points that anticolonial and critical race theories contribute to the understanding of youth violence in Toronto: (1) structural racism and manifestations of violence; (2) how violence dehumanizes the self and creates subhumanity; and (3) how violence can resist inferiority complex syndrome. The rest of the section expands on these three key points.

Structural Racism and Manifestations of Violence

Violence is endemic in society, and as such, it is manifested through multiple ways in private and public spaces. Donald Macedo, in his introductory chapter to Paulo Freire's *Pedagogy of the Oppressed,* argues that violence at the individual level cannot be adequately understood, explained, and analyzed without critically examining structural and institutional violence. Anticolonial and critical race theories help us to understand the link between individual violent behaviours and structural and systemic violence. We draw on Fanon's scholarship to elaborate on this point.

In the chapter "Colonial War and Mental Disorders" in *The Wretched of the Earth,* Fanon serialized disturbing cases of colonial violence and their psychical and emotional effects on people that were colonized. Each case shows a unique understanding of the effects of structural and institutional violence on victims and survivors of violence. Analogous to Fanon's colonized other, state representatives—such as those in the criminal (in)justice system, including public defenders and state prosecutors, judges, and police officers—implement harsh, inequitable, and discriminatory policies and practices that ensure Black youth are constantly surveilled, overpoliced, violated, and brutalized with a focus of protecting the white public. Fanon used stories and perspectives of the youth to demonstrate the pervasiveness of racism and the laws that fail to account for the Black experience. For the purpose of our present discussion, we review Series B, specifically "Case No. 1: The Murder of a European Boy by Two Algerian Playmates."

Two Algerians youth aged thirteen and fourteen were accused of killing one of their European schoolmates. What makes the story even more disturbing was that this European schoolmate was the only friend these youths had, yet they intentionally murdered him. Fanon, as one of the clinical psychiatrists handling the casefile, tried to understand the young Algerians' motivation for killing their only friend. From the account of the thirteen-year-old Algerian, they killed their European friend as an act of revenge against all Europeans:

> We weren't a bit cross with him. Every Thursday we used to go and play with catapults together, on the hill above the village. He was a good friend of ours. He isn't [sic] to go to school anymore because he wanted to be a mason like his father. One day we decided to kill him, because the Europeans want to kill all the Arabs. We can't kill big people. But we could kill ones like him, because he was the same age as us. (Fanon, *The Wretched of the Earth* 270-271)

The fourteen-year-old youth also tried to justify the killing of his European friend by citing instances in which European soldiers killed two of his family members. The following excerpts detail exchanges between Fanon and the fourteen-year-old youth:

> Fourteen-year-old: Two of my family were killed then. At home, they said that the French has sworn to kill us all [Algerians], one after the other I wanted to take to the mountains, but I was too young. So X—and I said we'd kill a European.
>
> Fanon: Why?
>
> Fourteen-year-old: In your opinion, what should we have done?
>
> Fanon: I don't know. But you are a child and what is happening concerns grown-up people.

Fourteen-year-old: But they kill children too....

Fanon: That is no reason for killing your friend.

Fourteen-year-old: Well, kill him I did. Now you can do what you like.

Fanon: Had your friend done anything to harm you?

Fourteen-year-old: Not a thing. (Fanon, *The Wretched of the Earth* 272)

Although the case seems disturbing, it also reveals how structural violence can influence violent behaviour in that the youths experienced the murder and beatings of their families and friends and their violence became a learned behaviour and one of survival. Fanon used this case and others to make a point that individual violent behaviours are not a product of biological and cultural defects but rather the manifestation of a violent and oppressive society.

Black people in Toronto are victims and survivors of harsh institutional policies and practices, such as carding, school suspension and expulsion, child welfare apprehension, and over-incarceration, which can create an impression that they are surplus bodies with little or no value to the Canadian state. Structurally, these practices and policies exemplify the perpetuation of anti-Black racism. When Black youth, their families and friends are treated as disposable, it motivates feelings of inferiority and lack of self-worth, which are catalysts to violent behaviour, as youth may use guns to feel a sense of security and protection. We use public reports and news publications to make transparent the insidiousness of anti-Black racism in Toronto (this will be expanded on below).

After the so-called Yonge Street Riots in the summer of 1992, then Premier Bob Rae appointed Stephen Lewis as his advisor on race relations and in his role, Lewis was mandated to consult widely with community stakeholders and politicians to determine the impetus for the violence and offer recommendations to address the problems. Lewis's *Report on Racism in Ontario to the Premier* highlighted the prevalence of anti-Black racism in Toronto. The report discussed some specific aspects of anti-Black racism, including high unemployment and underemployment, police brutality, and excessive racial profiling among Black youth. The report further suggested that such institutional and structural violence can contribute to Black youth's sense of alienation, isolation, and rejection:

> First, what we are dealing with, at root, and fundamentally, is anti-Black racism. While it is obviously true that every visible minority community experience the indignities and wounds of systemic discrimination throughout Southern Ontario, it is the Black community which is the focus. It is Blacks who are being shot, it is Black youth that is unemployed in excessive numbers, it is Black students who are being inappropriately streamed in schools, it is Black kids who are disproportionately dropping out, it is housing communities with large concentrations of Black residents where the sense of vulnerability and disadvantage is most acute, it is Black employees, professional and non-professional, on whom the doors of upward equity slam shut. Just as the soothing balm of "multiculturalism" cannot mask racism, so racism cannot mask its primary target. (1)

Other reports echo the findings of the *Lewis Report* including the Ontario Human Rights Commission's *Paying the Price: The Cost of Racial Profiling* (2003), which reported Blacks were among the racialized groups that experience racial profiling. Racial profiling also exists at the Toronto District School Board (TDSB) under the guise of the Ontario Safe Schools Act or "Zero Tolerance." The Ontario Human Rights Commission report *Ontario Safe Schools Act: School Discipline and Discrimination* found that "In the Greater Toronto Area (GTA) and other parts of Ontario there is a strong perception, which is supported by some independent evidence, that the Act and school board policies are having a disproportionate impact on racial minority students, particularly Black students, and students with disabilities" (4). Institutional anti-Black racism is further demonstrated in higher rates of school suspension among Black students so that one in every seven Black grade seven and eight students was suspended compared to one in every twenty white students in the same grades (Rankin and Winsa). Scholars report that institutional anti-Black racism is evident in Black youth disenfranchisement in school, where four out of ten Black students are pushed out of school through harassment, expulsion, and suspension, and many ultimately drop out of school before completing grade twelve (Adjei and Agyepong; Dei). The remaining ones are taught to despise themselves and everything about their race, history and culture by teachers, social workers, guidance counsellors, and administrators in the education system, which is riffed with anti-Black racist policies and practices When school administrators push Black youth out of school through expulsion and child welfare workers separate them from their families by apprehension, they are disconnected and dislocated from their families and friends. These actions socialize Black youth to hate themselves and everything that they represent; therefore, it becomes a self-fulfilling prophecy for them to self-destruct through gun violence that seeks to destroy other Black youth, which is similar to the Algerian youth who killed their only white friend.

Former Ontario Premier Mike Harris's administration cut many social services that supported working-class Black families. As many studies and committees reports show, the short, medium, and long-term consequences of these cuts have played a significant role in creating an environment for youth violence (Chadwick-Parkes; McMurtry and Curling; Walcott et al.). In addition, David Hulchanski's study found that the number of people living in poverty in Toronto has increased significantly over the last thirty years and that poor neighbourhoods are becoming more racially and geographically segregated and isolated. Hulchanski further cautions that if the trend continues, Toronto will witness the kinds of crime and violence that is common in some major urban centres in the United States. Dr. Samuel Getachew, in his interview with *Huffington Post Canada* after the second tragic shooting at the Toronto Eaton Centre, echoes Hulchanski's observation: "The shootings are not the issue; they are symptoms of larger issues of poverty, exclusion and stereotypes and racism. All the media's focus is on this one horrible criminal act, but the real story of what's going on in Toronto is consistently ignored" (Getachew par. 6).

Clearly, structural and institutional anti-Black racist and classist policies and practices cannot be decoupled from Black youth violence. Fanon diagnosed fratricide in the Black community in Algeria: "The [Black] man will first manifest this aggressiveness which has been deposited in his bones against his own people. This is the period when the ['n...'] beat each other up, and the police and magistrates do not know which way to turn" (*The Wretched of the Earth* 52).

Fanon's discussion about Black Algerian men can be extended to include the experiences of Black youth in Toronto, given the historical colonial trauma and violence they experience. The continuous violence among Black youth in Toronto is dubbed "Black-on-Black violence." The violence perpetuated towards each other in the Black community is exemplified by the gun violence being discussed in this chapter. However, in the case of Toronto's youth violence, the scenario is played out differently than in Fanon's description of what happened on the street of Algeria. In the Toronto context, police and magistrates have helped to create public discourses of fear and perceived savagery of Black youth.

To be clear, there is no suggestion that Black youth ought to interpret anti-Black racism and poverty as a license to be violent, nor are we suggesting that all Black youth, having experienced anti-Black racism and classism, will become involved in gun violence. However, we argue that one cannot fully address Black youth violence in Toronto without understanding systemic issues that influence how Black youth may behave. Isolation, exclusion, mental wellness, racism, sexism, and classism can have profound effects on Black youth. As Fanon argued, these experiences can promote negative attitudes towards oneself and others in similarly oppressed groups. Violence among Black youth is not normal as perceived by the larger society; rather, it is a chronic symptom of structural racism and other oppressions. Therefore, violence among Black youth in Toronto must be understood within the context of mundane brutality of institutional and systemic colonialism and anti-Black racism that exist in Toronto; it ought not be misrepresented as inherent defects of Black people.

How Violence Dehumanizes the Self and the Subhumanity of the Other

Violence is an act of self-destruction that dehumanizes both the perpetrator and its victims or survivors. Aime Cesaire offers an explanation: colonization "thingifies" human beings; it reduces humans to the level of things that the violent experiences of such humans are rendered invisible. Henry Giroux, using Michel Foucault's concept of "biopower" (Foucault) and events surrounding Hurricane Katrina, coined the term "bio-politics of disposability" to explain the neoliberal response to the crisis (Giroux 174). The biopolitics of disposability is when human lives are reduced to economic goods. In the environment of biopolitics of disposability, state institutions only respond to the needs of individuals based on their perceived economic and social values. People deemed valueless and worthless to the state are left on their own in times of crisis.

In Toronto, we are witnessing a new biopolitics of disposability in Black communities. Within the public schools in Toronto, neighbourhoods marked rich and affluent have their public schools well resourced and funded, whereas poor communities, where the majority of Black people live, have their schools underresourced and poorly funded. Furthermore, whereas parents in affluent communities can successfully advocate on behalf of their children's education, Black parents are often denied access to support their children's education (Dei and Seffa). In addition, when Black youth witness the disenfranchisement of their peers—"hear teachers tell Black students they wouldn't achieve their dreams and see themselves ostracized from their peers as a result of racist stereotypes" (Wabari par.3)—this can stir anger and resentment. Consequently, Black children are always at risk of school disengagements or dropouts (Dei). For example, states such as Arizona and California are able to use the number of youths at risk of school dropout to project prison beds needed in the future (CRESC; Nicholas).

Colonial violence marks certain regions for privilege and other regions for exploitation (Fanon, *The Wretched of the Earth*), which is done through the creation of a Manichean world between the white settlers and the colonized, Indigenous and Black people. Resources are distributed in favour of the white settlers. Therefore, every effort of the colonized people goes to enrich the pockets of white settlers:

> This world [the Manichean world] is divided into compartments, this world cut in two is inhabited by two different species. The originality of the colonial context is that economic reality, inequality, and the immense difference of ways of life never come to mask the human realities. It is evident that what parcels out the world is to begin with the fact of belonging to or not belonging to a given race, a given species.... The cause is the consequences; you are rich because you are white, you are white because you are rich (40).

However, the insidiousness of the Manichean world is not just the stolen land and resources from the colonized, but the system it leaves in place to normalize this violent colonial domination.

Fanon speaks of colonial violence that scripts the colonized as the quintessence of evil with no good qualities:

> As if to show the totalitarian character of colonial exploitation the settler paints the native as a sort of quintessence of evil. Native society is not simply described as a society lacking in values. It is not enough for the colonists to affirm that those values have disappeared from, or still better never existed in, the colonial world. The native is declared insensible to ethics; he represents not only the absence of values, but also the negation of values. He is, let us dare to admit, the enemy of values, and in this sense, he is the absolute evil. He is the corrosive element, destroying all that comes near him; he is the deforming element, disfiguring all that has to do with beauty or morality; he is the depository of maleficent powers, the unconscious and irretrievable instrument of blind forces. (*The Wretched of the Earth* 41)

The colonial racist scripting of Black people as the quintessence of evil has in many ways justified Black disposability in Toronto Canada. As previously discussed, Black people are disproportionately imprisoned with an incarceration rate that far exceeds their population. The prison bed projections solidify an understanding of the disposability and lack of humanity of Black bodies through the prison industrial complex. In addition, it signifies the level of anti-Black racism in the (in)justice system with respect to laying criminal charges and sentencing in which the state prepares to exploit the free labour of Black prisoners and violate Black bodies as subhuman.

In Toronto, many Committees' reports on youth violence have identified the loss of hope and helplessness among Black youth as major causes of Black youth violence (Chadwick-Parkes; McMurtry and Curling). For example, Statistics Canada reveals that although 94 per cent of Black youth (aged fifteen to twenty-five) compared to 93.9 per cent of the rest of Canada's population desire to get at least a bachelor's degree, only 60 per cent of Black youth compared to 82.4 per cent of the rest of Canada's population think it can be a reality ("Canada's

Black Population").

Reacting to the findings from Statistics Canada, Andrea Davis, the then chair of York University's Department of Humanities and coordinator of Black Canadian studies, argues that this finding is not surprising because the major threat to Black youth is the daily violence in the education system. By this, Davis is referring to teachers who do not believe in Black students, the negative stereotypes of Black students in schools, excessive discipline measures and punishments of Black students when they go wrong, and the perceived unfair and unequal treatments of Black students by teachers and school administrators (Slaughter and Singh). Some of the Black youth who cannot take this daily violence drop out or get pushed out from schools (Dei). Given these experiences, Black youth feel insignificant and materially and psychologically unwanted in many ways (James). Consequently, some Black youth may feel hopeless and be drawn to abandon their dreams, aspirations, and goals. Feelings of hopelessness can influence choices and actions that result in early deaths. Opportunities for Black youth to provide counter-stories and challenge anti-Black racism are few; however, Black youth have initiated the Black Muslim Youth Toronto organization to highlight racial inequity across Canada (Wabari). Contrary to pathologizing discourse perpetuated in society, aided by the media about Black families, we propose that Black youth violence is a manifestation of colonial racist terror that they experience daily. As W.E.B. Du Bois noted, the high crime rate in African American communities is "a symptom of countless wrong social conditions" (241-42). In many ways, Black youth violence exposes a deadly silence and profound apathy towards Black youth suffering in Toronto.

How Violence Can Resist Inferiority Complex Syndrome

As we previously discussed, Black youth's violence is a response to institutional alienation and perceived inferiority complex created by anti-Black racism in Canada. As Fanon argued: "At the level of individuals, violence is a cleansing force. It frees the native from his inferiority complex and from despair and inaction; it makes him fearless and restores his self-respect" (*The Wretched of the Earth* 94). Fanon's perception has been criticized for promoting violence as a cathartic release. In response, we propose that Fanon saw the pathological phenomena of violence in external factors, such as racism and colonialism and in their contributions to individuals' violent behaviour. Fanon saw how systemic racism and colonialism have made it possible for white settlers to steal and destroy the land, possessions, language, culture, values, worldviews, and identity of oppressed people. In fact, Albert Memmi describes white settlers as usurpers who through violent racism and colonialism have stolen the resources and possessions of colonized people:

> It is impossible for colonizers not to be aware of the constant illegitimacy of *their* statuses. It is, moreover, in a way, a double illegitimacy. Foreigners, having come to a land by the accidents of history, *they have* succeeded not merely in creating a place for *themselves*, but also in taking away that of the inhabitants, granting *themselves* astounding privileges to the detriment of those rightfully entitled to them. And not by virtue of local laws ... but by upsetting the established rules and substituting *their* own. They thus appear doubly unjust. *They are* privileged ones; that is, usurpers. (our emphasis to make it gender-neutral language, 8-9)

Memmi further argues that colonized people, being fully aware of their violent colonial conditions, are left with the option of rejecting those colonial conditions through violent confrontation:

> However, revolt is the only way out of the colonial situation, and the colonized realizes it sooner or later. *Their* conditions *are* absolute and *cry* for an absolute solution; a break and not a compromise. *They* have been torn away from *their* past and cut off from *their* future, *their* traditions are dying, and they lose the hope of acquiring a new culture. *They have* neither language, nor flag, nor technical knowledge, nor national or international existence, nor rights, nor duties. *They* possess nothing, is no longer anything and no longer hope for anything.... The colonial situation, by its own internal inevitability, brings on revolt. For the colonized conditions cannot be adjusted to; like an iron collar, it can only be broken. (our emphasis to make it gender-neutral language, 127-28)

Both Fanon and Memmi acknowledge that violence remains the necessary option to offset oppression and regain liberty and freedom from internalized inferiority. As Helmi Sharawy puts it, every oppressive relation produces material and moral violence that can only be confronted by revolutionary violence (6).

The works of these anticolonial scholars help us to explain the underlying causes of Black youth violence in Toronto. In environments of perceived injustices, institutional anti-Black racism, police brutality, and stakeholders in an education system that sees Black children as disposable, violence becomes a cathartic act for the Black youth. Fanon uses the phrase "the death wish among Negroes" (218) in *Black Skin, White Masks* to explain how alienation, invisibility, and a sense of rejection can push victims of anti-Black racism, colonialism, and classism to the point of doing things that will make death inevitable. Thus, Black youth violence is an expression of a suppressed fury that must find an outlet to recreate a sense of humanity and self-respect. Black youth in Toronto are left in deplorable and helpless situations through their continued experiences of structural and systemic anti-Black racism and colonialism in Toronto. As we have mentioned, Black youth unemployment is higher than the national average, access to postsecondary education remains a mirage for many young Blacks, and poverty is prevailing in the Black community. Some young Blacks, as an attempt to escape the vicious cycle of structural and systemic racism and colonialism, form or join street gangs for protection, money, respect, and a sense of hope (Esbensen, Deschenes and Winfree; Howell; Mirande). In the book *Suburban Gangs: The Affluent Rebels,* Danny Korem argues that street gangs function as a surrogate family for youths who have nonexisting support systems.

Anti-Black racism, poverty, and discrimination, compounded by institutional disregard for Black lives, leave Black youth with little or sometimes no choice to fend for themselves. The gang subcultures are always available to offer belongingness, protection, respect, and care—something state institutions have failed or refused to offer Black youth. Gang association has its own values and norms. The initiated gang member learns quickly to survive on the street. One must be ruthless and aggressively defend one's territories at all costs. Violent activities, such as gun violence, are used as a means to harness power and control one's territories. Realizing that they have minimal power and control in the larger society, similar to Fanon's case with the Algerian youth, they turn on their friends and people in their communities to garnish and exercise further power and control.

We are not by any means suggesting that Black youth are justified to join street gangs and engage in gun violence. However, we cannot fully discuss Black youth violence if we are reluctant to engage and confront complex and nuanced circumstances that push young Blacks to gun violence as a means of survival. If violence is cyclical, then Black youth learn violent habits and tendencies from their personal and vicarious contact with violence. Black youth violence is their way of resisting institutional disregard of Black lives. It is their way of fighting against the inherent anti-Black racism and colonialism in Canada.

A Way Forwards: Anticolonial and Critical Race Responses to Youth Violence

As we searched for theories to understand Black youth violence, our goal was not to simply search for theoretical clarity, since the worth of a social theory is measured in two ways: its philosophical grounding and its ability to offer a social and political corrective response. We employ anticolonial theory and CRT given their ability not only to provide philosophical clarity about Black youth violence but also to encourage measures that can bring about change.

Black youth violence is a concern in Toronto for everyone; however, the public, decisionmakers, and politicians seem to believe that increasing police presence where Black people reside by overpolicing Black communities and evoking the law-and-order agenda will solve the problem. For instance, after the shooting of Jane Creba outside the Eaton Centre of Toronto on Boxing Day 2005, the police raided and arrested many alleged gang members in Toronto; many of whom were released without being charged. They also increased patrolling and covert activities among racialized communities expecting to arrest and charge young Black people who were presumed to be involved with gun violence.

These strategies have not reduced gun violence among Black young people; Black youth's violence still prevails in Toronto. Six years after the Creba shooting, another gunman opened fire inside the Eaton Centre, killing two individuals and leaving several others injured. In response to the incident, Toronto Police Chief Bill Blair said, "Today harkens back to that horrible moment"—referring to the 2005 shootings (Scallan par.4). We argue that the colour-blind analysis and solutions to Black youth violence have failed to yield desired outcomes because the analyses of gun violence have failed to see Black youths as victims. The analyses have so far treated Black youths as criminals who need to be imprisoned to ensure public safety and security. None of the solutions has addressed systemic racism and colonialism that motivate a sense of alienation, hopelessness, and helplessness in the Black communities.

Therefore, a long-term sustainable, institutional, and community-based approach is needed in order to eliminate gun violence among young Black people. Thus, rather than blaming and pathologizing Black communities and Black people in general, when gun violent incidents occur, Torontonians, including politicians and government officials, need to interrogate institutional structures and systemic vices of power for a more nuanced answer. Those in positions of power must denounce anti-Black racist policies and practices and implement policies that are just and fair to avoid Black youth being at risk of internalized violence. When racist structural conditions that create despair and a sense of helplessness among Black youth are addressed in Toronto that would be an indication of a genuine commitment to seriously address and circumvent Black youth violence.

The following suggestions can help address anti-Black racism in Toronto: 1) Eliminate the scrutinizing and inequitable treatment of Black youth by stopping their excessive expulsion and suspension from public schools; 2) Provide culturally and racially responsive support to Black parents and families in crisis; 3) Stop dismantling the Black family through the child welfare system, wherein social workers continuously remove Black children from their families and place them in state care; 4) Abandon overpolicing, such as street checks (carding), and destroy all data collected under the policy; 5) Public officials, politicians, law enforcement officers, and authority figures who commit racist and colonialist actions, must be held accountable with criminal charges and job dismissal; 6) The school curricula and pedagogical practices must reflect Black people's history and experiences; 7) Teachers, guidance counsellors, and administrators must demonstrate belief in young Black people's abilities by encouraging them and introducing them to high achieving programs, including those in science, technology, engineering, and mathematics (STEM); and 8) Governments at all levels must fund recreational, summer, and after school programs to help introduce Black youth to academics in a playful way, provide a place for them to create and maintain community, and offer culturally relevant race-based counselling for those at risk of or engaging in gun violence. The implementation of these recommendations will help to reduce gun-violence among Black youth in Toronto.

Endnotes

1. We acknowledge that the gender binarism of the male/female dichotomy is limited; however, the scholarship to allow meaningful inclusion of lesbian, gay, bisexual, two-spirited, trans*, and queer (LGBTTQ) youth is limited, and we did not want to add on the acronym LGBTTQ without fully including the nuances of these populations in the discussion.
2. Priority neighbourhoods are those areas in Toronto that are predominantly populated by working-class Black, Indigenous, and white people. They are deemed a priority because of their vulnerability to drugs, gun violence, sex work, and other social vices.
3. In June 11, 2007, after the fatal shooting of a high school student at school alongside an upsurge of gun violence in Toronto, then Premier of Ontario, Dalton McGuinty appointed the Honourable Roy McMurtry and Dr. Alvin Curling to cochair activities to determine the root cause of youth violence in Ontario. The Honourable Roy McMurtry and Dr. Alvin Curling published a five volume report outlining the root cause of youth violence in Ontario and offered thirty recommendations aimed at structural and institutional reforms in Ontario. The recommendations have not been im-plemented to date.

Works Cited

Adjei, Paul Banahene. "Chapter Three: When Blackness Shows Up Uninvited: Examining the Murder of Trayvon Martin through Fanonian Racial Interpellation." *Counterpoints*, vol. 445, 2013, pp. 25-41.

Adjei, Paul, and Rosina Agyepong. "Resistance from the Margin: Voices of African-Canadian Parents on Africentric Education." *Breaching the Colonial Contract*, edited by Arlo Kempf, Springer, Dordrecht, 2009, pp. 137-58.

Adjei, Paul Banahene, and Eric Minka. "Black Parents Ask for a Second Look: Parenting Under 'White' Child Protection Rules in Canada." *Children and Youth Services Review*, vol. 94, 2018, pp. 511-24.

Adjei, Paul Banahene, et al. "The 'Fragility of Goodness': Black Parents' Perspective about Raising Children in Toronto, Winnipeg, and St. John's of Canada." *Journal of Public Child Welfare*, vol. 12, no. 4, 2018, pp. 461-91.

Aiken, Sharryn J. "From Slavery to Expulsion: Racism, Canadian Immigration Law and the Unfulfilled Promise of Modern Constitutionalism." *Interrogating Race and Racism*, edited by Vijay Agnew, University of Toronto Press, 2007, pp. 55-111.

Akers, Ronald L., and Gary F. Jensen. "The Empirical Status of Social Learning Theory of Crime and Deviance: The Past, Present, and Future." *Taking stock: The Status of Criminological Theory*, vol. 15, 2006, pp. 37-75.

Albert Bandura. *Social Learning Theory*. N.J. Prentice-Hall, 1977.

Alexander, Michelle. *The New Jim Crow: Mass Incarceration in the Age of Colorblindness*. New Press. 2010.

Austin, David. "Narratives of Power: Historical Mythologies in Contemporary Quebec and Canada." *Race & Class*, vol. 52, no. 1, 2010, pp. 19-32.

Barnes, Robin D. "Race Consciousness: The Thematic Content of Racial Distinctiveness in Critical Race Scholarship." *Harv. L. Rev.*, vol. 103, no. 8, 1989, pp. 1864-71.

Bell, Derrick A. "Serving Two Masters: Integration Ideals and Client Interests in School Desegregation Litigation." *The Yale Law Journal*, vol. 85, no. 4, 1976, pp. 470-516.

Bell Jr, Derrick A. "Brown v. Board of Education and the Interest-Convergence Dilemma." *Harv. L. Rev.*, vol. 93, no. 3, 1980, pp. 518-33.

Blatchford, Christie. "Judge Lashes Police for Racial Profiling." *The Globe and Mail. N.pub. 17 Sept. 2004,* www.theglobeandmail.com/news/national/judge-lashes-police-for-racial-profiling/article745800/. Accessed 25 Mar. 2022.

Bolan, Kim. "Former Biker Says Crimes Discussed at Hells Angels Clubhouse." *Vancouver Sun,* 4 May 2018, vancouversun.com/news/crime/former-biker-says-crimes-discussed-at-hells-angels-clubhouse. Accessed 25 Mar. 2022.

Bursik Jr, Robert J. "Social Disorganization and Theories of Crime and Delinquency: Problems and Prospects." *Criminology*, vol. 26, no. 4, 1988, pp. 519-52.

Bursik Jr, Robert J., and Harold G. Grasmick. "Economic Deprivation and Neighborhood Crime Rates, 1960-1980." *Law & Soc'y Rev.*, vol. 27, 1993, pp. 263-83.

Calliste, Agnes. "Canada's immigration policy and domestics from the Caribbean: The second domestic scheme." *Race, class, gender: Bonds and barriers*, vol. 5, edited by Jesse Vorst, Between the Lines, 1989, pp. 133-65.

Cardoso, Tom. "Toronto Sees Record Number of Shootings in 2019, but Fewer Deaths." *The Globe and Mail, 1 Jan. 2020,* www.theglobeandmail.com/canada/toronto/article-toronto-sees-record-number-of-shootings-in-2019-but-fewer-deaths/. Accessed 25 Mar. 2022.

Césaire, Aimé. *Discourse on Colonialism*. Monthly Review Press, 1972.

Chadwick-Parkes. S. *Youth Armed Violence Interventions: The Caribbean and Its Toronto Diaspora*. Project Ploughshares, 2012.

City News Toronto. "Murder 2007: The Grim List." *City News Toronto,* 17 Dec. 2007, toronto.citynews.ca/2007/12/19/murder-2007-the-grim-list/. Accessed 25 Mar. 2022.

Cole, Desmond. *The Skin We're In: A Year of Black Resistance and Power.* Random House, 2020.

Cooper, Afua. *The Hanging of Angelique: The Untold Story of Canadian Slavery and the Burning of Old Montreal*. University of Georgia Press, 2007. Print.

Crenshaw, Kimberle. "Mapping the margins: Intersectionality, identity politics, and violence against women of color." *Stan. L. Rev.*, vol. 43, no. 6, 1990, pp. 1241-99.

Crenshaw, Kimberlé. *Critical Race Theory: The Key Writings that Formed the Movement.* New Press, 1995.

CRESC. "Read, or Go to Jail." *Capital Region Ex-Offenders Support Coalition.* 7 Dec. 2011, www.reentrynow.org/blog/read-or-go-to-jail. Accessed 25 Mar. 2022.

Dei, George J. S. *Reconstructing "Dropout": A Critical Ethnography of the Dynamics of Black Students' Disengagement from School.* University of Toronto Press, 1997.

Dei, George J. S. *Removing the Margins: The Challenges and Possibilities of Inclusive Schooling.* Toronto: Canadian Scholars' Press, 2000.

Dei, George, and Jerry Sefa, editor. *Fanon and the Counterinsurgency of Education.* Sense Pub., 2010.

Dhillon, Sunny. "Toronto Council to Revisit Former Chief Justice's Youth-Violence Report." *The Globe and Mail, 20 Feb. 2013,* www.theglobeandmail.com/news/toronto/toronto-council-to-revisit-former-chief-justices-youth-violence-report/article8878350/. Accessed 25 Mar. 2022.

Doucette, Chris. "Where's Black Lives Matter When It Matters?" *Toronto Sun,* 8 July. 2018, torontosun.com/news/local-news/wheres-black-lives-matter-when-it-matters. Accessed 25 Mar. 2022.

Du Bois, William Edward Burghardt. *The Philadelphia Negro: A Social Study.* Published for the University, 1899.

Dunn, Trevor. "In Deadly Encounters with Toronto Police, More Than a Third of Victims Are Black." *CBC News,* 5 Apr. 2018, www.cbc.ca/news/canada/toronto/police-deaths-blacks-data-1.4599215. Accessed 25 Mar. 2022.

Edwards, Peter. "Alleged Hells Angels Affiliate Charged with Beating Rival with Bat in Broad Daylight Near St. Catharines Convenience Store." *The Star, 22 Jun. 2020,* www.thestar.com/news/gta/2020/06/17/alleged-hells-angels-affiliate-charged-with-beating-rival-with-bat-in-broad-daylight-near-st-catharines-convenience-store.html. Accessed 25 Mar. 2022.

Ellis, Lee. "A Theory Explaining Biological Correlates of Criminality." *European Journal of Criminology,* vol. 2, no. 3, 2005, pp. 287-315.

Englander, Elizabeth K. *Understanding Violence.* Lawrence Erlbaum Associates, 2003.

Esbensen, Finn-Aage, Elizabeth Piper Deschenes, and L. Thomas Winfree Jr. "Differences between Gang Girls and Gang Boys: Results from a Multisite Survey." *Youth & Society*, vol. 31, no. 1, 1999, pp. 27-53.

Fanon, Frantz. *Black Skin, White Masks.* Grove Press, 1967.

Fanon, Frantz. *The Wretched of the Earth.* Grove Press, 1963.

Feather, Norman T. "Economic Deprivation and the Psychological Impact of Unemployment." *Australian Psychologist*, vol. 32, no. 1, 1997, pp. 37-45.

Fishbein, Diana H. *Biobehavioral Perspectives in Criminology.* Wadsworth/ Thomson Learning, 2001.

Fitzgerald, John L. "Policing as Public Health Menace in the Policy Struggles Over Public Injecting." *International Journal of Drug Policy*, vol. 4, no. 16, 2005, pp. 203-06.

Foucault, Michel. *Birth of the Clinic: An Archaeology of Medical Perception.* Pantheon Books, 1973.

Freeman, Alan David. "Legitimizing Racial Discrimination through Antidiscrimination Law: A Critical Review of Supreme Court Doctrine." *Minn. L. Rev.*, vol. 62, no. 6, 1977, pp. 1049-1120.

Freeman, Alan David. "Truth and Mystification in Legal Scholarship." *The Yale Law Journal*, vol. 90, no. 5, 1981, pp. 1229-37.

Freire, Paulo. *Pedagogy of the Oppressed.* Continuum, 2000.

Gallant, Sigrid Nicole. "Perspectives on the Motives for the Migration of African-Americans to and from Ontario, Canada: From the Abolition of Slavery in Canada to the Abolition of Slavery in the United States." *The Journal of Negro History*, vol. 86, no. 3, 2001, pp. 391-408.

Gee, Marcus. "We Can't Keep Tiptoeing around Black-on-Black Violence." *The Globe and Mail*, 20 Feb. 2013, www.theglobeandmail.com/news/toronto/we-cant-keep-tiptoeing-around-black-on-black-violence/article8907404/. Accessed 25 Mar. 2022.

Getachew, Samuel. "Getachew Gets a Bite of a Rhodes Scholar's Noodle." *The Huffington Post*, 3 July, 2012, www.huffpost.com/

archive/ca/entry/eaton-centre-shooting_b_1581311. Accessed 25 Mar. 2022.

Giroux, Henry A. "Reading Hurricane Katrina: Race, Class, and the Biopolitics of Disposability." *College Literature*, vol. 33, no. 3, 2006, pp. 171-96.

Gittens, Margaret, David P. Cole, and Commission on Systemic Racism in the Ontario Criminal Justice System. *Report of the Commission on Systemic Racism in the Ontario Criminal Justice System.* Queen's Printer for Ontario, 1995.

Gordon, Andrea. "Black Students Hindered by Academic Streaming, Suspensions, Says Report from York University." *The Star, 24 Apr. 2017,* www.thestar.com/yourtoronto/education/2017/04/24/black-students-hindered-by-academic-streaming-suspensions-report.html. Accessed 25 Mar. 2022.

Hasham, Alysha. "When 'Systemic and Structural' Racism Is Considered in Sentencing." *The Star, 13 Jun. 2020,* www.thestar.com/news/gta/2020/06/12/when-systemic-and-structural-racism-is-considered-in-sentencing.html. Accessed 25 Mar. 2022.

Henry, Frances, and Carol Tator. *The Colour of Democracy: Racism in Canadian Society.* Thomson/Nelson, 2006.

Howell, James C. "Gang Prevention: An Overview of Research and Programs." *Juvenile Justice Bulletin.* Office of Juvenile Justice and Delinquency Prevention, 2010.

Hulchanski, John D., and University of Toronto. Cities Centre. "The Three Cities within Toronto: Income Polarization among Toronto's Neighbourhoods, 1970-2005." *Cities Centre* Press, 2010.

James, C. E. *We Rise Together.* Peel District School Board, 2019.

James, Katie, Jackson Bunch, and Jody Clay-Warner. "Perceived Injustice and School Violence: An Application of General Strain Theory." *Youth Violence and Juvenile Justice*, vol. 13, no. 2, 2015, pp. 169-89.

Khenti, Akwatu. "The Canadian War on Drugs: Structural Violence and Unequal Treatment of Black Canadians." *The International Journal of Drug Policy*, vol. 25, no. 2, 2014, pp. 190-95.

Kitossa, Tamari. "'Thugs' Is a Race-Code Word That Fuels Anti-Black Racism." *National Post, 18* Oct. 2010, nationalpost.com/pmn/news-pmn/thugs-is-a-race-code-word-that-fuels-anti-black-racism. Accessed 25 Mar. 2022.

Kohlberg, Lawrence. *Stages in the Development of Moral Thought and Action.* Rinehart and Winston, 1969.

Korem, Danny. *Suburban Gangs: The Affluent Rebels.* International Focus Press, 1994.

Ladson Billings, Gloria. "'But That's Just Good Teaching!' The Case for Culturally Relevant Pedagogy." *Theory into Practice,* vol. 34, no. 3, 1995, pp. 159-65.

Ladson Billings, Gloria. "Just What Is Critical Race Theory and What's It Doing in a Nice Field Like Education?" *International Journal of Qualitative Studies in Education,* vol. 11, no. 1, 1998, pp. 7-24.

Lawson, Erica. "Single Mothers, Absentee Fathers, and Gun Violence in Toronto: A Contextual Interpretation." *Women's Studies,* vol. 41, no. 7, 2012, pp. 805-28.

Lewis, Stephen. "Report of the Race Relations and Policing Task Force." *Canadian Police College Journal,* vol. 14, no. 3, 1990, pp. 202-14.

MacDonald, John, et al. "Race, Neighbourhood Context and Perceptions of Injustice by the Police in Cincinnati." *Urban Studies,* vol. 44, no. 13, 2007, pp. 2567-85.

MacLeod, Meredith. "A Deadly Year of Gun Violence in Toronto." *CTV News, 21 Dec. 2018,* www.ctvnews.ca/canada/a- deadly-year-of-gun-violence-in-toronto-1.4222566. Accessed 25 Mar. 2022.

Makin, Kirk. "Court Grants Blacks Special Sentencing." *The Globe and Mail, 13 Feb. 2003,* www.theglobeandmail.com/news/national/court-grants-blacks-special-sentencing/article18284544/. Accessed 25 Mar. 2022.

McMurtry, Roy, and Alvin Curling. *The Review of the Roots of Youth Violence: Literature Reviews.* Government of Ontario, 2008.

Memmi, Albert. *Colonizer and the Colonized.* Beacon Press, 1967.

Merali, Farrah. "Community Safety Minister Slammed for Saying He Wore a Bulletproof Vest at Jane and Finch." *CBC News,* 18 July. 2018, www.cbc.ca/news/canada/toronto/michael-tibollo-jane-finch-bulletproof-1.4752033. Accessed 25 Mar. 2022.

Mirandé, Alfredo. *Gringo Justice.* University of Notre Dame Press, 1987.

Montecinos, Carmen. "Culture as an Ongoing Dialog: Implications for Multicultural Teacher Education." *Multicultural Education, Critical Pedagogy, and the Politics of Difference*, edited by Christine E. Sleeter and Peter L. McLaren. University of New York Press, 1995, pp. 291-308.

Morgan, J. "Of 'Thugs,' 'Gangsters' and 'Sewer Rats': Why John Tory's Language on Gun Violence Is a Problem," *Now*, 14 Aug. 2018, nowtoronto.com/news/john-tory-gun-violence-racism. Accessed 25 Mar. 2022.

Mosher, Clayton James. *Discrimination and Denial: Systemic Racism in Ontario's Legal and Criminal Justice Systems, 1892-1961.* University of Toronto Press, 1998.

Mullings, Delores V. *Racism in Canadian Social Policy.* Wilfrid Laurier University Press, 2012.

Mullings, Delores V. "The Racial Institutionalisation of Whiteness in Contemporary Canadian Public Policy." *On Whiteness. Inter-Dis ciplinary Press,* 2012.

Ontario Human Rights Commission. *Paying the Price: The Human Cost of Racial Profiling: Inquiry Report*. Government of Ontario, 2003.

Ontario Human Rights Commission. *The Ontario Safe Schools Act: School Discipline and Discrimination*. Government of Ontario, 2003.

Owusu-Bempah, Akwasi, and Scot Wortley. "Race, Crime, and Criminal Justice in Canada." *The Oxford Handbook of Ethnicity, Crime, and Immigration*, edited by Sandra Bucerius and Michael Tonry, 2014, pp. 281-320.

Paperny, Anna. M. "Toronto Gangs Smaller, Looser—But Packing More Heat." *The Globe and Mail, 8 June 2012,* www.theglobeandmail.com/news/toronto/toronto-gangs-smaller-looser-but-packing-more-heat/article4243872/. Accessed 25 Mar. 2022.

Paradkar, Shree. "Why Black-on-Black Crime Continues to Be a Thing." *The Star,* 30 Jan. 2017, www.thestar.com/news/gta/2017/01/30/why-black-on-black-crime-continues-to-be-a-thing-paradkar.html. Accessed 25 Mar. 2022.

Principe, T. *Unpublished paper at the Department of Sociology and Equity*

Studies in Education. Ontario Institute for Studies in Education: University of Toronto. 2004.

Rankin, Jim. "Singled Out: A 2002 Star Series Based on Analysis of Police Crime Data Showed Justice Is Different for Blacks and Whites." *The Star, 2002,* www.thestar.com/news/gta/known topolice/2002/10/19/singled-out.html. Accessed 25 Mar. 2022.

Rankin, Jim, Kristin Rushowy, and Louise Brown. "Toronto School Suspension Rates Highest for Black and Aboriginal students." *The Star, 22 March 2013,* www.thestar.com/news/gta/2013/03/22/toronto_school_suspension_rates_highest_for_black_and_aboriginal_students.html. Accessed 25 Mar. 2022.

Rankin, Jim, and Patty Winsa. "Known to Police: Toronto Police Stop and Document Black and Brown People Far More Than Whites." *Toronto Star,* 12 Mar. 2012, www.thestar.com/news/insight/2012/03/09/known_to_police_toronto_police_stop_and_document_black_and_brown_people_far_more_than_whites.html. Accessed 25 Mar. 2022.

Reitz, Jeffrey, et al. *Multiculturalism and Social Cohesion: Potentials and Challenges of Diversity*. Springer Science & Business Media, 2009.

Russell, Margaret M. "Entering Great America: Reflections on Race and the Convergence of Progressive Legal Theory and Practice." *Hastings LJ*, vol. 43, 1991, pp. 749-67.

Sampson, Robert J., and W. Byron Groves. "Community structure and crime: Testing social-disorganization theory." *American journal of sociology* 94.4 (1989), pp. 774-802.

Scallan, Niamh. "Eaton Centre Shooting: Violence Recalls Jane Creba's Death on Boxing Day 2005." *Toronto Star, 2 June. 2012,* www.thestar.com/news/gta/2012/06/02/eaton_centre_shooting_violence_recalls_jane_crebas_death_on_boxing_day_2005.html. Accessed 25 Mar. 2022.

Sharawy, Helmi. "Frantz Fanon and the African Revolution, Revisited at a Time of Globalization." *Pambazuka News,* 2003, www.pambazuka.org/global-south/frantz-fanon-globalisation-and-african-revolution. Accessed 25 Mar. 2022.

Slaughter, Graham, and Mahima Singh. "Five Charts That Show What Systemic Racism Looks Like in Canada." *CTV News,* 4 June 2020, www.ctvnews.ca/canada/five-charts-that-show-what-systemic-racism-looks-like-in-canada-1.4970352. Accessed 25 Mar. 2022.

Solórzano, Daniel G., and Tara J. Yosso. "Critical Race Methodology: Counter-Storytelling as an Analytical Framework for Education Research." *Qualitative Inquiry*, vol. 8, no. 1, 2002, pp. 23-44.

Spaulding, H. B. "Wayward Youth. By August Aichhorn. (New York: The Viking Press, 1935)." *American Journal of Psychiatry*, vol. 92, no. 4, 1936, pp. 998-99.

Statistics Canada. *Population Estimates Program; Population Projections for Canada, Provinces and Territories. Statistics Canada*, 2012, www150.statcan.gc.ca/n1/en/catalogue/91-520-X. Accessed 25 Mar. 2022.

Statistics Canada. *Canada's Black Population: Education, Labour and Resilience. Statistics Canada*, 2020, www150.statcan.gc.ca/n1/pub/89-657-x/89-657-x2020002-eng.htm. Accessed 25 Mar. 2022.

Stovall, David. "A Challenge to Traditional Theory: Critical Race Theory, African-American Community Organizers, and Education." *Discourse: Studies in the Cultural Politics of Education*, vol. 26, no. 1, 2005, pp. 95-108.

Tanovich, David M. *The Colour of Justice: Policing Race in Canada*. Irwin Law, 2006.

Thobani, Sunera. *Exalted Subjects: Studies in the Making of Race and Nation in Canada*. University of Toronto Press, 2007.

Thornhill, Esmeralda MA. "So Seldom for Us, So Often Against Us: Blacks and Law in Canada." *Journal of Black Studies*, vol. 38, no. 3, 2008, pp. 321-37.

Thornhill, Esmeralda MA. "Focus on Racism. Legal Perspectives from a Black Experience." *Analytical Legal Study*, vol. 8, 1994, pp. 153-62.

United Nations News. "UN Expert Panel Warns of Systemic Anti-Black Racism in Canada's Criminal Justice System." *UN News*, 21 Oct. 2016, news.un.org/en/story/2016/10/543482-un-expert-panel-warns-systemic-anti-black-racism-canadas-criminal-justice. Accessed 25 Mar. 2022.

Valencia, Richard R.and Daniel Solórzano. "Contemporary Deficit Thinking." *The Evolution of Deficit Thinking: Educational Thought and Practice*, edited by Richard R. Valencia, The Falmer Press, 1997, pp. 160-210.

Vizenor, Gerald Robert. *Manifest Manners: Postindian Warriors of Survivance.* Wesleyan University Press, 1994.

Wabari, Osobe."Combating Anti-Black Racism in Canada Will 'Take More Than a Village,' Black Youth Say." *CBC News, 9 July 2020,* www.cbc.ca/news/canada/toronto/black-muslim-youth-toronto-racism-schools-ontario-1.5643154. Accessed 25 Mar. 2022.

Walcott, Rinaldo. "Shame: A Polemic." *The CLR James Journal*, vol. 20, no. 1-2, 2014, pp. 275-80.

Walcott, Rinaldo, et al. *Racial Minority Perspectives on Violence: A Report Prepared for the Review of the Roots of Youth Violence.* Ministry of Children and Youth Services, 2008.

Welch, Kelly. "Black Criminal Stereotypes and Racial Profiling." *Journal of Contemporary Criminal Justice*, vol. 23, no. 3, 2007, pp. 276-88.

Wigmore, Gregory. "Before the Railroad: From Slavery to Freedom in the Canadian-American Borderland." *The Journal of American History*, vol. 98, no. 2, 2011, pp. 437-54.

Winfree Jr, L. Thomas, Teresa Vigil Bäckström, and G. Larry Mays. "Social Learning Theory, Self-Reported Delinquency, and Youth Gangs: A New Twist on a General Theory of Crime and Delinquency." *Youth & Society*, vol. 26, no. 2, 1994, pp. 147-77.

Wortley, Scot. "Hidden Intersections: Research on Race, Crime, and Criminal Justice in Canada." *Canadian Ethnic Studies Journal*, vol. 35, no. 3, 2003, pp. 99-118.

Wortley, Scot, and Julian Tanner. "Immigration, Social Disadvantage and Urban Youth Gangs: Results of a Toronto-Area Survey." *Canadian Journal of Urban Research*, vol. 15, no. 2, 2006, pp. 18-37.

Chapter 3

Gun Violence: The Lyrics of the Street

Santana Stallberg

With the increasing news reports on mass shootings, gang-related deaths, and the need for gun control, gun violence has become a social epidemic, which has tarnished the general public's view of safety and security. In 2017, firearms caused almost half of all homicides worldwide (UNODC). To put this into perspective, there were approximately 464,000 homicides worldwide in 2017 (Lederer). Although it is not the leading cause of firearm-related homicides, gang-related homicides involving youth have contributed to issues of gun violence overall. In 2017, approximately 21 per cent of all homicides were gang-related and were committed with a firearm in Canada (Berthiaume). In the United States (US), gang-related firearm homicides account for 13 per cent of the total number of homicides each year (National Gang Survey).[1] As such, it has become a priority to understand and identify the reasons for the rise in gun violence, especially among gang-involved youth.

Although it is known that gun- and gang-related violence is rooted in a multitude of social and economic issues, it is important to understand that what appear to be peripheral issues often play a catalytic role in gun violence. One such catalyst that can be linked to an increase in gun violence is rap music. During the 1990s, gangsta rap was topping the charts with its explicit images of guns and violent behaviours. Rappers were idolizing the hustler lifestyle within their lyrics, which often included the portrayal of drug dealing, pimping, and violence as a way to increase their street credibility and to escape the poverty-stricken lifestyles that plagued their neighbourhoods. Due to its often vulgar and violent lyrics and images, parents and politicians began to blame gangsta rap for all society's problems, including firearm-related violence (Canton). Therefore, the question that must be addressed is why is gangsta rap a catalyst for the social issues occurring in the world, specifically gun violence?

The Evolution of Gangsta Rap

During the 1980s, rappers like NWA (Niggaz wit Attitudes) revolutionized the music industry with gangsta rap (Kennedy). This music genre began taking over mainstream media by romanticizing the street life in Los Angeles by depicting the violence, drug dealing, and crime that occurred on the streets. NWA used their music as an outlet for expressing their anger and frustration with living on the streets in one of the most dangerous cities in the US. These rappers acted like street reporters, highlighting their experiences with hardship, discrimination, and police brutality. NWA's violent lyrics—seen within their songs "Fuck the Police" and "Cop Killer"—created controversy that spiked riots by exposing the police brutality that young, African American men faced every day. In particular, the songs' messages were used as an outcry to the general public in Los Angeles in 1992, after white police officers were acquitted of brutally beating an unarmed black man named Rodney King (Kennedy). NWA raps:

> Fuck the police comin' straight from the underground
> A young nigga got it bad 'cause I'm brown
> And not the other color so police think
> They have the authority to kill a minority
> Fuck that shit, 'cause I ain't the one
> For a punk motherfucker with a badge and a gun
> To be beatin' on, and thrown in jail.

These lyrics along with others in the song emphasize the racial profiling by police officers that occurred in the streets of America. In the documentary *Straight Outta Compton*, Ice Cube, a member of NWA, can be seen in a press conference, after riots broke out at their concert in Detroit, telling reporters that "Their art reflects their reality" ("Straight Outta Compton"). NWA was using their lyrics to incite change by highlighting the realities of young, African American men growing up in the ghetto. The lyrics, though vulgar, were meant to change the narrative and invoke discussions about the problems within these disadvantaged neighbourhoods. However, as gangsta rap grew in popularity and more rappers joined the industry, the lyrics began to incite feuds and violence while trying to resolve conflicts with the police and between rival gangs on the streets. But how could vulgar rap lyrics result in real-life violence?

The East-West Rivalry

Gangsta rap became commercialized due to West Coast rappers, such as NWA and Snoop Dogg (*Hip-Hop Evolution*). However, rap culture was first developed in the East Coast streets of New York, which led to conflicts between the two coasts. The feuds began when West Coast rappers entered into the rap game, which was primarily composed of East Coast rappers (*Hip-Hop Evolution*). Rap, as a music genre, was competitive, and, therefore, certain labels, media platforms, and rappers did not appreciate the success of rappers from the opposite coast. The documentary *Hip-Hop Evolution* highlights the fact that the East Coast never appreciated or recognized the success of the West Coast, which was seen in their use of subliminal messages to draw attention to their feud and disapproval of the West Coast rappers. This can be seen in one of Tim Dog's songs, "Fuck Compton," where he disses West Coast rappers, such as NWA, Snoop Dogg, and Dr. Dre. Tim Dog raps:

> Well I'm from the South Bronx
> Fuck Compton
> Tim Dog and I'm the best from the East
> And all this Compton shit must cease
> So keep your eyes on the prize and
> Don't jeopardize my arrive 'cause that's not wise
> You really think that you can rhyme
> Well come and get some of this loaded tech-nine
> Bo bo bo shots are cold gunning.

These types of lyrics emphasized the hatred coming from both coasts. Although most of the rivalry was contained within the lyrics, it was not until a feud between two prominent rappers Tupac and Biggie took place that the rivalry developed into more than just a battle of words.

The biggest rivalry in the music industry was between Tupac and Biggie (Chang). Tupac entered the music scene in 1991, whereas Biggie's first record was released in 1993. Although entering the music scene at different times, Tupac and Biggie became friends (Chang). Tupac's music, like NWA's, exemplified the injustices he experienced. As Tupac's popularity grew, he often interacted with the criminal justice system, and therefore he sought the support of his fellow rappers, one of them being Biggie (*Hip-Hop Evolution*). The feud between Tupac and Biggie only began after an incident occurred at a recording studio in 1994, where Tupac was robbed and shot five times while visiting some rappers including Biggie and Puff Daddy (Chang). This did not sit right with Tupac, as he believed his friend had set him up. As highlighted in *Hip-Hop Evolution,* Cheo Hodari Coker, a journalist, explained how Tupac believed Biggie and the other rappers knew about the robbery and were involved in setting him up. Unfortunately, tension in Biggie and Tupac's relationship spiralled from there on.

The tension continued to grow until it came to a head in 1995, when Suge Knight, and Snoop Dogg called out the East Coast during the Source Awards for not showing love to the West Coast rappers and West Coast gangsta rap (*Hip-Hop Evolution*). This event at the Source Awards revolutionized the rap industry as the music became a source of illuminating the gang lifestyle by calling out other rappers, dissing one another and inciting violence. On the West Coast, gangsta rap was considered real and authentic only when rappers' lyrics imitated their gangbanging lifestyles. In *Hip-Hop Evolution,* Coker explains that Suge Knight, the CEO of Death Row Records, "had this notion that if you weren't really a gangster, if you were writing about this stuff and you weren't really living it, then you weren't real you were a studio gangster." This type of mantra solidified the fact that rappers not only had to be hard and violent in their music but also on the streets, especially when conflict presented itself. Therefore, rap became a mechanism for inciting violence, and hatred towards the opposite coast.

The two major players in the feud between the East and West coast was Death Row Records [2] and Bad Boy Records.[3] The turning point in

Tupac and Biggie's relationship was solidified once Tupac signed with Death Row Records, which was the competing label to Bad Boy Records, where Biggie was signed (Chang). The change in record labels was Tupac's way of getting back at Biggie, since Tupac believed that Biggie set up the armed robbery against him. In 1995, approximately three months after Tupac was shot, Biggie released a song, titled "Who Shot Ya", which he had been working on for months (Hip-Hop Evolution). However, to Tupac this track was evidence of Biggie's involvement in the armed robbery that previously took place. As the feud heightened, songs and lyrics were used as a mechanism to disrespect and threaten one another. In response to "Who Shot Ya", Tupac released his song titled, "Hit 'Em Up", which detailed violent acts against Bad Boy Records rappers, and the claim that Tupac slept with Biggie's wife (Chang). Tupac raps:

> First off, fuck your bitch and the click you claim
> Westside when we ride come equipped with game
> You claim to be a player but I fucked your wife
> We bust on Bad Boy niggaz fucked for life
> Plus Puffy tryin' ta see me weak hearts I rip
> Biggie Smalls and Junior M.A.F.I.A. Some mark-ass bitches
> We keep on comin' while we runnin' for yo' jewels
> Steady gunnin, keep on bustin at them fools, you know the rules
> Lil' Ceaser, go ask ya homie how I leave ya
> Cut your young ass up, leave you in pieces, now be deceased
> Lil' Kim, don't fuck around with real G's
> Quick to snatch yo' ugly ass off the streets, so fuck peace
> I let them niggaz know it's on for life
> So let the Westside ride tonight
> Bad Boy murdered on wax and killed
> Fuck wit' me and get yo' caps peeled, you know, see.
> ("Hit Em Up")

One after another, both labels released dis tracks, and eventually the East-West feud ended up on the streets (*Hip-Hop Evolution*).

Ultimately, the feud between these coasts led to the murder of both Tupac and Biggie within a six-month gap of one another (Chang). The issue of gun violence does not end here; as it does not live only within the confines of the music industry; it is an epidemic issue worldwide and is highly visible within gang culture.

Gang Formation

Within poorer neighbourhoods, like the ghetto, often referenced in rap music, there is an increased amount of violence and crime. In these neighbourhoods, social and economic factors contribute to the presence of gangs, crime, and violence. Gangs are defined as

> any denotable adolescent group of youngsters who (a) are generally perceived as a distinct aggregation by others in their neighbourhood, (b) recognize themselves as a denotable group (almost invariably with a group name), and (c) have been involved in sufficient number of delinquent incidents to call forth a consistent negative response from neighbourhood residents and/or law enforcement agencies. (Klemp-North 13).

The formation of gangs, particularly youth gangs, is one of the ways that young, usually ethnically diverse men deal with the social and economic hardships they encounter (Dunbar). In Canada, it was found that approximately 94 per cent of gang members were male,[4] 25 per cent were African Canadian,[5] and 48 per cent were under the age of eighteen[6] (Astwood Strategy Corporation). In the US, the composition of gangs is similar with ethnically diverse populations accounting for the majority of gang members; 35 per cent of gangs are composed of African Americans and 46 per cent are composed of Hispanic members (Lozon and Bensimon). These populations disproportionately experience social and economic disadvantages that contribute to the formation of gangs as a way to build resistance mechanisms in order to survive. In particular, the overarching social determinants—such as poverty, unemployment, family disruption and isolation—are key elements present within these inner-city neighbourhoods (Kurbin). Gang formation also helps individuals handle strenuous events through bonding with one another.

Gang formation can be explained through strain theory, which posits that individuals will be more likely to react in deviant ways when strain is presented because there is a failure to achieve positively valued goals, removal of positively valued stimuli, and the presentation of noxious stimuli (Slocum and Simpson). There are varying types of strain that can lead individuals to become involved in deviant behaviour. For instance, adolescents that experience economic strain may be more likely to join a gang to achieve financial stability that would not have been readily available beforehand (Klemp-North). Another type of strain that can negatively affect an individual is the removal of positively valued stimuli, which can occur, for example, through the social disorganization of the family by divorce or separation (Klemp-North). This type of strain is highly indicative of gang formation, since gangs provide a protective, cohesive support system, which ultimately acts as a family unit. The third type of strain that one can experience is the presentation of negatively valued stimuli, which can occur through negative labels, or the presence of delinquent peers (Klemp-North). Youths that have been previously involved in delinquent behavior increases the likelihood that they will join a gang (Gatti et al.). Gang membership occurs through this type of strain, when individuals receive negative labels, and thus can only form relationships with fellow deviant peers. Ultimately, youths are at risk of joining a gang when they are unable to cope with strenuous events in a positive, legal manner, which ultimately leads to violence and criminal activity.

Guns, Gangs, and the Street Code

Between 1999 and 2006, homicide using a firearm was the leading cause of death for minority youth in the US (Centers for Disease Control and Prevention).[7] There are multiple risk factors that are correlated with minority youth carrying a weapon, particularly a firearm. For instance, gang membership, violent behaviour, and violence within the community are all risk factors correlated with youths carrying guns (Spano and Bolland). As gun violence became a global epidemic, researchers began to analyze the reasons for which youths carried guns. One study conducted by Richard Spano and John Bolland in the US analyzed data from the Mobile Youth Survey conducted in 2000 and 2001 to determine the risk factors that contributed to first-time gun carrying among youths. The study determined that gang members were approximately 1.6 times more likely to be exposed to violence than their counterparts[8] (Spano and Bolland). These risk factors, in turn, were a significant indicator of engaging in violent behaviour. Specifically, the study found that gang members are 2.1 times more likely to participate in violent behaviour than nongang members.[9] In Canada, there were similar findings regarding the risk factors that increase the likelihood of youths carrying a gun. In 2012, "30% of the youths that were accused of murder were involved in a gang-related homicide", which was almost double the rate of adults accused (Austin and Lane 38). These statistics indicate that there is a correlation between being in a gang and using a firearm to perpetrate a homicide. This phenomenon has been particularly evident in Toronto, Canada, where the police chief has blamed the recent spike in gun violence on street gang activity (The Canadian Press). For instance, in 2019, 492 shootings occurred in Toronto, Canada, with 292 people being killed or injured, which was the highest number in approximately fifteen years (Gillis). In both Canada and the US, there are issues with the prevalence of not only gun violence but also gang-related homicides. This begs the question: Why are there exceptionally high rates of violence associated with gang membership?

Albert Cohen's subcultural theory asserts that youths adjust to social and economic problems by forming subcultures,[10] which are antisystems of society that have their own set of attitudes, norms, and rules, which are contradictory to societal ones (Cohen). In lower-economic areas, such as the ghetto, young adolescents, as well as adults, are presented with fewer legitimate opportunities to obtain wealth, status, and power, which leads to the formation of deviant subcultures such as gangs.[11] Gang members gain their wealth, status, and power through illegitimate means, usually of a violent nature. Gang violence entails expressive and/or instrumental crimes: Expressive crimes pertain to altercations arising from anger-inducing situations such as rivalries between gangs,[12] whereas instrumental crimes pertain to incidents developing from economic factors, such as drug crimes (Youngs, Ioannou and Eagles). In order to maintain wealth, power, and status, gang members must cultivate tough personas that highlight their ability to respond and react in a violent nature when needed. In the ghetto, people are able to advance their status and power by attacking others, and thus it is important to maintain respect from others in order to protect oneself from being attacked.

Within the inner-city neighbourhoods, violence is perpetuated through the street code, which is a set of principles that govern and conduct interpersonal social relations within a given area (Kubrin).

Expressive crimes, which are common among gangs, tend to occur when individuals fail to act in accordance with the street code, thus leading to conflicts of a violent nature. One of the main causes of violent conflicts between gangs is disrespect. Respect is one of the main features of the street code and is defined as "being treated right or granted the deference one deserves" (Kubrin 363). Unlike individuals who possess a plethora of opportunities, members of low-status groups obtain their self-worth through the respect of other members in their community (Brezina et al.). In order to protect this self-worth, the street code defines how individuals should act when others try to attack their status and, ultimately, their self-worth. For instance, within inner city neighbourhoods, rival gangs assert their dominance through acts of disrespect, which are usually of a criminal and violent nature, including "tagging"[14] rival gangs' territories, fighting, and using a firearm (Lozon and Bensimon). Through violent, criminal acts, individuals are able to gain respect by promoting themselves as violent. A study conducted in the inner-city neighbourhoods of Philadelphia found that adolescents would create conflict through altercations with others in order to build respect (Anderson). In gang culture, one of the most common ways to develop respect is through violence, usually perpetrated using a firearm.

As highlighted throughout mass media, guns are a pivotal mechanism for settling scores and asserting dominance over others. As previously mentioned, both Biggie and Tupac referenced the use of guns to settle their conflicts with one another. This is also a common feature of many rap songs as well as an unwritten rule in the ghetto. Since many rappers grew up in poverty-stricken neighbourhoods, the street code is identified and idolized within their lyrics to assert how to deal with conflicts. As noted, rap lyrics emphasize that individuals must adhere to the street code, not only by following the rules of the street but also by immersing themselves in the street culture and adopting a specific persona.

One of the ways this occurs is by building a social identity as a gangster. In order to do so, one must create a demeanour that discourages others from disrespecting or challenging them; this is usually accomplished by acting violently towards another gang (i.e., by stealing from other gangs, marking their territories through tagging, or killing a rival gang member) (Kubrin). The street code entices violence as a means of resolving conflict, especially when disrespect is involved. The street code justifies violence through three propositions: (1) "to retain respect and deter future transgressions, it is necessary to respond to public assaults against the self with physical retaliation"; (2) "given the first proposition, public attacks or shows of disrespect can be expected to elicit a violent response from streetwise persons"; (3) "everyone has the opportunity to know and learn [the propositions]" (Brezina et al. 306). In these instances, violence is deemed to be the only appropriate response and there is an assumption that the instigator deserves any payback that comes to them. As such, due to the risk of victimization within the ghetto, minority youths are more likely to carry a gun for the first time once they become members of a gang due to the increased risk of exposure to violence through retaliation or initiation. In the end, these acts of violence play out like a ping-pong game, bullets going back and forth between opposing gangs, ultimately until more deaths accumulate. Therefore, there is a correlation between gang membership, experiencing violence and carrying a gun. So, how could rap music be correlated with increased gun violence among youth gangs?

Learned Behaviour

Ronald Aker's social learning theory is pivotal to understanding the correlation between gangsta rap and gun violence. Social learning theory posits that crime is learned through observed behaviours, and the likelihood of modelling this behaviour is based on the observed rewards or punishment of the action (Akers). The main purpose of this theory is to explain how individuals learn deviant behaviour, which can be linked to their peer groups:

> The probability that persons will engage in criminal and deviant behaviour is increased and the probability of their conforming to the norm is decreased when they differentially associate with others who commit criminal behaviour and espouse definitions favourable to it, are relatively more exposed in-person or symbolically to salient criminal/deviant models, define it as desirable or justified in a situation discriminative for the behaviour, and have received in the past and anticipate in the current or future situation relatively greater reward than punishment for the behaviour (Akers 50).

Akers argues that there are four key components to learning criminal behaviour: differential associations, definitions favouring the violation of the law, imitation, and differential reinforcements. Differential association and definitions are components of differential association theory. The social learning process begins with the association of deviant peers, who then provide individuals with the definitions that determine the "attitudes, perceptions and justifications for deviance that might neutralize the potential negative consequences of traditional offending" (Burruss et al. 1162). Imitations and differential reinforcement were added as part of the revision to differential association theory. Differential reinforcement occurs during the social learning process when individuals weigh the rewards and punishments of their actions. Akers states the following: "Whether individuals will refrain from or initiate, continue committing, or desist from criminal and deviant acts depends on the relative frequency, amount, and probability or past, present, and anticipated rewards and punishments perceived to be attached to the behaviour" (66).

This is an important part of the social learning process, since individuals will use their experiences with rewards or punishments received for committing criminal acts in order to determine their persistence or desistance in criminal activities. Finally, imitation can be defined as following the behaviours of those observed by others based on the already determined consequences (Akers). Imitation is vital to the social learning process because individuals may be more likely to commit criminal acts if they see others committing the act without receiving punishment. Therefore, criminal behaviour is learned through the association with deviant peers who are rewarded rather than punished for the criminal acts they commit.

Social learning theory can be used to explain gang membership through the process of mentoring. Mentors play an important role in the social learning process, since individuals learn from other members in society that they associate with. For example, if an individual associates mostly with gang members, there will be an increased likelihood that the individual becomes part of the gang. Often people join gangs due to peer pressure (Walker-Barnes and Mason), and according to social learning theory, this means that having delinquent friends or family is the first step to getting involved in a gang. Once individuals have immersed themselves into the gang environment, the gang provides individuals with the tools and justifications to commit criminal acts in an effort to prove their dedication to the gang (Winfree Jr, Mays and Vigil-Bäckström). The next part of the process involves assessing the rewards and punishments in relation to the others in the gang. This can reinforce the benefits of joining a gang, especially when criminal acts result in instant gratification without punishment (Winfree Jr, Mays and Vigil-Bäckström). Therefore, adolescents are more likely to become involved with gangs when they learn through the process of mentoring and favourable reinforcements.

One of the main influences growing up in impoverished neighbourhoods is the presence of criminal mentors for young adolescents. As noted, many families living within these neighbourhoods are unable to retain gainful employment due to the lack of resources and opportunities that are afforded within these locations (Klemp-North). Since there is a lack of opportunities, families may turn to illegitimate avenues in order to not only make money but also handle the stress. As such, young adolescents are surrounded by mentors who are highly immersed in the street lifestyle and, in turn, are taught specific lessons about growing up on the streets from a young age. For instance, these mentors (e.g., their family members, close relatives, and friends) teach youths about the tactics needed to avoid getting caught while committing criminal acts, how to be initiated into a gang and once initiated, how to use violence on others who disrespect them, which can and does involve the use of a firearm (Winfree Jr, Mays and Vigil-Bäckström). As explored previously, there is a correlation between gang membership and carrying a gun for the first time. Due to peer imitation, the involvement in a gang emphasizes and reinforces the persona of a gangsta and as such youths, are able to learn from their mentors about how to effectively use a firearm as a means of resolving conflict. Since there is a lack of diversity within the different mentors in these areas, youths quickly learn the values that are desired within these neighbourhoods. Thus, these adolescents are taught by their peers that survival comes first, respect cannot be taken for granted, and one must fight at all costs for their place in the world (Anderson). For these children, the most valuable lessons are not the ones that are taught in schools, but the ones taught from the people around them on how to thrive and survive in a location centred around violence.

Rap Music and Gang Culture

The main genre of music that exemplifies much of modern gang culture is rap music. Gangsta rap is commonly used to communicate or represent the gangster lifestyle: "Gangsta rap is known for its vivid sexist, misogynistic, and homophobic lyrics as well as its violent depiction of urban ghetto life" (Lozon and Bensimon 1244). Rap lyrics are the expression of the gangster lifestyle, attitudes, and the lived experience of growing up, living, and dying on the streets. A common theme in rap music is the options used by many marginalized youths to survive while living in disadvantaged neighbourhoods, with little to no opportunities for social and economic progression. The truth about the hardships faced by these rappers appeals to marginalized youth because they are living similar experiences.

Gangsta rap, in particular, depicts life growing up in crime-filled streets (Lozon and Bensimon). For some, rap music can draw in listeners by creating an emotional connection to the rapper's lived experience and identity, ultimately transforming the rapper from just a performer to a mentor. This connection is important especially for marginalized youth because it promotes and creates a collective unit, one that connects people with similar lived experiences. Some rappers, such as Tupac and Biggie, use their music to highlight the misfortunes of growing up on the streets, the systemic impacts of racism, political and social injustices, as well as issues relating to drugs, gangs, and gun violence. These are the realities of many marginalized groups, particularly Black youths: "[Black] adolescents have been consistently harassed by the local police, subjected to prejudice and discrimination and often struggle to procure respectable [life opportunities]" (Lozon and Bensimon 1247). Rappers are essentially rapping about what they know, their lived experiences, just as other artists do. However, the problem with any celebrity in any music genre is that their lyrics have power; these artists become role models and youths ultimately want to act and behave like them. Since many rap lyrics portray gun violence as an appropriate means of ending a conflict on the streets, it leads impressionable youth to believe and act in accordance with messages favouring gun violence. This is where the issue lies within the rap industry: The gangster lifestyle is embodied by many of the rappers on and off camera, which makes it hard to differentiate the real from the fake. As a result, what do young, impressionable adolescents take away from rap music?

Idolized Mentors

Social learning theory emphasizes the role of imitation. Imitation occurs when individuals act in similar ways to the behaviour they observe (Akers). The importance of this theory is the recognition that individuals will learn to act criminally from mentors that promote the beneficial consequences of criminal behaviour. Craig Anderson et al. argue that the likelihood that an individual will acquire an observed behaviour is increased when the model performing the behaviour is similar to the viewer, the context is realistic, and the viewer is able to see the perceived benefits of the action. Rappers are idols and models for marginalized youth because of their shared lived experiences. Many of the early rappers were former gang members; as such, their lyrics heavily relied on their previous experiences of growing up in the streets (Lozon and Bensimon). Rappers such as Tupac, Biggie, and Snoop Dogg are known for their violent lyrics; however, their gangster identities are also recognized. For example, in 1993, Snoop Dogg was charged with murder after an altercation with another gang member (Daunt). Although Snoop Dogg was acquitted, his lyrics continued to portray a violent, criminal lifestyle, where guns must be carried to resolve issues. In many rap songs, it is not only recommended but also required that young Black adolescents use guns in order to protect themselves and to assert their dominance over others. These types of lyrics teach young gang members the code of the streets and the importance of using a firearm in different circumstances in order to emphasize and bolster a gangster persona. To many adolescents growing up in the ghetto, the messages of gun violence are the main takeaways from the music they listen to everyday.

The majority of the content described in gangsta rap emphasizes violent, tough lifestyles that rely on guns to solve problems. These lyrics portray a reality that is all too real to members living in the ghetto. Adolescents look up to these rappers because they survived on the same streets, in the same conditions, and with similar struggles, creating a collective identity. Through these identities, both in the streets and in the music industry, there is a consensus that violent behaviour is condoned in certain circumstances (i.e., to resolve conflict, to demand respect, and to show dominance). Why does a shared identity lead to an influence of rap music on gun violence?

Shared Identity, Shared Set of Codes to the Streets

Rap lyrics are an educational tool for some marginalized youth by reiterating the street code that must be observed and learned. As argued in social learning theory, criminal behaviour is a learned behavioural code that is reinforced by one's peers. Jeffrey Lozon and Moshe Bensimon argue gangsta rap teaches the street code and is used as a guide to educate gang members. The lyrics in many of the most notoriously known rap songs involve positive messages about the use of gun violence as a means of ending conflict. Unfortunately, not only do the lyrics emphasize a positive message for gun use, but they also essentially argue for the motive and need for payback through violent actions such as shooting up a rival gang member. For instance, in Nas's song "Shoot 'Em Up", gun violence is portrayed as a way of ending conflict with rival gangs:

> One 44, two 45's/Three loaded clips, four niggas roll, one nigga drives/500 Benz, six reasons why this kid should die/We shooting every mothafucka outside/Pulled on his block, jumped out the car/Guns in our hand, at the same time everybody ran/There that nigga go, hiding in the crowd/Let the trigger blow, seven shots now he lying on the ground.

These lyrics dictate how one must handle a conflict, ultimately by shooting another gang member. Gang rivalry exists heavily in disadvantaged neighbourhoods because different gangs fight over territory in order to increase their ability to commit criminal acts, such as drug dealing (Brezina et al.). For many gang members, this is not just a song; it is their reality, one that they will experience on a day-to-day basis.

Rap music also educates the newcomers on the life they are about to enter. Lozon and Bensimon use the example of Nipsey Hussle and Snoop Dogg's song "Gangsta's Life," which explains in detail the personal life experiences of these rappers when they lived in the urban ghetto. Rappers use these lyrics as an educational tool for how to survive and the proper way to act on the streets, which emphasizes gun violence. As such, these rappers become mentors for marginalized youth because of the connection between the similar lifestyles; hence the mentality becomes one of 'If he can escape the ghetto, so can I, as long as I follow the street code." In order to survive, youths within gangs must learn and adapt to the street code. In essence, their lives depend on their ability to develop social respect within the ghetto and react when that social respect is disregarded. Therefore, in order to do so, youth gangs turn to the street code exemplified in gangsta rap in order to know how to act and react to social situations within the ghetto. The gun, therefore, becomes one of the only mechanisms for staying alive while they are living in the ghetto, as it enables these youths to protect themselves in the face of danger and enables them to maintain the power and dominance needed to keep thriving in order to escape these circumstances.

How to Use Gangsta Rap for Change

Although gangsta rap is a catalyst for gun violence due to the constant portrayal of guns as a means to solving conflict, gangsta rap can also be used to change the narrative for these marginalized youths. Rap music highlights the disparities occurring in low-income neighbourhoods, the struggles to survive, and the systemic racism that plagues these communities each and every day. The issue of systemic racism keeps Black people in an endless cycle of constant gang violence, imprisonment, and low socioeconomic status. Tupac said it best: "THUG LIFE: The hate you give little infants fucks everyone." Tupac was a rapper known for his lyrics that portrayed gun violence as the answer to conflicts. He was a heavily recognized individual among the music industry and a role model for young Black adolescents. Tupac's songs represented and displayed the epitome of gun violence, gangs, hustling, and a lifestyle surrounded by danger and violence. However, Tupac, along with many other rappers, used their lyrics to portray the reality of the world they live in everyday—one that is plagued with gun violence, gangs, low economic status, and few opportunities. Tupac's motto, "Thug Life," identifies the need for change on a greater scheme: the need for policymakers to take action, for systemic racism to end, and for communities to work together to foster a better life for young Black adolescents. The reality is what society teaches and fosters in these children is what they will grow up to be and give back to the community. Music has the power to create change and to start conversations regarding issues such as gun violence, and without this change gun violence will continue to plague the streets.

This is where government officials need to start to change the influence of the media on gun violence. Policymakers need to holistically address all issues that contribute to the increase in gun violence. One way to do this is to target the issues contributing to gun violence, one being the increasing presence of youth gangs. In order for this to occur, systemic racism, issues of disadvantage, and the inability to advance through legal opportunities, such as gainful employment and education, need to be addressed. The narrative for so many ethnically diverse adolescents needs to be one of opportunity, growth, support, and change. Therefore, by providing these youths with opportunities to cope with strenuous situations in legal, positive ways, it will decrease the need for guns, gangs, and violence. These efforts can bring about positive change for many young adolescents growing up in the ghetto so that their lives are not plagued with gun violence and upcoming rappers have better life experiences to draw upon when they are writing their lyrics.

Conclusion

In conclusion, this analysis explored the nexus between gangsta rap and gun violence among youth gangs. Gangsta rap is known for its vulgar and violent imagery related to gang wars and gun violence. The presumption that guns solve all problems is one that is heavily emphasized within gangsta rap and the street code. As such, youth gangs rely on their rapper mentors, such as Tupac and Biggie, to teach them how to survive and thrive within the ghetto. Through their lyrics, these rappers provide a guide for growing up on the inner-city streets, ultimately teaching these marginalized youth to become gangsters, to demand respect, and to believe that gun violence is an acceptable and required response to disrespect. The reality is that the issue of gun violence is not within lyrics but in the social and economic issues that plague the streets of the ghetto. In order to understand the catalytic role of gangsta rap on gun violence among youth gangs, one must understand that following the street code, so often articulated in rap lyrics, is the difference between staying alive and dying within the ghetto. Therefore, in order to reduce the presence of gun violence among youth gangs, policies need to address the economic and social hardships that promote gang membership.

Endnotes

1. The National Youth Gang Survey data encompasses information from 1996 to 2011. This is the most up to date analysis conducted on gang-related firearm homicides in the US.
2. Death Row Records was the main record label on the West Coast, which signed many famous rappers, such as Snoop Dogg, NWA, and Tupac (*Hip-Hop Evolution*).
3. Bad Boy Records was the main record label on the East Coast, which consisted of such rappers as Puff Daddy and Biggie (*Hip-Hop Evolution*).
4. According to the 2002 Canadian Police Survey on Youth Gangs, 6 per cent of gang members are female.
5. During the 2002 Canadian Police Survey on Youth Gangs, it was determined that First Nations represented 22 per cent of the gang population; Caucasians made up 18 per cent; East Indians accounted for 14 per cent; Asians made up 12 per cent; 6 per cent were Latinos; and 3 per cent were Arab.
6. According to the 2002 Canadian Police Survey on Youth Gangs, 10 per cent of the population were younger than sixteen; 39 per cent ranged between sixteen and eighteen years old; 37 per cent were between nineteen and twenty-one years old; and 14 per cent were over twenty-two years old.
7. The Astwood Strategy Survey conducted in 2002 was the first and most recent survey that analyzed the characteristics of youth gangs in Canada.
8. In Canada, from 2008 to 2012, among young adolescents, 55 per cent of firearm deaths were homicides (Austin and Lane).
9. The results of Spano and Bolland's (850) study determined that approximately "71% of youth who were gang members were also exposed to violence compared to 45% of non-gang members."
10. To determine this, Spano and Bolland divided the percentage of gang members engaged in violent behaviour versus nongang members.
11. Essentially for Cohen, individuals formed groups to deal with strenuous events rather than dealing with these events individually.
12. Cohen would argue that gangs are a delinquent subculture because

they have their own set of rules about how they react to the given problems that they face; these rules are known as the street code.

13. For the purpose of this chapter, we will be focusing on expressive crimes.
14. A graffiti tag is basically a signature, an individual identifier adopted by writers, and that the tagger will be known by in the graffiti culture (Hardin et al.).

Works Cited

Akers, Ronald L. *Social Learning and Social Structure: a General Theory of Crime and Deviance.* Northeastern University Press, 1998.

Anderson, Craig A., et al. "The influence of media violence on youth." *Psychological Science in the Public Interest,* vol.4, no.3, 2003, pp. 81-110.

Anderson, Elijah. *Code of the Street: Decency, Violence, and the Moral Life of the Inner City.* W. W. Norton & Company, 2000.

Astwood Strategy Corporation. *Results of the 2002 Canadian Police Survey on Youth Gangs. Public Safety,* 2003, www.securitepublique.gc.ca/cnt/cntrng-crm/plcng/cnmcs-plcng/rsrch-prtl/rslts-en.aspx?a=%22Astwood+Strategy+Corporation%22. Accessed 7 Apr. 2022.

Austin, Katherine, and Margo Lane. "The Prevention of Firearm Injuries in Canadian Youth." *Paediatrics & Child Health,* vol.23, no.1, 2018, pp. 35-42.

Berthiaume, Lee. "Statistics Canada Blames Gang Violence, Shootings as Homicide Rate Hits 10-Year High." *CTVNews. Bell Media,* 21 Nov. 2018, https://www.ctvnews.ca/canada/statistics-canada-blames-gang-violence-shootings-as-homicide-rate-hits-10-year-high-1.4186494. Accessed 7 Apr. 2022.

Brezina, Timothy, et al. "The Code of the Street: A Quantitative Assessment of Elijah Anderson's Subculture of Violence Thesis and Its Contribution to Youth Violence Research." *Youth Violence and Juvenile Justice,* vol. 2, no. 4, 2004, pp. 303-28.

Burruss, George W., Adam M. Bossler, and Thomas J. Holt. "Assessing the Mediation of a Fuller Social Learning Model on Low Self-Control's Influence on Software Piracy." *Crime & Delinquency,* vol.

59, no.8, 2013, pp. 1157-84.

Canton, David A. "The Political, Economic, Social, and Cultural Tensions in Gangsta Rap." *Reviews in American History,* vol. 34, no.2, 2006, pp. 244-57.

Centers for Disease Control and Prevention. *National Center for Injury Prevention and Control: Web-based Injury Statistics Query and Reporting System* (WISQARS), 2006, www.cdc.gov/injury/wisqars/index.html. Accessed 7 Apr. 2022.

Chang, Rachel. "How Biggie and Tupac Went from Friends to Music's Biggest Rivals." *Biography, A&E Networks Television,* 12 Sept. 2019, www.biography.com/news/biggie-tupac-friends-rivals-east-coast-west-coast. Accessed 7 Apr. 2022.

Cohen, Albert K. *Delinquent Boys: The Culture of the Gang.* Free Press, 1955.

Daunt, Tina. "Rapper Snoop Doggy Dogg Is Acquitted of Murder." *Los Angeles Times.* 21 Feb. 1996, www.latimes.com/archives/la-xpm-1996-02-21-mn-38322-story.html. Accessed 7 Apr. 2022.

Dog, Tim. "Fuck Compton." *YouTube,* www.youtube.com/watch?v=n5lLiI-M3aY. Accessed 7 Apr. 2022.

Dunbar, Laura. "Youth Gang Exit: A Canadian Perspective." *Global Perspectives on Youth Gang Behavior, Violence and Weapons Use,* edited by Simon Harding, and Marek Palasinki, Information Science Reference, 2016, pp. 133-57.

Gatti, Uberto, et al. "Youth Gangs, Delinquency and Drug Use: A Test of the Selection, Facilitation, and Enhancement Hypotheses." *Journal of Child Psychology and Psychiatry,* vol. 46, no.11, 2005, pp. 1178-90.

Gillis, Wendy. "GTA Mayors and Police Chiefs Call for Smarter Investment on 'Unacceptable' Youth Gun Violence." *The Toronto Star,* 28 Jan. 2020, www.thestar.com/news/gta/2020/01/28/gta-mayors-and-police-chiefs-call-for-smarter-investment-on-unacceptable-youth-gun-violence.html. Accessed 7 Apr. 2022.

Hardin, Rod, et al. "Are You the Parent of a Tagger?" *Saskatoon Police,* saskatoonpolice.ca/pdf/brochures/Are_You_The_Parent_of_a_Tagger.pdf. Accessed 7 Apr. 2022.

Kennedy, Gerrick D. "The Moment N.W.A Changed the Music

World." *Los Angeles Times,* 9 Dec. 2017, www.latimes.com/entertainment/music/la-et-ms-nwa-parental-discretion-20171205-htmlstory.html. Accessed 7 Apr. 2022.

Klemp-North, Michael. "Theoretical Foundations for Gang Membership." *Journal of Gang Research,* vol. 14, no. 4, 2007, pp. 11-26.

Kubrin, Charis E. "'I See Death around the Corner': Nihilism in Rap Music." *Sociological Perspectives,* vol. 48, no. 4, 2005, pp. 433-59.

Lederer, Edith M. "464,000 People Killed in Homicides around the World in 2017: UN Report." *Global News,* 9 July 2019, globalnews.ca/news/5473422/un-report-homicides-2019/. Accessed 7 Apr. 2022.

Lozon, Jeffrey, and Moshe Bensimon. "A Systematic Review on the Functions of Rap Among Gangs." *International Journal of Offender Therapy and Comparative Criminology,* vol. 6, no. 11, 2015, pp. 1243-61.

Nas. "Shoot 'Em Up." *YouTube,* www.youtube.com/watch?v=xuQv5Culpbs. Accessed 7 Apr. 2022.

National Gang Centre. "Frequently Asked Questions about Gangs." *Institute for Intergovernmental Research,* nationalgangcenter.ojp.gov/about/faq#:~:text=%20Frequently%20Asked%20Questions%20About%20Gangs%20%201,How%20extensive%20is%20the%20gang-drug-violence%20connection%3F%20More%20. Accessed 7 Apr. 2022.

NWA. "Fuck Tha Police." *YouTube,* www.youtube.com/watch?v=5lt1OsPSdBc. Accessed 7 Apr. 2022.

Public Safety Canada. *Gun and Gang Violence. Public Safety Canada,* 8 Jan. 2019. www.publicsafety.gc.ca/cnt/cntrng-crm/gn-crm-frrms/index-en.aspx. Accessed 7 Apr. 2022.

Public Safety Canada. *Youth Gangs in Canada: What Do We Know? Public Safety Canada,* 1 Jan 2018. www.publicsafety.gc.ca/cnt/rsrcs/pblctns/gngs-cnd/index-en.aspx. Accessed 7 Apr. 2022.

Rodrigo Bascunan et al. Directed by Darby Wheeler et al. *Hip-Hop Evolution,* Netflix, 2016.

Shakur, Tupac. "Hit Em Up." *YouTube,* www.youtube.com/watch?v=41qC3w3UUkU. Accessed 7 Apr. 2022.

Shakur, Tupac. "T.H.U.G.L.I.F.E. (The Hate U Give Little Infants

Fuck Everybody)." *YouTube*, www.youtube.com/watch?v=128ao5Xl_VY. Accessed 7 Apr. 2022.

Slocum, Lee A., and Sally S. Simpson. "Strained Lives and Crime: Examining Intra-Individual Variation in Strain and Offending in a Sample of Incarcerated Women." *Criminology*, vol. 43, no. 4, 2005, pp. 1067-10.

Spano, Richard, and John M. Bolland. "Is the Nexus of Gang Membership, Exposure to Violence, and Violent Behavior a Key Determinant of First Time Gun Carrying for Urban Minority Youth?" *Justice Quarterly*, vol. 29, no. 6, 2011, pp. 838-62.

Straight Outta Compton. Directed by F. Gary Gray, with O'Shea Jackson Jr., Corey Hawkins, Jason Mitchell, Neil Brown Jr., Universal Pictures, 2015.

The Canadian Press. "Toronto Police Chief Says Recent Strong Gun Violence in City Related to Street Gangs." *Global News*, 9 Aug. 2019, globalnews.ca/news/5746070/toronto-police-chief-mark-saunders-gun-violence/. Accessed 7 Apr. 2022.

Tita, George E., Emily Troshynski, and Michelle Graves. "Strategies for Reducing Gun Violence: The Role of Gangs, Drugs and Firearm Accessibility." *Public Safety Canada*, 2007, www.publicsafety.gc.ca/cnt/rsrcs/pblctns/rdcng-gn-vlnc/index-en.aspx . Accessed 7 Apr. 2022.

UNODC. *Global Study on Homicide 2019: Executive Summary*. The United Nations Office on Drugs and Crime, 2019.

Walker-Barnes, Chanequa J., and Craig A. Mason. "Ethnic Differences in the Effect of Parenting on Gang Involvement and Gang Delinquency: A Longitudinal, Hierarchical Linear Modeling Perspective." *Child Development*, vol. 72, no. 6, 2001, pp. 1814-31.

Winfree Jr., L. Thomas, G. Larry Mays, and Teresa Vigil-Bäckström. "Youth Gangs and Incarcerated Delinquents: Exploring the Ties between Gang Membership, Delinquency, and Social Learning Theory." *Justice Quarterly*, vol. 11, no. 2, 1944, pp. 229-256.

Youngs, Donna, Maria Ioannou, and Jenna Eagles. "Expressive and Instrumental Offending: Reconciling the Paradox of Specialisation and Versatility." *International Journal of Offender Therapy and Comparative Criminology*, vol. 60, no.4, 2016, pp. 1-26.

Chapter 4

A Public Health Approach to Toronto's Black Homicide Victimization is Long Overdue

Akwatu Khenti

Canada has long been a global leader in the areas of public health and health promotion. Such leadership was internationally recognized when the COVID-19 pandemic emerged, and the Public Health Agency of Canada acted proactively to sustain collective action and multisectoral coordination to contain it (Chattu, Anil and Yaya). This longstanding leadership attribute has not yielded similar results in addressing racialized risks or disparities in mortalities related to COVID-19 or gun violence. For instance, some public health leaders have not considered race-based data in public health responses to these issues and have appeared insensitive to the significant risks and consequences they bring to racialized groups (Khenti; Yaya et al.).

A crucial criterion for public health leadership is the understanding that health for every citizen, regardless of the community to which they belong, cannot be achieved without certain necessary conditions being met. Conditions, such as adequate income and education, are assumed to be critical resources for health preservation and for tempering issues affecting socially marginalized people in all contexts (Hankivsky and Christoffersen; Raphael). The work of public health is not equitably realized across social risks and populations. Despite three decades of mortality disparity in gun homicide victimization among Black residents of Toronto, Ontario, a major public health shift towards reducing and eliminating preventable harms associated with this disparity remains imminent (Khenti). Indeed, their citizenship entitlement to healthy conditions—which should involve access to targeted prevention and informed care related to gun violence risks and harms—continues to hang in the balance, despite accumulating international evidence that such considerations can effectively reduce victimization (Krisch, Eisner, and Mikton; Richardson).

Indeed, the conditions that Black Canadians need to be healthy are far from ideal. Education and employment are key determinants of health, yet evidence shows that young Black males and females who were between thirteen and seventeen in 2006 were less likely than their non-Black peers to have attained a postsecondary certificate, diploma, or degree by 2016. Similarly, Black job seekers in 2014 were more than twice as likely as non-Black peers to encounter racial discrimination when looking for work (13 per cent vs 6 per cent respectively) and thus more likely to be unsuccessful in their efforts (Turcotte). The lower likelihood of both high school graduation and a successful job search is the result of experiences of structural violence that involve a range of factors—namely, low educational expectations, academic streaming, and overreliance on expulsions and/or suspensions in the school system. For example, Black children and youth are more likely to be suspended or expelled from schools in jurisdictions such as Peel and Toronto than their white peers (James and Samaroo). Such disparities undoubtedly account for a significant proportion of variations in morbidity and mortality (Khenti; Satcher and Higginbotham). The disparity in school dropout rates among Black youth may well be the primary environmental driver of a persistent gun homicide epidemic in Toronto that engenders huge disparity in emergency room visits for related injuries and excess mortality rates.

The negative impact of school dropout on gun carrying by both Black and white youth has been well documented (Butters et al.; Kahn). However, for Black youth, their outcomes with guns following school dropout are further complicated by experiences of systemic racism as well as distrust with and victimization by the police (Khubchandani and Price). Consequently, although Blacks and whites have equal capacity to achieve academically and/or make correct choices about violence involvement, Black youth and young adults in Toronto experience public stigmatization that undermines both their life potential as well as decision making related to harmful behaviours (Welch). The scope of this problem is huge. But where the problem is amplified by higher rates of school dropout among Black youth, the resolution lies in resources and efforts to prevent dropouts. It is no surprise that funds devoted to keeping Black youth enrolled in school is a fraction of the resources applied to gun reduction in Ontario (Butters et al.). A public health conceptualization of the collaboration and coordination required to reorient educational efforts in gun violence reduction is therefore justifiable. The following data underscore why a public health approach is sorely needed.

Stark Numbers in Toronto Homicide

The past fifteen years reveals some deeply disturbing patterns. The following table (1) lists all homicides in Toronto between 2004 and 2019.Of the 1,042 victims, 828 were males, and 214 were females. Blacks comprised only about 7.5 per cent of the total population during this fifteen-year period in Toronto (Maheux and Do), but 523 of the victims (50 per cent) were Black: 485 males and 38 females. Given their population, only about seventy-eight victims should have been Black over the course of the fifteen years. Instead, Toronto's Black community bore an excess mortality burden of approximately 445 homicides over the fifteen-year period.

Category	Total Homicides	Total Males	Total Females	Total Black	Black Male	Black Female
Number	1042	828	214	523	485	38
% of total	100%	79%	21%	50%	93%	7%

Table 1. Homicides in Toronto between 2004 and 2019

Both male and female data present disparities, but the male disparity is especially pronounced; more pointedly, only thirty-eight Black males should have been homicide victims according to their share of the city's population.[2] Instead, Toronto had at least 485 Black male victims, since I excluded racially ambiguous victims. These disparities situate Toronto in the ranks of US cities, such as New York and Detroit, with respect to excess Black male deaths, reflecting the broader geographic scope of this serious North America-wide public health problem (Geronimus). It would not be an unreasonable speculation, in the absence of race-based data, to assume that Black Torontonians share a firearm-related disparity in life expectancy that is akin to African American males (Sharkey and Friedson). According to a recent study, Black males in the US are experiencing a total life expectancy loss of 4.14 years due to gun violence (Kalesan et al.).

Could Black male Torontonians be experiencing the same? Without the application of race-based data to health information (including mortality data) in Ontario, we may never be able to fully answer this question.

The mean age for Black male victims was approximately 26.48 compared, with an average age of 33.8 for all male victims. The mean age was 35.04 for Black female victims compared to 40.4 for all female victims. The fact that Black victims tend to be younger than their non-Black counterparts suggests that years of life lost by Toronto's Black communities constitute a significant demographic harm that lends additional urgency to the longstanding need for a public health approach. Indeed, reducing the racialized homicide rate could represent a significant public health accomplishment by adding years to life expectancy at birth for Black males. The age disparity for Black male victims also suggests the need for much more intensive targeted efforts aimed at mitigating disparities in health outcomes as well as education, employment, and criminal justice.

The Problem of Gun Homicide

Most of the homicides during the fifteen-year period discussed above, including all Black homicides, were the result of shootings, stabbings, and assault or trauma ending in death (manslaughter). The following Table (2) lists the causes of all homicides, indicating that most Black persons were killed by guns, unlike the relatively even distribution observed among non-Black male victims. Additionally, of the 409 shooting victims, a staggering 78 per cent were Black males, and the vast majority involved illegal handguns smuggled from the US (Ezeonu; Sheptycki; Thompson). Given the longstanding focus on reducing illegal gun supply from the US, the need for effective equity-based demand reduction and harm-reduction strategies regarding guns could not be starker. The risks and harms associated with gun possession and gun carrying have to be brought home to at-risk young Black men in messaging that resonates culturally and speaks to their racialized vulnerability in Toronto and Canadian life.

Category	Total Shot	Total Stabbed	Total Assault/ Trauma	Black Male Shot	Black Male Stabbed	Black Male Assault/ Trauma
Number	409	67	47	401	55	29
% of total	78%	13%	9%	77%	11%	6%

Table 2. Causes of Black homicides in Toronto between 2004 and 2019

The prevalence of gun use has persisted despite additional public resources for criminal justice approaches following every major shooting outrage. Such practices as carding or street checks, which inevitably exacerbate racial profiling, have been the go-to response following acts of racialized violence and homicide in Toronto (Siciliano). The *Toronto Star* has repeatedly confirmed that Blacks, especially Black males, were subject to racial profiling through higher rates of stops and carding and experienced harsher treatment by police during stops, searches, and arrests (Rankin). Such practices have been applied across Toronto's many Black communities despite infringing upon Canada's Charter of Rights and Freedoms. Moreover, there is no scientific evidence of positive impact on the phenomenon across the fifteen years under consideration. I could find no statistical association between carding practices and numbers of homicide within Toronto's 140 neighbourhoods during the period from 2004 to 2014, and I expect the same empirical result holds for subsequent years, 2015 to 2019 (Khenti; Csete et al.).

Municipalities that have adopted public health approaches have effectively reduced their rates of homicide mortality, regardless of the type of public health intervention or the type of violence. For instance, Boston used group violence interventions (GVI) to avoid violent escalations of disputes and provide educational and mentoring pathways out of crime and witnessed declines in racialized gun fatalities, whereas Glasgow created an integrated public health and policing crime reduction unit—the Scottish Crime Reduction Unit—to tackle knife violence and saw significant declines in related mortality (Henderson, Peterson and Engel; Skott and McVie). These cities have succeeded through the broadening of efforts to address these issues from approaches centred on policing to ones rooted in public health. Engaging and building truly meaningful partnerships with community residents in vulnerable neighbourhoods has also been key to effectively addressing the gun violence and homicide victimization problems. Black gun possession, gun carrying, and gun use are serious public safety and public health problems. Effectively addressing overarching risk factors requires both a more effective public safety approach as well as the public health prevention and intervention strategies that have yet to be fully tried.

Conclusion

Although racialized school dropout rates and gang involvement and/or victimization by peers may be proximal causes of racialized gun violence and Black homicide victimization, it is systemic anti-Black racism across Toronto and Canadian society that are fundamental causes of the problem (Phelan and Link). A completely futile war on drugs, launched when illicit drug use was already in decline, has amplified the exposure to structural violence among Toronto's Black youth and young adults—leading to oversurveillance of Black boys/youth in both elementary and secondary schools, overreliance by educators on police to resolve issues in school settings, and neglect for the school to prison pipeline that has doubled Black representation in both provincial and federal prisons (Khenti). By contrast, Toronto's white youth and young adults have been largely spared intrusive policing and detentions for use of illegal drugs, especially cannabis, and are increasingly underrepresented in correctional settings (Owusu-Bempah, Luscombe, and Finlay).

Anti-Black racial stigmatization within schools is reinforced by similar experiences in interactions with child welfare workers, healthcare providers, community housing, and public transportation. A violent temperament and criminal proclivity are behaviours that are disseminated widely as Black cultural characteristics (Welch). Not surprisingly, some Black youth and young adults acquire a sense of powerlessness as a result of their discriminatory experiences and begin to self-stigmatize—expressing behaviours that confirm the negative stereotypes (Khenti; Rankin). Inevitably, intensification of marginal socioeconomic conditions engenders social frustrations and anger that may lead to fatal interpersonal violence, especially because institutional decisionmakers are well beyond reach or influence in contrast to their peers. The precipitants can be experiences of victimization or even perceptions of disrespect by peers. Such experiences multiply risks of anxiety, depression, and even posttraumatic stress disorders (PTSD) and can fuel violent behaviours (Anderson; Nyborg and Curry; Sanders-Phillips). Although there is a need for research into various dimensions of this public health problem, the immediate imperative should be governmental actions to reduce the health harms. It is critically important to implement evidence-based public health initiatives that have proven efficacy in reducing the violence such as Cure Violence, GVI, or the Scottish Violence Reduction Unit.

Toronto, with provincial and federal support, can implement adequately resourced and targeted public health interventions aimed at reducing both racialized gun violence and Black homicide victimization. Evidence of successful public health approaches reducing such outcomes are now well established (Atienzo, Baxter and Kaltenthaler). Keeping at-risk Black youth in school acquiring meaningful knowledge and skills for the world of work is eminently doable, given a range of successful pilots that various school boards, including the Toronto District School Board, have tried but been unable to sustain (Howard and James; Murray). The Province of Ontario can bring an end to racialized streaming and suspensions while providing needed training and educational support across the school life cycle, including peer mentoring to divert Black youth and young adults out of high risk lifestyles and behaviours. The province's race-based data standard can also be effectively applied across education, child welfare, criminal justice, and healthcare to ensure the targeted success of such efforts; such data can also highlight those initiatives that are working well, or having limited impact, at important intersections in Black youth's lives.

The racialized behaviours that Black male youth and young adults are exhibiting in Toronto (and other Canadian cities) have more to do with public stigmatization within Canadian society than with anything intrinsic to Black and/or Caribbean or African culture. Many non-racialized subpopulations, such as marginalized youth and young adults in Glasgow, have exhibited similar problems of interpersonal violence among their peers because of a combination of socioeconomic marginalization and class stigma. Notably, such problems have been effectively addressed with public health approaches involving many sectors of society, including the criminal justice system.

All stigma, especially the racial stigma that is expressed within institutions, can be reduced, and harms can be mitigated, following the growing evidence of stigma reduction in mental health (Szeto et al.). Black and racialized communities can support public education efforts designed to reduce stigma (which have been found to have a positive impact on self-stigmatization) as well as engage with institutions, such as boards of education and police boards, to initiate and sustain organizational efforts to reduce the racial stigma and implicit bias that exist in these settings (Brown and Russell). Communities and families can also put in place efforts to instill African-centred resiliencies in their youth and young adults, since such attributes can strengthen their protective factors and reduce key risk factors (Khenti, "Homicide Among Young Black Men in Toronto"). What communities cannot do is change the institutions' cultures that sustain systemic anti-Black racism within key institutions—such as education, health, and criminal justice—across the Western world, nor can they lead public health campaigns. That remains the purview of boards of directors, leaders and decisionmakers, senior management teams and middle management as well as organizational champions across all levels of an institution. Health and criminal justice leaders in particular are urged to recognize that a comprehensive public health effort addressing gun violence is long overdue and needs no further justification.

Endnotes

1. Data about homicides occurring between January 1, 2004, and December 31, 2019, were taken from media sources in Toronto, including the *Toronto Star, CP24, National Post, Toronto Sun*, and other major print and online news outlets. In many cases, perpetrator information was undisclosed, unknown, or speculative, and media reports about perpetrators tended to be unreliable and inconsistent, so perpetrator data were omitted. The following analysis focuses

only on data about victims, including name, age, gender, race, and method of murder. Coding for race was based on published articles and publicly available police releases as well as photographs of victims available online and was verified by two independent coders. A Black/non-Black classification scheme is known to be crude and inherently problematic (Thompson), but it was necessary for this analysis.

2. According to a recent Statistics Canada report, *Diversity of the Black Population* (2019), Black males account for 48.4 per cent of the Black population.

Work Cited

Anderson, Katherine F. "Diagnosing Discrimination: Stress from Perceived Racism and the Mental and Physical Health Effects." *Sociological Inquiry*, vol. 83, no. 1, 2013, pp. 55-81.

Atienzo, Erika E., Susan K. Baxter, and Eva Kaltenthaler. "Interventions to Prevent Youth Violence in Latin America: A Systematic Review." *International Journal of Public Health*, vol. 62, no. 1, 2017, pp. 15-29.

Brown, Kirsten L., and Alex M. T. Russell. "Exploration of Intervention Strategies to Reduce Public Stigma Associated with Gambling Disorder." *Journal of Gambling Studies*, vol. 36, no. 2, 2020, pp. 713-33.

Bryant, Wesley W. *African American Male Youth Violence and Internalized Racism*. Bryn Mawr College, 2009.

Butters, Jennifer E., et al. "Guns and Sublethal Violence: A Comparative Study of At-Risk Youth in Two Canadian Cities." *International Criminal Justice Review*, vol. 21, no. 4, 2011, pp. 402-26.

Caughy, Margaret O'Brien, Patricia J. O'Campo, and Carles Muntaner. "Experiences of Racism among African American Parents and the Mental Health of their Preschool-Aged Children." *American Journal of Public Health*, vol. 94, no. 12, 2004, pp. 2118-24.

Census. "2011 National Household Survey: Immigration, Citizenship, Place of Birth, Ethnicity, Visible Minorities, Religion and Aboriginal Peoples." *City of Toronto*, 2013, www150.statcan.gc.ca/nl/daily-quotidien/130508/dq130508b-eng.htm. Accessed 27 Mar. 2022.

Chattu, Vijay Kumar, Anil Adisesh, and Sanni Yaya. "Canada's Role in Strengthening Global Health Security during the COVID-19 Pandemic." *Global Health Research and Policy*, vol. 5, no. 1, 2020, pp. 1-3.

Csete, Joanne, et al. "Public Health and International Drug Policy." *The Lancet*, vol. 387, no. 10026, 2016, pp. 1427-80.

Ezeonu, Celestine I. *The Social Construction of "Black-on-Black" Violence in Toronto*. PhD dissertation, University of Toronto, 2005.

Geronimus, Arline T. "The Health of Urban African American Men: Excess Mortality and Causes of Death." *Presentation, Comprehensive Community Initiatives Roundtable, Aspen Institute*, 1998, www.aspeninstitute.org/wp-content/uploads/files/content/upload/19Geronimus.pdf. Accessed 27 Mar. 2022.

Hankivsky, Olena, and Ashlee Christoffersen. "Intersectionality and the Determinants of Health: A Canadian perspective." *Critical Public Health*, vol. 18, no. 3, 2008, pp. 271-83.

Hayle, Steven, Scot Wortley, and Julian Tanner. "Race, Street Life, and Policing: Implications for Racial Profiling 1." *Canadian Journal of Criminology and Criminal Justice*, vol. 58, no. 3, 2016, pp. 322-53.

Henderson, Samantha M., Samuel S. Peterson, and Robin S. Engel. "Pulling Levers to Prevent Violence: 'The Boston Miracle,' Its Adaptations, and Future Directions for Research." *Preventing Crime and Violence*, Springer, Cham, 2017, pp. 281-96.

Hunte, Haslyn E., et al. "Interpersonal Discrimination and Depressive Symptomatology: Examination of Several Personality-Related Characteristics as Potential Confounders in a Racial/Ethnic Heterogeneous Adult Sample." *BMC Public Health*, vol. 13, no. 1, 2013, p. 1084.

Howard, Philip S.S., and Carl E. James. "When Dreams Take Flight: How Teachers Imagine and Implement an Environment That Nurtures Blackness at an Africentric School in Toronto, Ontario." *Curriculum Inquiry*, vol. 49, no. 3, 2019, pp. 313-37.

James, Carl E., and Julia A. Samaroo. "Alternative Schooling and Black Students: Opportunities, Challenges, and Limitations." *Alternative Schooling and Student Engagement*, edited by Nina Bascia, Esther Fine, and Michael A. Levin, Palgrave Macmillan, 2017, pp. 39-54.

Kahn, Laura, et al. "Youth Risk Behavior Surveillance—United States, 2015." *MMWR Surveill. Summ*, vol. 65, 2016, p. 119.

Kalesan, Bindu, et al. "Cross-Sectional Study of Loss of Life Expectancy at Different Ages Related to Firearm Deaths among Black and White Americans." *BMJ Evidence-Based Medicine*, vol. 24, no. 2, 2019, pp. 55-58.

Khenti, Akwatu A. "Homicide Among Young Black Men in Toronto: An Unrecognized Public Health Crisis?" *Canadian Journal of Public Health*, vol. 104, no. 1, 2013, pp. e12-e14.

Khenti, Akwatu A. "The Canadian War on Drugs: Structural Violence and Unequal Treatment of Black Canadians." *International Journal of Drug Policy*, vol. 25, no. 2, 2014, pp. 190-95.

Khenti, Akwatu A. *Three Decades of Epidemic Black Gun Homicide Victimization in Toronto: Analyzing Causes and Consequences of a Criminological Approach*. PhD dissertation, York University, 2018.

Khubchandani, Jagdish, and James H. Price. "Violent Behaviors, Weapon Carrying, and Firearm Homicide Trends in African American Adolescents, 2001–2015." *Journal of Community Health*, vol. 43, no. 5, 2018, pp. 947-55.

Krisch, Maria, Manuel Eisner, and Chris Mikton. "Global Strategies to Reduce Violence by 50% in 30 Years: Findings from the WHO and University of Cambridge Global Violence Reduction Conference 2014." *University of Cambridge*, 2015, www.vrc.crim.cam.ac.uk/system/files/documents/violencereductionreport.pdf. Accessed 27 Mar. 2022.

Maheux, Hélène, and Deniz Do. "Diversity of the Black Population in Canada: An Overview." *Statistics Canada*, 27 Feb 2019, www150.statcan.gc.ca/n1/pub/89-657-x/89-657-x2019002-eng.htm. Accessed 27 Mar. 2022.

Murray, Karen, et al. "Symposium: Driving Black Student Success on a System-Wide Level." *Journal of the Canadian Association for Curriculum Studies*, vol. 18, no. 1, 2020, pp. 57-59.

Nyborg, Vanessa M., and John Curry. "The Impact of Perceived Racism: Psychological Symptoms among African American Boys." *Journal of Clinical Child and Adolescent Psychology*, vol. 32, no. 2, 2003, pp. 258-66.

Owusu-Bempah, Akwasi, Alex Luscombe, and Brandon M. Finlay. "Unequal Justice: Race and Cannabis Arrests in the Post-Legal Landscape." *High Time: The Legalization and Regulation of Cannabis in Canada*, 2019, pp. 114-31.

Phelan, Jo C., and Bruce G. Link. "Is Racism a Fundamental Cause of Inequalities in Health?" *Annual Review of Sociology*, vol. 41, 2015, pp. 311-30.

Rankin, Jim. "Race Matters: Blacks Documented by Police at High Rate." *The Star*, 6 Feb. 2010, www.thestar.com/news/crime/raceandcrime/2010/02/06/race_matters_blacks_documented_by_police_at_high_rate.html. Accessed 27 Mar. 2022.

Rankin, Jim. "Singled Out." *The Star*, 19 Oct. 2002, www.thestar.com/news/gta/knowntopolice/2002/10/19/singled-out.html. Accessed 27 Mar. 2022.

Raphael, Dennis. "Grasping at Straws: A Recent History of Health Promotion in Canada." *Critical Public Health*, vol. 18, no. 4, 2008, pp. 483-95.

Richardson, Monte-Angel. "Framing Community-Based Interventions for Gun Violence: A Review of the Literature." *Health & Social Work*, vol. 44, no. 4, 2019, pp. 259-70.

Sanders-Phillips, Kathy. "Racial Discrimination: A Continuum of Violence Exposure for Children of Color." *Clinical Child and Family Psychology Review*, vol. 12, no. 2, 2009, pp. 174-95.

Satcher, Daniel, and Eve J. Higginbotham "The Public Health Approach to Eliminating Disparities in Health." *American Journal of Public Health*, vol. 98, no. 3, 2008, pp. 400-03.

Sharkey, Patrick, and Michael Friedson. "The Impact of the Homicide Decline on Life Expectancy of African American Males." *Demography*, vol. 56, no. 2, 2019, pp. 645-63.

Sheptycki, James. "Guns, Crime and Social Order: A Canadian Perspective." *Criminology & Criminal Justice*, vol. 9, no. 3, 2009, pp. 307-36.

Siciliano, Amy. *Policing Poverty: Race, Space and the Fear of Crime After the Year of the Gun (2005) in Suburban Toronto*. PhD dissertation, University of Toronto, 2011.

Skott, Sara, and Susan McVie. "Reduction in Homicide and Violence in Scotland Is Largely Explained by Fewer Gangs and Less Knife Crime." *Applied Quantitative Methods Network Research Briefing*, vol. 13, 2019, www.research.aqmen.ac.uk/wp-content/uploads/sites/27/2020/02/S-Skott-Types-of-Homicide-28.1.19.pdf. Accessed 27 Mar. 2022.

Szeto, Andrew, et al. "Workplace Antistigma Programs at the Mental Health Commission of Canada: Part 2. Lessons Learned." *The Canadian Journal of Psychiatry*, vol. 64, 1_suppl, 2019, pp. 13S-17S.

Thompson, Sara K., and Rosemary Gartner. "The Spatial Distribution and Social Context of Homicide in Toronto's Neighborhoods." *Journal of Research in Crime and Delinquency*, vol. 51, no. 1, 2014, pp. 88-118.

Turcotte, Martin. "Results from the 2016 Census: Education and Labour Market Integration of Black Youth in Canada. Insights on Canadian Society." *Statistics Canada*, 2020, www150.statcan.gc.ca/nl/en/catalogue/75-006-X202000100002. Accessed 27 Mar. 2022.

Welch, Kelly. "Black Criminal Stereotypes and Racial Profiling." *Journal of Contemporary Criminal Justice*, vol. 23, no. 3, 2007, pp. 276-88.

Williams, David R. "Race, Socioeconomic Status, and Health: the Added Effects of Racism and Discrimination." *Annals of the New York Academy of Sciences*, vol. 896, no. 1, 1999, pp. 173-88.

Yaya, Sanni, et al. "Ethnic and Racial Disparities in COVID-19-Related Deaths: Counting the Trees, Hiding the Forest." *BMJ Global Health*, vol. 5, no. 6, 2020, p. e002913.

Chapter 5

Race, Trauma, and Gun Violence: A Case for Public Health

Annette Bailey, Renee Bailey, Divine Velasco, and Michelle Jubin

Gun violence occurs in a complex system of social and structural factors, with progressive social, economic, psychological, and physical health consequences (Sharpe, Joe, and Taylor; Smith and Patton). Addressing this complex social issue in an effective and sustainable manner has been the focus of ongoing, and sometimes contentious, debate. No one disagrees that gun violence is an unwelcoming social havoc. The contention lies within the solution—whether to focus on how guns are accessed or why people shoot others. This essentially is a debate about gun control versus gun violence prevention. Yet the common objective for both sides is gun violence reduction, which makes these positions more complementary than different. Gun violence thrives in an interlocking, discursive, and sociopolitical web, which calls for both control and prevention efforts. Although gun violence solutions are increasingly focused on law enforcement efforts to manage criminality (Eizadirad), the best outcomes in gun violence will no doubt involve an investment in both gun control and prevention measures; with the latter targeting social equality in areas of education, employment, and family support.

With increased immigration and urbanization in the global context, the disproportionate burden of gun violence has been made more visible along racial and cultural lines (de Coster, Heimer, and Wittrock;

Stewart and Simons). Young marginalized Black males residing in disadvantaged neighbourhoods—who are exposed to neighbourhood violence, neighbourhood stigma, and lack of access to social resources—bear the unequal burden of exposure to and death by gun violence, as well as the unequal burden of disenfranchised grief and trauma from losing multiple friends and family members to gun violence (Granek and Peleg-Sagy; Smith and Patton; Spano). They grapple with continuous disintegration of their social networks due to gun violence deaths, which creates further disparities in their lifelong experiences with traumatic grief, vicarious trauma, and posttraumatic stress disorder symptoms (Smith and Patton). This intersection of neighbourhood, psychological response, and poverty in Black youth's disproportionate experiences with gun violence invariably elevates race as a spatial (neighbourhood segregation), psychological (trauma susceptibility), and social (social inequality) driver in gun violence, which requires social justice considerations.

Multiple social pressures exerted on disadvantaged Black youth in society, as well as solutions that prioritize law enforcement interventions over public health prevention approaches, only work to limit opportunities to deconstruct social inequalities and contextual impacts that underpin their experiences. Meanwhile, the contemporary complexities faced by these youth and the burden of historical and present-day racial oppression ensure their continual disproportionate involvement with gun violence (Bastomski and Duane; Lawson, "Disenfranchised Grief and Social Inequality"). A shift to a social justice perspective will however require understanding of how race intersects with social inequities to influence the impact of gun violence among this group.

This chapter is meant to challenge traditional patterns of thinking that have influenced patterns of actions and reactions to gun violence solutions. This is accomplished through discussions of how racialized youth's disproportionate involvement in gun violence frames current gun violence discourse and solutions. With the alarming evidence linking social disparities to the proliferation of gun violence, this analysis calls for solutions rooted in public health perspectives. A public health approach acknowledges violence prevention as a complex issue requiring diverse expertise and intersectoral collaboration. Furthermore, this approach recognizes the importance of addressing underlying risk factors linked to gun violence and identifying protective factors for mitigating the impact of gun violence.

Race and Gun Violence

In Canada, racialized groups residing in disadvantaged communities, where poverty and violence are concentrated, are disproportionately affected by gun homicide as perpetrators, victims, and witnesses (Butters et al.; Kalesan et al.). As stated in previous chapters, racialized youth are not inherently predisposed to gun violence, nor is it a normalized expectation in this demographic. Yet gun violence poses a significant threat to their survival (Resnick et al.; Sheats et al.). The absence of systematic race-based and race-crime data collection in Canada limits understanding of the epidemiological impact of gun violence on Black youth (Khenti, "Three Decades of Epidemic"; Thompson). However, intersectionality scholars and advocates have broadened our understanding of the cumulative and compounding effects of social inequities linked to gun violence proliferation (Quimby et al.; Sheats et al.). Although, this association is consistently wrought with criticisms from those claiming that not everyone dealing with social disparities engages in gun violence. There is legitimacy to this observation; however, it is important to further explore how the workings of social deprivations among Black youth are experienced and translated differently. Research shows that Black youths' experience with gun violence involves the dynamic wrestling between such factors as anti-Black racism, generational stagnation, trauma, fatherless homes, and exposure to neighbourhood violence (Gaylord-Harden et al.; Lawson, "Single Mothers"). Their experiences with racism have compelling effects on their mindset, aspirations, and their social progression, which are critical pathways to gun violence. Wesley Bryant has identified that the effects of internalized racism have overall implications on aggressive behaviours and propensity towards gun violence, which demonstrates that Black youth's immense social struggles present harsh realities for violence involvement.

As a disenfranchised group, Black youth identities have been shaped by media, contentious debates, and discriminatory patterns of thinking (Braga and Brunson; Bryant). Black youth, especially those living in poverty-stricken neighbourhoods, are often viewed as underachievers, unintelligent, vicious, and thugs (Parham-Payne). Largely, their construction of self-value, their potential, and their contributions to society are often predicated on these views. This problematic ideology has successfully seeped into public consciousness and attitude towards gun violence among Black youth. Consequently, public discussions about Black youth and gun violence are never void of racial biases and social stigma. The contentious nature of public and political discourse around their involvement in gun violence, combined with deprived social circumstances, can force Black youth to reconceptualize how they represent themselves in their environments. The resulting identity, representing the construction of social injustices, is one built from feelings of abandonment, anger, resentment, and hopelessness, that can be translated into the holding or carrying of a gun (Fagan and Wilkinson; Smith & Patton). Anger and hopelessness are elicited from interactions that make youth feel that their self-dignity and their potential do not matter. Without intervention, this feeling of hopelessness infiltrates their paradigm of worthiness to the extent that they begin placing limitations on their longevity (Bolland et al.).

Despite the racial disparities in gun violence involvement among youth, the dominant trends have positioned, analyzed, and treated gun violence as a Black issue, as dominant narratives spotlight Black shooters as the source of this public health problem (Eizadirad; Ezeonu, "Gun Violence in Toronto"; Khenti, "Three Decades of Epidemic"). Such trends appear to be consistent across jurisdictions, with Black shootings discussed as a matter of morality and white shootings (mainly mass shootings) as an issue of mental health (Parham-Payne). As would be expected, these discussions yield disparate responses to gun violence, none of which focus on racial injustices as points of public health intervention in gun violence reduction. Although moral aberrance as a cause of Black youth violence has been contested, this perspective remains deeply rooted in social consciousness. For example, in a 2018 *CBC* report, Angela Wright acknowledges the critical role of racism in shaping gun violence analysis and the criminalization of Black shooters in Canada. This came after the Mayor of Toronto's public denigration of Black shooters as "profoundly antisocial sewer rats." The 2008 Roots of Violence Report cautioned against gun violence being viewed as a Black problem, but rather a societal problem rooted in poverty and mental-health issues (McMurtry and Curling). Without concession, this representation of nuisance and delinquency has effectively stigmatized gun violence and Black youth in such a manner that the racial disparities underpinning their involvement in gun violence have remained largely overlooked. Concomitantly, addressing gun violence among this group has primarily focused on controlling criminality and delinquency and less about social development and health equity, which are key social justice approaches for reducing the burden and the complexity of racial inequalities in gun violence victimization and survivorship among Black youth.

Trauma and Gun Violence

Although social and racial inequalities and a maligned self-identity are central to the occurrences of gun violence among Black youth, research shows that trauma represents their greatest vulnerability in their experience with gun violence (McGibbon, Bailey, and Lukeman; Smith; Smith and Patton). Trauma is broadly defined as the psychosocial experience of witnessing, or being exposed to, traumatic events that are intense, painful, and emotionally distressing (Cohen, Mannarino, and Deblinger). Multiple experiences feed into Black youth's trauma at different transitional stages in their lives. The cumulative nature of the traumas they experience over time—such as historical trauma, childhood trauma, and environmental trauma—coupled with the intricate interweaving of contextual factors into their upbringing, shape their complex relationship with gun violence. As Rinaldo Walcott et al. have recognized, more than four hundred years of historical evolution have left a permanent demarcation across cultures and generations. And the most obvious and lasting evidence of this history is observed in the ecological and economic distinctions across neighbourhoods. Black youth's most primitive experience with trauma resides in reconciling the unrelenting presence of police in marginalized neighbourhoods, negotiating with deteriorating neighbourhood infrastructure, and contending with differential treatment in the educational system (Khenti, "Homicide Among Young Black Men in Toronto"; Levy, Ansara, and Stover; Walcott et al.). Within marginalized neighbourhoods, their trauma blooms with frequent exposure to gun violence and the premature deaths of friends and/or family members to gun violence, which potentiate racial and gendered disparities in life expectancy for Black youth (Smith and Patton; Spano; Umberson).

We see that cumulatively, over the years, guns have killed hundreds of Black males primarily between the ages of fifteen and twenty-five in marginalized neighbourhoods in Toronto (Butters et al.; Owusu-Bempah and Wortley). Lower life expectancy due to frequent exposure to death among young Black males dramatically illustrates their collective disadvantage and personal vulnerability along racial and socioeconomic lines. Media coverage of these deaths tend to focus on the racial context of the neighbourhoods where they live, reinforcing gun violence as a problem occurring mainly in communities inhabited by racialized groups. As the social devastation of these deaths remains largely contained in these susceptible neighbourhoods, the racial stigmatization of affected neighbourhoods, as opposed to the influence of social depravities, continues to influence public perceptions and discourse of gun violence. Tendencies of media representations and racist discourses in relation to gun violence and Black youth have not only resulted in the racialization of violent crimes (Galabuzi, "Social Exclusion") but have also fuelled fear of Black youth in the general public (Butters et al.; Owusu-Bempah and Wortley). This socially patterned burden also exposes Black youth to higher levels of stress associated with racial discrimination, labelling, and stigmatization of gun violence deaths, which further subject them to disenfranchised and complicated grief, as well as complicated trauma responses (Lawson, "Disenfranchised Grief and Social Inequality"). Furthermore, the accumulation of environmental context stressors and the racial stigma of gun violence deaths have been shown to complicate posthomicide experiences, hinder posttraumatic growth, and prolong posttraumatic stress reactions (Smith and Patton). Being subjected to continuous exposure to gun violence, without resources and support, reveals even more risks for acute and long-term psychosocial impacts, which can lead to gun carrying for self-protection and defense (Bania; Span).

Living in socioeconomically disadvantaged communities also means that Black youth bear witness to the death of multiple friends, peers, and family members to gun violence throughout their life course, leaving them at disproportionate risk for traumatic stress (Johnson; Smith and Patton; Umberson). It has been shown that the experience of homicide loss for Black youth begins early in childhood, peaks in the adolescent years, and persists in adulthood (Smith). In Smith's study, Black youth knew an average of three homicide victims between childhood and early adulthood. The tremendous disparities in the repeated loss of close relationships to gun violence death position socioeconomically vulnerable Black youth with unique and devastating lifelong stressors and associated adverse effects on relationships, overall health, wellbeing, and longevity (Umberson; Smith). Because friendships in particular, serve prominent psychosocial roles in the lives of youth, mourning the sudden loss of friends to murder results in traumatic distress symptoms, complex grief, and difficulty finding meaning in the loss (Johnson; Salloum, Avery, and McClain). With the continued and cumulative trauma of witnessing and experiencing the death of loved ones to gun violence, it is expected that these youths will be compelled to redefine their meaning of life, question their own fate, and struggle to adjust to a new social milieu. While adapting to the traumatic deaths of their loved ones to gun violence, these youth also negotiate with the racial stigma attached to the deaths and the microaggressions that such racial stigma interjects in gun violence debate and management. In light of these impacts, it is reasonable to assume that the magnitude of Black youth survivors' grief is cataclysmic. Yet their grief is continuously curtailed by the racial stigma of gun violence, which victimizes them as accomplices in their plight and proprietors of their loss, while quelling the worthiness of their survivorship experiences (Bailey, Clarke, and Salami; Khenti). This curtailing is most apparent in Black-on-Black shootings.

The majority of the gun violence deaths of Black youth in urban cities, like Toronto, is committed by other Black youth (Ezeonu, "Gun Violence in Toronto"). The most common explanations for these deaths are gang wars, Black hatred, and even economic and territorial greed. These come without recognition of the indelible legacy of death and destruction woven by racial injustice and racial oppression. Without fail, the most inerasable legacy is the stamp of perceived powerlessness, which has prompted a heightened need for protection among marginalized Black youth. Several scholars have theorized that in an attempt to ameliorate powerlessness, the gun is constructed as a symbol of power and superiority as well as a tool for aligning control and gaining respect (e.g., Bania; Black, and Hausman; Fagan and

Wilkinson). And without the tools and skills of education to understand and situate their powerlessness, it is manifested laterally in Black-on-Black shootings. Some scholars postulate this visual expression of powerlessness as the ever-evolving weight of trauma from exposure to neighbourhood violence and from loss of loved ones to gun violence (e.g., Smith and Patton). From this perspective, it is saddening to surmise that without possibilities for social justice, Black youth struggling with trauma may continue to see killing other Black youth as a less accountable option to combatting entrenched structural and racial oppression. Of most concern is the fact that when Black youth are implicated in their own deaths, the involvement of social disparities is easily dismissed or replaced with alternate explanations of blame (Braga and Brunson). Hence, before gun violence becomes a taken-for-granted reality for Black youth, understanding how their differential and unique trauma expressions fit into a public health framework for gun violence reduction is critical.

The multiple and unrelenting impact of issues such as racial profiling, exposure to violence, police brutality, and neighbourhood stigma can have distinctive trauma impacts for Black youth. The impact of these experiences is not well understood. As well, the ways in which Black youth situate and express trauma from these experiences and other traumatic events are grounded in social and racialized contexts and may equally be misunderstood. Trauma for racialized youth may be expressed in a myriad of ways, including aggression, fear, altered identity, and hypermasculinity (Fagan and Wilkinson; Smith). Although trauma experiences and responses are unique, the trauma of gun violence loss and exposure is a shared and widespread experience among Black youth and their families. If Black youths' trauma is left unrecognized and unaddressed, it becomes complicated and prolonged (Smith and Patton), facilitating widespread trauma in Black families and furthering social degradation of Black communities.

The nature of gun violence in itself is already stigmatizing, oppressive, and demoralizing to survivors and their families. The issue of race adds profoundly to the disproportionate representation of secondary trauma and mental health needs of Black youth and their gun homicide survivorship. And although trends of secondary survivorship pose a public health crisis for these youth, there remains little community support and other resources focused on addressing their mental health needs. This inertia may surround the politics of race in gun violence—the idea that investing resources to help a racialized group deal with the predicaments of a problem they are responsible for is futile. To avoid this view, the role of racism in the cycle of violence cannot be attempted from a political perspective but from a social justice viewpoint. Analyzing the proliferation of gun violence death and gun violence trauma among Black youth from a social justice perspective gives credence to the mechanisms of racial inequality in heightening their vulnerability to gun violence exposure and death and in complicating their disenfranchised grief experiences (Smith and Patton). As Ruth Wilson Gilmore explains, racism is "the state-sanctioned and/or extralegal production and exploitation of group-differentiated vulnerability to premature death" (247). Walcott and colleagues point to racism as "a form of violence that gives rise to other kinds of violence" (329). Both definitions of racism give support to a public health approach for gun violence prevention and survivorship among Black youth. From a prevention perspective, efforts can focus on personal empowerment of Black youth as well as equity policies and diversity training in systems such as schools, employment, and social agencies. Addressing the outcomes of vicarious trauma, posttraumatic stress disorder, and other mental health concerns from exposure to gun violence may require trauma-informed supports that are situated at the family, school, and community level.

Black youth have been subjected to debates through a Universalist research framework, historically based on knowledge and perspectives of Eurocentrism, which at its core juxtaposes the Black and coloured identity to the White one. The epistemological dimension of the Eurocentric worldview evolved the norm upon which histories, cultures, experiences and expressions of non-European groups and societies have been implicitly and explicitly compared and interpreted. Since the inception of European sociology, different degrees of Eurocentrism have been embedded in the patterns of thinking, values, assumptions, methodologies, and content of academic traditions (Alvares). Black youth experiences with trauma and gun violence may not be congruent with a universalist understanding. The multiple, fragmented and varied narratives that exist to frame the topic of gun violence and posthomicide experiences (Ezeonu, "Dudes, Let's Talk About Us") make it difficult to move towards a universalist discourse on the connections between trauma, racialized youth, and violence.

Scholars recognize that the narratives on gun violence in Black communities—including the discourse on intersecting precursors, complexities, and traumatic grief responses—are contextually bound (Ezeonu, "Dudes, Let's Talk About Us"; Granek and Peleg-Sagy; Smith). As trends in gun violence and gun-related trauma are not evenly distributed, we cannot rely on universalist research frameworks and views to critically understand the intersection of trauma, race, and gun violence. Researchers recognize that Black survivors' racial appraisal of the posthomicide experience and associated race-based structural inequalities hold serious implications for their social interactions, mental health, and use of coping resources (McGuffey and Sharpe). Therefore, Black youth's relationship with trauma cannot be understood in isolation from the social and psychological context of their existence. Understanding Black youth's lived experiences requires sensitization to the subtle and invasive impacts of the intersection of race and power on their actions and responses. These intersections are best unravelled by social justice frameworks that are designed to go beyond individual behaviours to understand how social and structural nuances inform people's thinking and their behaviour patterns.

The Policing of Gun Violence

Gun violence is as much a social issue as it is a political issue. Politics is embedded in all aspects of gun violence discussions—from the way it is framed to influence public opinion to the motivation behind decisionmakers' choice of actions. Unlike other emerging social crises situated within a public health framework, gun violence—with its deeply rooted connections to health inequalities, social injustices, and social stagnation—has not progressed towards a sustainable, multidimensional public health strategy (Butts et al.; Parham-Payne). In fact, the politics inherent in the racial stigmatization of gun violence has profoundly infiltrated decisions to prioritize emotive responses, such as law enforcement strategies, over more suitable public health initiatives (Butts et al.).

In August 2019, three levels of government committed 4.5 million dollars to advance the City of Toronto's efforts to address its ongoing gun violence crisis. This was followed by an unprecedented gathering of political leaders and a subsequent public announcement that the priority of focus for this funding would be increased police surveillance in affected neighbourhoods and security cameras to catch violent criminals (Gillis and Pagliaro). The reason given for the lavish investment into these short-term measures in the City of Toronto is to improve community safety. However, evidence shows that standalone law enforcement actions may reduce gun crimes in the short term, but they have little sustainable impact in preserving community safety (Shaw). Intensive law enforcement strategies serve to illustrate the ongoing focus on controlling criminality, using measures that produce more immediate responses. Although this funding presented an opportunity for new, expanded, and more promising solutions to gun violence reduction in Toronto, there was an instinctive fall back on the usual law enforcement strategies. This is not because law enforcement is the more effective strategy but because it is most familiar. The implicit truth may be that there are political gains to be made from demonstrating efforts to combat gun violence, even in the short term. But the best political gains come from social justice efforts to understand the underlying root causes of gun violence to find solutions aimed at meaningful, sustainable outcomes. Social justice approaches steeped in public health concepts, social services, broad collaboration, and family and community resilience may take longer to achieve change, but they fit well within effective and sustainable policy frameworks.

Perhaps the strong focus on the use of policing is also a response to the stigmatizing manner in which Black youth and gun violence are portrayed in the media (Braga and Brunson). Because the public, the media, and political interests are often intertwined, gun violence is largely interpreted from the perspectives and opinions presented by the media (Eizadirad). Thus, a problem that is thought to stem from the delinquent behaviour of Black youth may inevitably lead to efforts thought to be effective in containing and controlling them. In essence, the nuances of race in gun violence discourse may very well serve as a factor in stagnating progress towards public policies (Braga and Brunson). Indeed, the public's understanding of gun violence goes as far as their proximity to it, and if this proximity goes as far as race and criminality, then the scope of political debates, political advocacy, and political action will remain limited.

As a social issue, gun violence has wide social consequences and far-reaching ripple effects that require collective and concerted social responsibility. With a primary focus placed on increased policing to counteract criminality and delinquency, structural resolutions to address gun crimes in marginalized communities and among racial minorities are rarely included in political discourse. Yet it is important to realize that criminality is a social consequence of the complexities of people's lives rather than an innate propensity towards delinquency. Criminality emerges out of chronic and concentrated social chaos that breeds immense trauma and shapes poor self-worth among racialized youth (Gaylord-Harden et al.). Therefore, gun violence will endure in conditions that foster the growth of criminal mindsets. We can equate this to managing an incessant field of dandelions. We can continue to cut off the heads of dandelions, but as long as the roots remain, they will grow and spread. Similarly, gun crimes have seen fluctuations over the years, with no sustainable reduction. This may account for the fact that the circumstances that create shooters have persisted and have continued to give rise to other shooters. Increasing police presence in vulnerable communities may be effective in quieting crimes in the short term, but without effectively ameliorating underlying causes, it may have adverse effects that stem from residents' distrust and suspicion of police objectives (Shaw).

A Public Health Approach to Gun Violence

Gun violence grows out of systems of poverty and trauma; thus, a goal to reduce violence requires shifting social norms that incite and sustain trauma and ignite the need for guns (Smith and Smith-Lee). The issue of gun violence among racialized youth is multifaceted and requires a social justice response that is balanced, holistic, and tackles varied dimensions of the problem. A public health approach seeks to accomplish this by encouraging a shift in understanding how the intersection of race, social inequities, and trauma influences gun violence proliferation among racialized youth. However, with gun violence control focused so heavily on punishment, the scale of justice is tipped in favour of consequences. Balancing the scale of justice means improving public health's role in facilitating communities' control over social circumstances that stifle their capacities and impede their resilience and healing. Law enforcement efforts serve as an important part of this balanced approach but as a standalone cannot advance deep social change. For the best results in the prevention and reduction of gun violence, the goals and mandate of law enforcement must be organized in a complimentary partnership with public health.

A comprehensive public health approach to gun violence is imperative to inform violence prevention efforts, motivate policy changes, influence programs and services improvement, and ignite innovative partnerships to address the consequences of gun violence loss on Black youth and other survivors (Butts et al.). By recognizing that gun violent death and survivorship experiences are underpinned by an active interplay of racism, criminality, and stigma (Bailey, Clarke, and Salami; Hannays-King, Bailey, and Akhtar), public health is well situated in social justice values to build communities in ways that law enforcement has not. With a focus on social inequalities, public health represents an objective partner to give unbiased recognition to the structural issues that keep gun violence alive. Gun violence among Black youth, with its multifaced consequences, requires public health activities that focus on predictors of race, trauma, and social inequalities (Smith and Smith-Lee).

A Focus on Race

A public health focus on race and gun violence requires efforts to alleviate racial predicaments of gun violence. An important part of this effort is assisting Black youth to see themselves as citizens and change makers in gun violence, even while they navigate the social circumstances of their lives. Helping Black youth to rebuild their identity and reshape their self-image is a priority to decreasing their involvement in gun violence. Achieving this requires an understanding of how the history of trauma and oppression implicate the culture and identities of Black youth. For public health, this will necessitate partnerships with Black families, community stakeholders, and advocates to facilitate initiatives that effectively link Black children and youth to resources and mentors that can help them thwart negative stereotypes and prejudices. Specifically, these may include the following:

1. ***Advocate for Race-Based Gun Violence Data:*** There is an absence of systematic race-based and race-crime data collection in Canada to substantiate Black youth's disproportionate involvement in gun violence. Public health can play a significant role in advocating for race-based data to assist with funding advocacy efforts and to jumpstart initiatives that explicate key factors in their disparity, such as anti-Black racism, race-based trauma, racial oppression, and exposure to neighbourhood violence.
2. ***Support Black Youth Identity Development:*** Gun violence loss among racialized youth is especially significant in influencing their basic assumptions about their self-worth, their meaning of life, and their view of the world (Boyraz, Horne, and Sayger). Public health can facilitate the development of community programs to support Black youths' identity building and improve their self-image. These programs can also include mentorship establishment with caring adults and entrepreneurial partners who can work closely with Black youth to build their social agility and shape their identity. These are important protective barriers against gun violence involvement.
3. ***Support Black Family Capacity Building:*** The efforts of economically disadvantaged Black families to protect Black youth from violence can become easily weakened by their social circumstances. Public health can target early years services and other family development programs towards building parenting skills and facilitate access to psychological resources for Black families struggling with grief, loss, and trauma.
4. ***Build Strategic Partnerships with the Black Community:*** A partnership between public health and youth, stakeholders, decisionmakers, and parents in the Black community can help to clarify and enhance efforts for Black youth development, family support, community services, and school policy reform. This partnership can also include the police, school officials, and representatives from different levels of governments—all working together to systematically enact a strategic and progressive course of action against gun violence.

A Focus on Trauma

Trauma exaggerated to the point of violence is the dual and synchronic pressure from persisting social forces of powerful structural barriers and socioeconomic risk factors.

Understanding Black youth's cumulative experiences with traumas (i.e., intergenerational and contextual traumas) may stir social justice opportunities for policy discussions and strategies for youth development and reduction in gun violence (Smith and Smith-Lee). Discussions of gun violence consequences for Black youth are rarely framed from a mental health perspective. That so little attention is paid to the bereavement challenges and psychosocial needs of this population also points to the disenfranchised nature of their grief. The first point of understanding in public health's efforts to influence social change in gun violence involving Black youth is to recognize the source of their trauma and how their trauma translates into gun violence. The next step calls for trauma-focused initiatives implemented in affected communities, which are made possible by galvanizing the collaborative efforts and resources of community groups, mental health services, and youth development experts. With little existing interventions to help Black youth cope with gun violent loss, a public health focus on protective factors to facilitate trauma adaptation may inform policy development and interventions to address the trauma needs of this population. This can be approached as follows:

1. ***Conduct Community Trauma Assessment:*** There is increasing evidence of the social impact of trauma. Trauma from racial oppression affects Black youths' perspectives and their actions in ways that may not be congruent with our usual understanding of trauma. It is crucial to explore the conditions that bring about trauma for Black youth and how trauma persists in social issues like gun violence. From a public health perspective, broad situational assessments of trauma in Black youth and Black families are important to develop targeted and unique trauma-informed programs in communities.

2. ***Facilitate Trauma-Informed Care for Black youth and Family:*** There is an accumulation of grieving Black youth in violence-prone neighbourhoods, who continue to struggle with trauma

from loss of multiple loved ones to gun violence over years. Without support, this trauma impacts on youth stagnation and recurring incidents of gun violence. Public health can partner with community organizations to facilitate the development of culturally relevant and accessible trauma support for Black youth and their families. Trauma support focusing on targeted strategies for self-expression, sharing of experiences, and expression of trauma-related emotions can be incorporated into school curriculum and other community-based youth programs.

Conclusion

Black youth affected by gun violence loss or exposure represent the fullest impact of the complexities of social depravities and the greatest deprivation of social support. The social and racial constraints endured by these youth do not afford them the social resources and supports to further their growth and community contribution. By working to improve these factors, public health can improve Black youth psychologically, socially, economically, and educationally. It is believed that even among existing and unyielding poverty, a public health intervention can help to facilitate feelings of respect, connection to community, security, and a reassuring sense of worth among Black youth (Gaylord-Harden et al.). Roy McMurtry and Alvin Curling recognize that Canadian public health attention to gun violence is limited and may explain why funding and public policy are extensively focused on incarceration and a tough-on-crime approach rather than a comprehensive health promotion approach. Given public health's limited involvement in gun violence currently, they will first need to recognize their role in gun violence, reorganize services to reach affected communities, and break through the political barriers that have kept police at the forefront of gun violence. It is acknowledged, to the simplest degree possible, that the more public health works to eliminate the conditions related to gun violence, the more likely the ripple effects on communities will be noticed. Hence, a collective public health response to gun violence in Canada is critical in understanding the causes and prevention of gun violence.

Works Cited

Alvares, Claude. "A Critique of Eurocentric Social Science and the Question of Alternatives." *Economic and Political Weekly,* vol. 46, no. 22, 2011, pp. 72-81.

Bailey, Annette, and Divine Velasco. "Canada." *Gun Violence, Disability and Recovery,* edited by Cate Buchanan, Surviving Gun Violence Project, 2014, pp. 207-21.

Bailey, Annette, Jennifer Clarke, and Bukola Salami. "Race-based Stigma as a Determinant of Access and Support in Black Mothers' Experience of Loss to Gun Violence." *Roots and Routes of Displacement and Trauma: From Analysis to Advocacy & Policy to Practice,* edited by Soheila Pashang and Sheila Gruner, Rock's Mills Press, 2015, pp. 262-76.

Bania, Melania. "Gang Violence Among Youth and Young Adults: (Dis) Affiliation and the Potential for Prevention." *IPC Review,* vol. 3, 2009, pp. 89-116.

Bastomski, Sara, and Marina Duane. "Losing a Loved One to Homicide: What We Know About Homicide Co-victims from Research and Practice Evidence." *Centre for Victim Research,* July 2019, ncvc.dspacedirect.org/bitstream/handle/20.500.11990/1384/CVR%20Research%20Syntheses_Homicide%20Covictims_Report.pdf?sequence=1&isAllowed=y. Accessed 9 Apr. 2022.

Black, Sally, and Alice Hausman. "Adolescents' Views of Guns in a High-Violence Community." *Journal of Adolescent Research,* vol. 23, no. 5, 2008, pp. 592-610.

Bolland, John M., et al. "Development and Risk Behavior Among African American, Caucasian, and Mixed-race Adolescents Living in High Poverty Inner-city Neighborhoods." *American Journal of Community Psychology,* vol.40, no. 3-4, 2007, pp. 230-49.

Boyraz, Güler, Sharon G. Horne, and Thomas V. Sayger. "Finding Meaning in Loss: The Mediating Role of Social Support Between Personality and Two Construals of Meaning." *Death Studies,* vol. 36, no. 6, 2012, pp. 519-40.

Braga, Anthony Allan, and Rodney Brunson. "The Police and Public Discourse on 'Black on Black' Violence." *National Institute of Justice,* May 2015, www.ojp.gov/pdffiles1/nij/248588.pdf. Accessed 9 Apr. 2022.

Bryant, Wesley W. "Internalized Racism's Association With African American Male Youth's Propensity for Violence." *Journal of Black Studies,* vol. 42, no. 4, 2011, pp. 690-707.

Butters, Jennifer E., et al. "Guns and Sublethal Violence: A Comparative Study of At-risk Youth in Two Canadian Cities." *International Criminal Justice Review,* vol. 21, no. 4, 2011, pp. 402-26.

Butts, Jeffrey A., et al. "Cure Violence: A Public Health Model to Reduce Gun Violence." *Annual Review of Public Health,* vol. 36, 2015, pp. 39-53.

Cohen, Judith A., Anthony P. Mannarino, and Esther Deblinger. *Treating Trauma and Traumatic Grief in Children and Adolescents.* The Guilford Press, 2006.

De Coster, Stacy, Karen Heimer, and Stacy M. Wittrock. "Neighborhood Disadvantage, Social Capital, Street Context, and Youth Violence." *The Sociological Quarterly,* vol. 47, no. 4, 2006, pp. 723-53.

Eizadirad, Ardavan. "Is It 'Bad' Kids or 'Bad' Places? Where is All the Violence Originating From? Youth Violence in the City of Toronto." *Review of Education, Pedagogy, and Cultural Studies,* vol. 38, no. 2, 2016, pp. 162-88.

Ezeonu, Ifeanyi. "Dudes, Let's Talk About Us: The Black "Community" Construction of Gun Violence in Toronto." *Journal of African American Studies,* vol. 12, no. 3, 2008, pp. 194-214.

Ezeonu, Ifeanyi. "Gun Violence in Toronto: Perspectives From the Police." *The Howard Journal of Criminal Justice,* vol. 49, no. 2, 2010, pp. 147-65.

Fagan, Jeffrey, and Deanna L. Wilkinson. "Guns, Youth Violence, and Social Identity in Inner Cities." *Crime and Justice,* vol. 24, 1998, pp. 105-88.

Galabuzi, Grace-Edward. "Social Exclusion." *Social Determinants of Health: Canadian Perspectives,* edited by Dennis Raphael, Canadian Scholar's Press, 2004, pp. 235-51.

Gaylord-Harden, Noni K., et al. "Understanding Development of African American Boys and Young Men: Moving from Risks to Positive Youth Development." *American Psychologist,* vol. 73, no. 6, 2018, pp. 753-67.

Gillis, Wendy, and Jennifer Pagliaro. "Police Plan Won't Curb Causes of Gun Violence, Researchers Say. *The Star,* 14 Aug. 2019, www.thestar.com/news/gta/2019/08/14/toronto-police-chief-to-detail-plan-to-fight-gun-violence.html. Accessed 9 Apr. 2022.

Gilmore, Ruth Wilson. *Golden Gulag: Prisons, Surplus, Crisis, and Opposition in Globalizing California*. University of California Press, 2007.

Granek, Leeat, and Tal Peleg-Sagy. "Representations of African Americans in the Grief and Mourning Literature from 1998 to 2014: A Systematic Review." *Death Studies,* vol. 39, no.10, 2015, pp. 605-32.

Hannays-King, Camille, Annette Bailey, and Mahlon Akhtar. "Social Support and Black Mothers' Bereavement Experience of Losing a Child to Gun Homicide." *Bereavement Care,* vol. 34, no.1, 2015, pp. 10-16.

Johnson, Celeste M. "African-American Teen Girls Grieve the Loss of Friends to Homicide: Meaning Making and Resilience." *OMEGA-Journal of Death and Dying,* vol. 61, no. 2, 2010, pp. 121-43.

Kalesan, Bindu, et al. "Cross-sectional Study of Loss of Life Expectancy at Different Ages Related to Firearm Deaths Among Black and White Americans." *BMJ Evidence-Based Medicine,* vol. 24, no. 2, 2018, pp. 55-58.

Khenti, Akwatu A. "Homicide Among Young Black Men in Toronto: An Unrecognized Public Health Crisis?." *Canadian Journal of Public Health,* vol. 104, no.1, 2013, pp. e12-e14.

Khenti, Akwatu A. "Three Decades of Epidemic Black Gun Homicide Victimization in Toronto:Analyzing Causes and Consequences of a Criminological Approach." *York Space Institutional Repository,* Aug. 2018, yorkspace.library.yorku.ca/xmlui/bitstream/handle/10315/34979/Khenti_Akwatu_A_2018_Phd.pdf?sequence=2&isAllowed=y. Accessed 9 Apr. 2022.

Lawson, Erica. "Disenfranchised Grief and Social Inequality: Bereaved African Canadians and Oppositional Narratives About the Violent Deaths of Friends and Family Members." *Ethnic and Racial Studies,* vol. 37, no.11, 2014, pp. 2092-109.

Lawson, Erica. "Single Mothers, Absentee Fathers, and Gun Violence in Toronto: A Contextual Interpretation." *Women's Studies,* vol. 41, no. 7, 2012, pp. 805-28.

Levy, Jennifer, Donna Ansara, and Andi Stover. *Racialization and Health Inequities in Toronto. Toronto Public Health,* 2013.

McGibbon, Elizabeth, Annette Bailey, and Sionnach Lukeman. "Violence and Health." *Community Health Nursing: A Canadian Perspective,* edited by Lynnette Leeseburg Stamler et al. Pearson Canada Inc., 2020, pp. 503-20.

McGuffey, C. Shawn, and Tanya L. Sharpe. "Racial Appraisal: An Integrated Cultural and Structural Response to African American Experiences with Violent Trauma." *Journal of Sociology and Social Work,* vol. 3, no. 2, 2015, pp. 55-61.

McMurtry, Roy, and Alvin Curling. "The Review of the Roots of Youth Violence." *Ministry of Children, Community and Social Services,* 2008, children.gov.on.ca/htdocs/English/professionals/oyap/roots/index.aspx. Accessed 9 Apr. 2022.

Owusu-Bempah, Akwasi, and Scot Wortley. "Race, Crime, and Criminal Justice in Canada." *The Oxford Handbook of Ethnicity, Crime, and Immigration,* edited by Sandra Bucerius and Michael H. Tonry, Oxford University Press, 2014, pp. 321-59.

Parham-Payne, Wanda. "The Role of the Media in the Disparate Response to Gun Violence in America." *Journal of Black Studies,* vol. 45, no. 8, 2014, pp. 752-68.

Quimby, Dakari, et al. "Gun Exposure Among Black American Youth Residing in Low-income Urban Environments." *Journal of Black Psychology,* vol. 44, no. 4, 2018, pp. 322-46.

Resnick, Shelby, et al. "Firearm Deaths in America: Can We Learn from 462,000 Lives Lost?" *Annals of Surgery,* vol. 266, no. 3, 2017, pp. 432-44.

Salloum, Alison, Lisa Avery, and Ronald P. McClain. "Group Psychotherapy for Adolescent Survivors of Homicide Victims: A Pilot Study." *Journal of the American Academy of Child & Adolescent Psychiatry, vol.* 40, no.11, 2001, pp. 1261-67.

Sharpe, Tanya L., Sean Joe, and Katie C. Taylor. "Suicide and Homicide Bereavement Among African Americans: Implications for Survivor

Research and Practice." *OMEGA-Journal of Death and Dying,* vol. 66, no. 2, 2013, pp. 153-72.

Shaw, Margaret. "Youth and Gun Violence: The Outstanding Case for Prevention." *International Centre for the Prevention of Crime,* Sept. 2005, citeseerx.ist.psu.edu/viewdoc/download?doi=10.1.1.1062.462&rep=repl&type=pdf. Accessed 9 Apr. 2022.

Sheats, Kameron J., et al. "Violence-Related Disparities Experienced by Black Youth and Young Adults: Opportunities for Prevention." *American Journal of Preventive Medicine,* vol. 55, no. 4, 2018, pp. 462-69.

Smith, Chauncey D., and Jocelyn R. Smith-Lee. "Advancing Social Justice and Affirming Humanity in Developmental Science Research with African American Boys and Young Men." *Applied Developmental Science,* vol. 24, no. 3, 2020, pp. 208-14.

Smith, Jocelyn R. "Unequal Burdens of Loss: Examining the Frequency and Timing of Homicide Deaths Experienced by Young Black Men Across the Life Course." *American Journal of Public Health,* vol. 105, no. S3, 2015, pp. S483-90.

Smith, Jocelyn R., and Desmond U. Patton. "Posttraumatic Stress Symptoms in Context: Examining Trauma Responses to Violent Exposures and Homicide Death Among Black Males in Urban Neighborhoods." *American Journal of Orthopsychiatry,* vol. 86, no. 2, 2016, pp. 212-23.

Spano, Richard. "First Time Gun Carrying and the Primary Prevention of Youth Gun Violence for African American Youth Living in Extreme Poverty." *Aggression and Violent Behavior,* vol. 17, no.1, 2012, pp. 83-88.

Stewart, Eric A., and Ronald L. Simons. "Race, Code of the Street, and Violent Delinquency: A Multilevel Investigation of Neighborhood Street Culture and Individual Norms of Violence." *Criminology,* vol. 48, no. 2, 2010, pp. 569-605.

Thompson, Sara K. "Black Homicide Victimization in Toronto, Ontario, Canada." *The Oxford Handbook of Ethnicity, Crime, and Immigration,* edited by Sandra Bucerius and Michael H. Tonry, Oxford University Press, 2013, pp. 430-53.

Umberson, Debra. "Black Deaths Matter: Race, Relationship Loss, and Effects on Survivors." *Journal of Health and Social Behavior,* vol. 58, no. 4, 2017, pp. 405-20.

Walcott, Rinaldo et al. "Racial Minority Perspectives on Violence. Review of the Roots of Youth Violence." *Ontario Ministry of Children, Community and Social Services,* June 2008, children.gov.on.ca/htdocs/English/professionals/oyap/roots/volume4/minority_perspectves.aspx. Accessed 9 Apr. 2022.

Wortley, Scot et al. "Social Disorganization Theory. Review of the Roots of Youth Violence." *Ontario Ministry of Children, Community and Social Services,* June 2008, children.gov.on.ca/htdocs/English/professionals/oyap/roots/volume5/chapter04_social_disorganization.aspx. Accessed 9 Apr. 2022.

Wright, Angela. "How Racism Fuels Ineffective Gun Control." *The Walrus,* 14 Nov. 2019, thewalrus.ca/how-racism-fuels-ineffective-gun-control/. Accessed 9 Apr. 2022.

Chapter 6

A Tale of Two Justice Systems: Competing Narratives about Gun Crime and Links with Social Engagement and Access to Justice

Thomas S. Harrison

> It was the best of times, it was the worst of times, it was the age of wisdom, it was the age of foolishness, it was the epoch of belief, it was the epoch of incredulity, it was the season of Light, it was the season of Darkness, it was the spring of hope, it was the winter of despair
>
> —Charles Dickens, *A Tale of Two Cities*, 1

Modern stories about crime and guns present two competing narratives. We live, it sometimes seems, in either the best or the worst of times. Just as Dickens presented the confusion resulting from contrasting stories in his *A Tale of Two Cities*, modern tales reflect a similar dichotomy in the portrayal of violence. In this respect, the popular perception that contemporary society is violent is undermined by more nuanced assessments indicating that things are improving. Of these two characterizations, the more dominant narrative is focused on contemporary challenges that continue to exacerbate criminality and the need for guns. The topic of gun violence has demonstrated capacity to provoke intense reactions about a wide range of issues, including government regulation, rights, safety and security, and the role of the justice system. And as such, it is safe to say that no other form of violence has so foundationally struck the core of our sociopolitical structure.

Although I present understandings of the conflicting perspectives surrounding gun violence, my focus in this chapter is to demonstrate how and why gun violence is perceived as it is, how this view is reinforced by public policy responses and media in Canada, and the implications connected to longer term legal and social trends. Essentially, I emphasize the critical question of why gun violence is perceived and portrayed in different ways than other violent crimes. I then situate the different narratives about crime and guns in a broader context, both historically and in light of contemporary social issues. I conclude that the perception and public response to crime and gun violence are based on some misapprehensions. However, its erroneous portrayal may also be connected to a breakdown in social ordering and part of the justice crisis in Canada today. Effectively, addressing questions about social violence related to guns will therefore likely require a broader perspective that holistically addresses these issues, which have both legal and social dimensions.

Perceptions of Crime and Gun Violence

Many would say that crime is increasing (Mussa; Quinn). We live in a dangerous world as constantly told by the media, news, and entertainment industries. Drug crises, youth and gang violence (Public Safety Canada), and, more recently, perceived social tensions arising out of racial injustice are said to aggravate pervasive social conflicts. Some might say that our society is full of ill-intentioned individuals who pose direct and personal threats, so there is therefore good reason to be wary.

The contrasting, and perhaps underappreciated perspective, is that the world has never been safer, more prosperous, or provided more opportunities (Pinker, *The Better Angels*). Overall social violence is not only down but has been decreasing for decades. Aspects of this larger challenge, such as violent crime rates, have reached historical lows. There is some reason to be concerned about a recent rise in firearms related offences, but most Canadians have a strong sense of personal security and believe their communities are safe and, with a few exceptions, are getting safer (McPhail, Olver, and Brooks).

Which of these narratives are adopted by people depends somewhat on their particular social situations and on individual perspectives rooted in personal opinions. Women tend to feel less personally safe than men. Generally, visible minorities also feel less secure, as do those living in western provinces and in Canada's three largest cities.[1] Across the board though, the dominant narrative supports a pervasive perception that crime is increasing and also becoming more severe (Scotti). The organizing question in this inquiry is why are there two narratives and why does the more threatening perception dominate? The next sections situate the current Canadian experience within a broader context, before considering it in light of its historical context, to assess the current reality and rhetoric associated with crime and guns in Canada.

Background: Social Violence, the Justice System, and Rights

The modern narrative about increasing crime and gun violence should be considered in light of the wider reality of social violence. Perceived heightened social tensions and increased conflict are viewed at both the systemic and individual level, including increases in crime and gun violence. Across place and time, there is significant evidence showing that we live in one of the most peaceful times ever. In fact, there is substantial evidence that over several centuries, there has been demonstrably less social violence, especially between international states. At the same time, there are also some indicators that conflict has decreased at the personal level, in many neighbourhoods and families, and between individuals.

In a well-known article a few years ago, legal scholar Lon Fuller suggests that our system of laws is one of many forms of social ordering that manages human behaviours (Fuller and Winston). From this perspective, some of our social governance mechanisms, including the justice system, have proven successful in reducing violence over the last few generations. Much of the decrease in violence is at least partly attributable to the identification of the importance of human rights and its articulation in the justice system, especially since the Second World War. Part of the postwar realizations about rights included recognition that the relatively civilized and modern German legal system had been complicit in Hitler's rise and the subsequent Holocaust, which murdered millions (Müller and Juristen). What followed were complementary and worldwide developments to better protect the legal rights of individuals, in conjunction with enhanced efforts to address root causes of social conflict. Although various rights revolutions focused on substantive legal rights (Harrison, "Between"), at the same time, there was widespread investment in public policies that sought to improve systems of social justice in its broadest sense. For example, through the 1950s and 1960s, Canada established several national programs to provide assistance to individuals to better ensure social security in such areas as healthcare (Maioni). In the legal system, the initial focus on substantive rights was later reinforced by widespread procedural and structural reforms, starting in the 1970s. There was a recognized need to maintain and increase the capacity of individuals to engage with both broader forms of social justice and with the legal system.

The most prominent example of these legal changes, encompassing both the substantive and procedural dimensions of the new focus on rights, was probably the fundamental reworking of the Canadian Constitution. The entrenchment of the *Charter of Rights* in 1982 was, in fact, the crest in a longer-term wave of social and legal change (Harrison, "The Statute"). All these efforts sought to ensure people had a better ability to enforce and defend basic rights by accessing justice (McCormick).

Today's Reality: Crime Decline in Canada

Whatever the final assessment on past efforts to improve social and legal justice, one correlative factor has been a generational decline in crime over the last quarter century. As discussed further below, these declines in criminality are connected to perceptions about social functioning, including the severity of offences and ideas about the current challenge of gun violence. There is little doubt that overall crime in Canada is now at historically low levels.

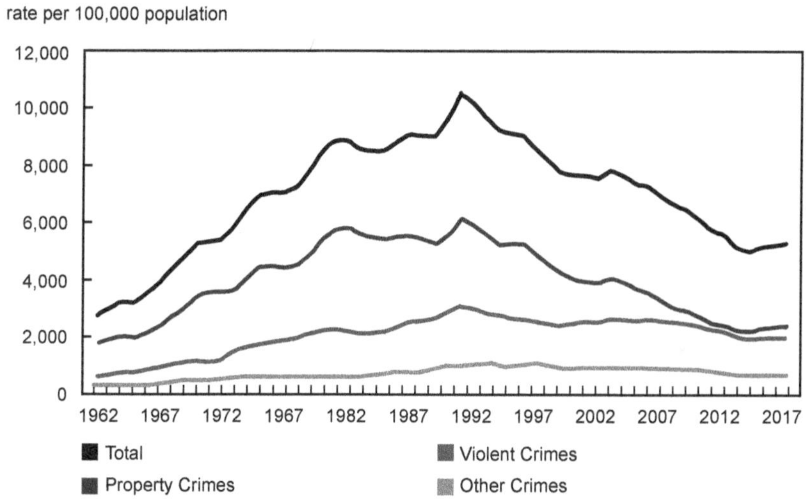

Figure 1. Total Canadian Crime Rate 1962–2017 (Statistics Canada, *Chart 2*)

However, one potential criticism of traditional crime rate statistics is that they inadequately distinguish between more and less serious criminal offences. It could be, for example, that even if the number of crimes is decreasing, the severity of those occurring is nonetheless becoming more extreme. In this respect, although actual rates might change over time, statistical representations of total crimes might not adequately capture the qualitative reality of the nature of the crimes committed. For example, the inclusion of aggravating factors in criminal offences, such as increased violence or the involvement of a gun, could mean that even if actual numbers of crimes were going down, those that did occur could be characterized as more serious under current criminal laws. To address this, the Canadian government developed a new tool to assess crime in 2009.

At that time, it introduced the Crime Severity Index, based on the principle that more serious crimes—such as murder or assaults that were aggravated by the inclusion of a weapon—should carry a higher weight in statistical representations (Wallace). The measure combines the quantitative volume of crimes with agreed qualitative measures to estimate seriousness. This measure can then be used as a benchmark to further compare changes in crime levels in terms of absolute occurrences but is also adjusted to better attend to differences year over year in more serious offences.

In comparison to the crime rate, the estimate of crime severity has also trended down over the last two decades. There has been uptick in the seriousness of offences since 2015, but the historical comparison suggests comparatively far less severe criminal conduct compared to the past.

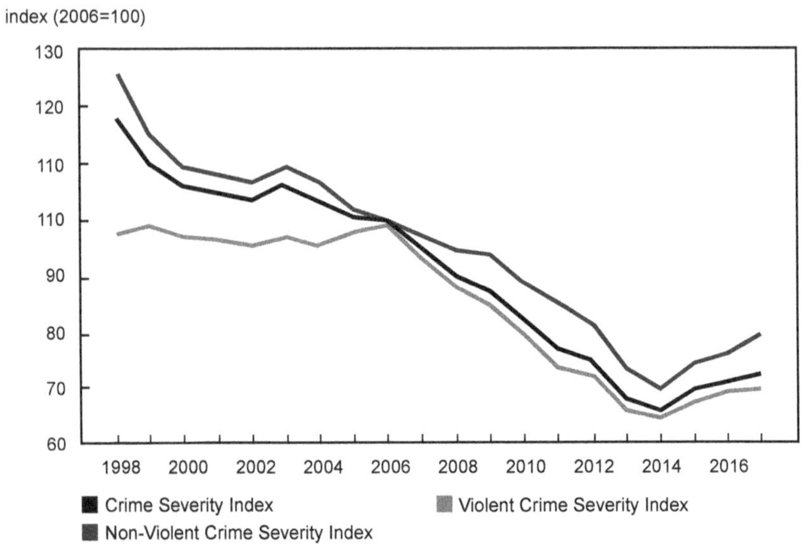

Figure 2. Police-Reported Crime Severity Indexes, 1998–2017 (Statistics Canada, *Chart 1*)

Misapprehensions about crime are symptomatic of a ubiquitous phenomenon. Despite attempts to improve social justice over the last two generations, many have the sense that things are not improving and that crimes are getting worse. It is also true that underlying causes of social injustice and crime are highly contested. Though largely outside the scope of this examination, there is a longstanding debate about the significance of social factors—such as poverty, education, and health—versus the emphasis in criminal law to hold people individually morally culpable for breaches of the law.

Yet despite misapprehensions about its prevalence and debate about its cause, it appears that most Canadians have historically had a reasonably nuanced understanding of the multivariate social, economic, and other factors usually associated with higher levels of criminal behaviour. This includes many of the underlying circumstances that past social and legal changes were intended to address.[2] More recent measures of crime severity show limited justification for people's current perceptions of increased violent crime. Perhaps related to this recent perception is a relative and recent increase in the rate of violent crime involving firearms. On this point, current occurrences of serious gun offences like homicide match, although they have not exceeded historical levels (Berthiaume).

In the end, the current reality of social violence, crime, and gun-related offences in Canada may represent neither the best nor the worst of times. In fact, the ultimate truth largely corresponds to a tale that falls somewhere between the two contrasting narratives. In this respect, the idea that there are only two opposite points of view—that crime is on the rise and becoming more serious or that criminality and social violence is decreasing—is really a false dichotomy.

Although the two stories about crime and gun violence in Canada may appear as mutually exclusive, on closer inspection, the middle ground between these two alternatives presents a much more integrated and holistic understanding of the reality and perception of gun violence. While overall violence is not increasing as noted, concerns about gun-related violence have some basis in the statistics reported in more recent years in the crime severity index. In the broader context though, some of these fears may be exaggerated in the popular perceptions. There is a web of interrelated contributors likely influencing public perceptions about crime and gun violence. The next section looks at concerns about guns expressed through public policy and often based in politics, which has deep roots in Canadian history.

Guns and Public Policy in Canada

Throughout Canadian history, public policy about crime and guns has been linked. Concerns about crime and gun violence in Canada have long led to public criticism and legislative responses (Brown, "Gun Control"). Following Confederation in the nineteenth century, there were frequent public expressions of concern about accidental shootings, murder, and suicide, which raised alarms (Brown, "Pistol Fever"). Reports of alcohol abuse by youth and men who carried guns as a sign of "bravado" were not uncommon.

Not unlike today, Canadian newspapers printed cautionary tales of the Americans' misuse of firearms and suggested our southern neighbours might be more inclined to commit mass murder or to resolve their disputes using handguns. In 1877, one senator observed warily that the habit of carrying pistols had become all too prevalent, prompting some of Canada's earliest legislation to ban the practice. In addition to its historical association with social problems, gun violence regulation in Canada has often been explicitly connected to political issues.

Early Canadian efforts to manage guns were often associated with fears about labour unrest and immigration (Pelletier). High levels of immigration early in the nineteenth century, together with a belief that new arrivals were "inherently violent" (Brown, "Every Boy Ought to Learn"), led to provincial legislation requiring sellers to keep records of purchases. These laws also required people to report foreigners with illegal weapons for the purposes of deportation, which was mirrored in the 1913 changes to the federal Criminal Code.

As was true in the past, modern Canadian public policy in relation to gun violence continues to touch on wider social issues and politics. Civil unrest in Quebec related to the wish of a few to separate from Canada starting in the 1960s gave rise in Parliament to new gun laws that required authority to restrict and prohibit certain weapons (Stanbury and Smithies). Later legislative reactions to gun violence also followed. So, for example, 1995 changes to laws included increasing mandatory minimum penalties for firearms-related offences, following the mass shooting at Montreal's Ecole Polytechnique (Boissoneault). In that case, the male perpetrator harboured extreme antifeminist sentiments and murdered fourteen female engineering students.

Further reforms were implemented in Conservative justice reforms in 2008, as part of its tough on crime agenda (Comack, Burgher, and Fabre). Here the criminal law was changed not only in light of declining crime but also despite significant research suggesting that harsher sanctions are not effective deterrents. Some political and social leaders now likely find emphasis on retributive reactions to crime politically expedient, even where, as it turns out, recent legislative responses are ultimately inconsistent with fundamental rights.

Despite decreasing crime, apparent drops over time in crime severity, and a sustained downwards trend of offences involving firearms, political leaders rely on recent increases in gun crime to underscore it as a significant issue of public policy (Naumetz). This political message has supported the dominant story that crime is increasing, which may also be encouraged by narratives conveyed through various media, which is examined in the next section.

News Narratives and Social Media

Traditional news reporting is often criticized for encouraging false perceptions about crime and guns. Just like narratives in the popular conception of issues and events, journalistic structure follows a pattern as well. Negative news, and conflicts in general, are frequently foregrounded in traditional media and journalism, and may now be further exacerbated by contemporary social media.

News media frequently highlights conflict, including serious criminal breaches, even where such disputes may be unusual, and belie a greater underlying functionality. This approach to conveying events is inherently somewhat pessimistic (Seto). The focus on stories of pathological exceptions in human social interactions may create a cognitive distortion that feeds many misperceptions. This includes an exaggerated understanding of the frequency of events such as social violence, including those related to crime and gun violence (Pinker, "The Media Exaggerates Negative News").

Recent studies quantifying negative sentiments in news reports over time show a steady, decades-long trend towards more negativity in news reporting (Leetaru). It is probably too early in the internet age to draw any definitive conclusions about its further influence. However, one recent survey also suggests that the vast majority of Canadians, seven out of ten, now believe that social media has similarly had a negative or somewhat negative impact on the news (Nanos).

We live in a version of what Marshall McLuhan foresaw as a "global village" (31), connected across a planet by modern communications. Technology has provided most with access to the vast majority of accumulated human historical knowledge and for individuals to communicate simultaneously virtually anywhere on the planet. Yet despite the hope that this would foster closer social relations, today's communicative powers have instead led many to perceive the state of the world and their place in it with increased discomfort and anxiety. This increasing unease is also reflected in several other broader measures of social engagement, such as access to justice and distrust in other forms of governance, which I turn to in the next section.

Politics of Distrust and Access to Justice

Postwar efforts to address social justice and protect rights in the justice system began to face significant challenges starting in the 1970s. Widespread distrust in political institutions is commonly traced to the shock of the American political Watergate scandal. Along with economic challenges of high unemployment, inflation, and fiscal constraints at that time, governments were also forced to reassess their previous commitments to a wide range of policies and programs related to social justice. In the legal system, people increasingly noted gaps in access to justice and touted a range of public and private alternatives to formal courts.[3]

There is now a widespread perception of an access to justice crisis in Canada, and it has become a substantial public policy issue (*Expanding Horizons*). Most everyone agrees that people should have access to the legal system, and some facilities to engage with broader systems of social justice, as part of an integrated effort to address interrelated social challenges. However, there has been little sustainability in the larger scope of social justice to address gun violence. In law, what access to justice even means to this issue remains open to debate.

Conceptually, the overall idea of access to justice is sometimes said to be a value that supports the rule of law (Rankin). In this framework, people must understand both their legal obligations and entitlements. Such a system relies on a conception of law that emphasizes the certainty afforded by a legal system. In this case, people must be able to access legal services, which can serve to guide and manage their affairs. On a practical basis, access to justice may also promote complementary democratic values, such as equal opportunity for participation in legal governance (Sommerlad).

For his part, Lon Fuller took the position that moving towards rule of law means "formal institutions are established guaranteeing to the members of the community some participation in the decisions by which their interests were affected" (5). However, there is now some recognition that those who cannot access justice—often because of inequalities arising from such factors as poverty, race or gender—may face practical limits on their ability to participate in the system of legal and social governance (Froc; Etherington; Mossman). Today, decreasing access to courts, constraints imposed on programs of social justice, and widespread disengagement from other forms of social ordering may be contributing to social distancing, encouraging negative views and pessimism, which are also affecting the perception of gun crime.

By several measures, there has been a long-term trend in both Canada and the United States towards decreasing social capital (Putnam). Despite some variability, political engagement is still at historic lows.[4] Other traditional measures of community involvement, like church attendance, union memberships, participation in parent-teacher associations and even local bowling leagues have seen widespread declines. While the spread of social media might have initially appeared to have potential to build community, as noted earlier, public perceptions of these online platforms in Canada now appear to have largely soured.

Perhaps unsurprisingly, in light of these broader trends there is some evidence that people also have a low level of trust in the formal justice system.[5] This despite consistent international measures that have placed Canada in the top cadre of countries in terms of the rule of law.[6] Paradoxically, although crime is at historic lows, Canada's criminal court system is clogged to the point that the Supreme Court has intervened to impose maximum procedural timelines, after which matters must be dismissed (Standing Senate Committee). The effectiveness and efficiency of the civil justice system are also in doubt, as some have resorted to private or alternative means to address their legal problems.

Misperceptions that crime is increasing may also be part of a larger social problem in which established social structures supporting constructive community interactions are fraying. A more worrying prospect may be that perceptions of increased crime and gun violence are also related to the increased social distancing, declining social capital, and the perceived need for individuals to independently seek justice (Black). Adverse social factors—such as poverty, racism, and other factors related to the broader decline in social justice—may also lead some to turn to guns for protection and justice ("Protection Is the Key Reason"). Some research also shows that decreased confidence in the justice system increases vigilantism (Haas, Keijser, and Bruinsma).

In other cases, the fear engendered by the dominant narrative about crime may provoke extraordinary reactions of frustration by those who feel justified in using extreme force to protect themselves (Hamilton). As one recent high profile and controversial example, a Saskatchewan farmer interceded in the commission of a property crime with a weapon. Part of the context of the 2018 case were concerns about the increasing criminal conduct of rural residents in Western Canada. The farmer used a gun to try to stop an Indigenous youth at his property; he killed the teenager and was ultimately acquitted of criminal charges in the death.

The breakdown in trust of traditional social conflict resolution mechanisms has enabled a growing kind of digital vigilanteeism (Trottier). This phenomenon is likely apparent to anyone who participates in social media. It has been described as an alternate and private form of criminal justice, in which people eschew long held principles of justice, such as the presumption of innocence, and use modern technologies to hold people accountable in online forums.[7] Some people's perception of the need to seek individual justice through technology may be just one more piece of a bigger story about declining social relations and decreased access to justice.

In defense of guns, it is common to hear the expression "Guns don't kill people; people kill people." Such sentiments diminish the complex nature of the context of people's lives and the simultaneous issues that impact criminality and the use of firearms. These issues are, in fact, associated with a number of broader social trends. This includes an exaggerated perception of social violence, crime and guns, a long-term trend in declining social engagement, a breakdown of some of the broader mechanisms of social justice, distrust in courts, and a widespread view that access to the formal justice system is declining. Ultimately, effectively addressing social violence, perceptions of criminality involving guns, and social justice itself may depend on the success of a broader approach that acknowledges and seeks to address interrelated issues of racism, poverty, and access to justice more holistically.

Conclusion

The competing stories about social violence and guns in our society are in part a tale of two justice systems. In the dominant narrative, there is significantly more crime and gun violence, reflected at the local level and in individual perceptions. However, when the main story is examined closely, it appears that most popular perceptions about conflict, especially about crime and gun violence, are exaggerated. Some of the causes of modern misperceptions can be traced to public policy. Other negative views are likely encouraged by the effects of traditional and new media.

Attitudes and beliefs about crime and guns may be correlated with other long-term trends related to declining civic engagement, reduced social infrastructure, and overall perceptions of access to legal and social justice. The perceived challenge with respect to violence and gun crime, though not substantiated by the numbers nationally, is consistent with a broader sense of malaise associated with a decades-long shift away from traditional systems of social ordering. People are less engaged in their communities and have less trust in many of the groups and institutions, which have commonly been seen to positively strengthen social participation.

Despite the evidence of decreased crimes in Canada over time, we must not ignore the fact that groups, such as the Black community, are disproportionately impacted by gun violence death and exposure. Therefore, the national statistics of crime rates must be considered alongside the disproportionate impacts of specific crimes on communities, which are facilitated by broader social issues, less political engagement, and less access to justice. These trends in relation to firearm use in Canada are better seen as part of wider efforts to continue to reduce social violence while striving to enhance access to social and legal justice. The challenges these issues present, along with how they are perceived, appear more complicated than suggested by simple narratives, and are not likely amenable to simple solutions or quick policy fixes. Ultimately, to come to grips with social conflict, crime, and guns, public policy needs to integrate a wider and more holistic perspective that better takes into account both the reality and rhetoric of violence, crime, and guns.

Endnotes

1. Although they reported feeling safer as compared to the past, only 38 per cent of women in 2014 felt "very safe" walking alone in their neighbourhood after dark, compared to sixty-four percent of men. Though crime severity in Toronto, Montreal and Vancouver was lower than the national average, urban residents in those cities also felt less secure (Perreault).
2. This includes poor parenting and availability of illegal drugs, which rated higher in a 1998 survey than other common factors: a soft justice system, poverty, low moral standards, unemployment, tv violence, discipline in schools, lack of family and childcare, and, ranking lowest amongst these, insufficient police (Stein).
3. By outsourcing traditional adjudication to alternative dispute resolution, devolving matters to other bodies like administrative tribunals, and through private resolution. In the US, Judith Resnik and Dennis Curtis have stated the following:

   The questions are whether courts will remain available to ordinary persons seeking to engage in the democratic practices of adjudication; whether the courts will continue to attend to individuals as equal and dignified members of a polity; and whether polities will authorize disputants to contest state authority and to use courts to foster debate about both the content and the application of norms. (307)
4. In Canada, 2015 federal voter turnout rose to 69 per cent, the highest level since 1993, but followed on the heels of the 2011 federal election which had one of the lowest turnouts in Canadian history (Johnston).
5. One poll published in 2018 found only 41 per cent of Canadians have complete or a lot of confidence in their provincial courts. Expressions of faith and trust in the system vary considerably by region, group, and amongst elements of the justice system. For example, only 32 per cent of visible minorities had complete or a lot of confidence in provincial courts, in BC only

   28 per cent had complete or a lot of confidence in provincial criminal courts, whereas the Supreme Court of Canada rated a 51 per cent overall of complete or a lot of confidence ("Confidence in the Justice System")

6. Out of 113 jurisdictions ranked annually by the World Justice Project's "Rule of Law Index 2017–2018" (2018), Canada ranked ninth, improving three spots over the previous year.
7. Often through "doxing" (Douglas).

Works Cited

Berthiaume, Lee. "Statistics Canada Blames Gun, Gangs as Homicide Rate Hits 10 Year High." *CBC*, 21 Nov. 2018, www.cbc.ca/news/politics/stats-can-homicide-rate-1.4914646. Accessed 12 Apr. 2022.

Black, Donald. "Crime as Social Control." *American Sociological Review*, vol. 48, no. 1, 1983, pp. 34-35.

Boissoneault, Lorraine. "The Mass Shooting that Reshaped the Canadian Debate about Guns and Political Identify." *Smithsonian Magazine*, 2 Feb. 2017, www.smithsonianmag.com/history/mass-shooting-reshaped-canadian-debate-about-guns-and-political-identity-180962013/. Accessed 12 Apr. 2022.

Brown, Blake R. "'Every Boy Ought to Learn to Shoot and to Obey Orders.' Guns, Boys, and the Law in English Canada from the late Nineteenth Century to the Great War." *Canadian Historical Review*, vol. 93, no. 2, 2012, pp. 196-226.

Brown, Blake R. *Gun Control: Filling-in the Missing History in Canada*. University of Toronto Press, 2013.

Brown, Blake R. "Pistol Fever: Regulating Revolvers in the Late-Nineteenth Century Canada." *Journal of the Canadian Historical Association*, vol. 20, no. 1, 2009, pp. 107-38.

Comack, Elizabeth, S. Burgher, and Cara Fabre. "The Impact of the Harper Government's 'Tough on Crime' Strategy: Hearing from Frontline Workers." Canadian Centre for Policy Alternatives, 2015.

"Confidence in the Justice System: Visible Minorities Have Less Faith in Courts than other Canadians." *Angus Reid Institute*, 20 Feb. 2018, angusreid.org/justice-system-confidence/. Accessed 12 Apr. 2022.

"Criminal Gun and Gang Violence in Canada." *Public Safety Canada*, 8 Mar. 2018, www.canada.ca/en/public-safety-canada/news/2018/03/criminal-gun-and-gang-violence-in-canada.html. Accessed 12 Apr. 2022.

Dickens, Charles. *A Tale of Two Cities*. Chelsea House Publishers, 1987.

Douglas, David M. "Doxing: A Conceptual Analysis." *Ethics and Information Technology*, vol. 18, no. 3, 2016, pp. 199-210.

Etherington, Brian. "Promises, Promises: Notes on Diversity and Access to Justice." *Queen's LJ*, vol. 26, no. 1, 2000, pp. 43-66.

Expanding Horizons: Rethinking Access to Justice in Canada, Proceedings of a National Symposium. Department of Justice Canada, 2000.

Froc, Kerri A. "Is the Rule of Law the Golden Rule? Accessing 'Justice' for Canada's Poor." *Can. Bar Rev.*, vol. 87, 2008, p. 459.

Fuller, Lon L. "Adjudication and the Rule of Law." *American Society of International Law*, vol. 54, 1960, pp. 1-8.

Fuller, Lon L., and Kenneth I. Winston. "The Forms and Limits of Adjudication." *Harvard Law Review*, vol. 92, no. 2, 1978, pp. 353-409.

Haas, Nicole E., Jan W. de Keijser, and Gerben J. N. Bruinsma. "Public Support for Vigilantism, Confidence in Police and Police Responsiveness." *Policing and Society*, vol. 24, no. 2, 2014, pp. 224-41.

Hamilton, Charles. "Frustrated and Helpless: Rural Residents Say Stanley Trial Highlights Crime, Police Response Time Concerns." *CBC*, 14 Feb. 2018, www.cbc.ca/news/canada/saskatoon/stanley-verdict-again-raising-concerns-over-rural-crime-1.4535146. Accessed 12 Apr. 2022.

Harrison, Thomas Stuart. "Between Principle and Practicality: A Dynamic Realist Examination of Independence in the Canadian Justice System. Diss." *New Legal Realism*, 2016, newlegalrealism.org/wp-content/uploads/2017/12/Harrison-Between-Principle-and-Practicality-A-Dynamic-Realist-Examination-of-Inde pendence-in-the-Canadian-Justice-System.pdf. Accessed 12 Apr. 2022.

Harrison, Thomas S. "The Statute of Westminster is Canada's Neglected Declaration of Independence." *Essays in Celebration of Canada 150*, edited by H. McIvor and A. Milnes. LexisNexis, 2017.

Johnston, Richard. "Political Participation." *The Canadian Encyclopedia*, 2015, www.thecanadianencyclopedia.ca/en/article/political-participation. Accessed 12 Apr. 2022.

Leetaru, Kalev. "Mapping World Happiness And Conflict Through Global News and Image Mining." *Forbes*, 13 Jan. 2016, www.forbes.

com/sites/kalevleetaru/2016/01/13/mapping-world-happiness-and-conflict-through-global-news-and-image-mining/?sh=4840 8d64e224. Accessed 12 Apr. 2022.

Maioni, Antonia, and Miriam Smith. "Health Care and Canadian Federalism." *New Trends in Canadian Federalism*, edited by Francois Rocher and Miriam Smith, Broadview Press, 2003, pp. 300-03.

McCormick, Peter. *Judicial Independence and the Judicial Governance in the Provincial Courts*. Canadian Association of Provincial Court Judges, 2004.

McLuhan, Marshall. *The Gutenberg Galaxy*. University of Toronto Press, 1962.

McPhail, Ian V., Mark E. Olver, and Carolyn Brooks. "Taking the Pulse: Perceptions of Crime Trends and Community Safety and Support for Crime Control Methods in the Canadian Prairies." *Journal of Community Safety and Well-Being*, vol. 2, no. 2, 2017, pp. 43-50.

Mossman, Mary Jane. "Shoulder to Shoulder: Gender and Access to Justice." *Windsor YB Access Just.*, vol. 10, 1990, pp. 351-63.

Müller, Ingo, and Furchtbare Juristen. *Hitler's Justice: The Courts of the Third Reich*. Harvard University Press, 1991.

Mussa, Idil. "Spike in Gun and Gang Violence in Canada has Experts Worried." *CBC*, 7 Mar. 2018, www.cbc.ca/news/politics/spike-in-gun-and-gang-violence-in-canada-has-experts-worried-1.456 4643. Accessed 12 Apr. 2022.

Nanos. "Impressions of Canadians on Social Media Platforms and Their Impact on the News." *Nanos*, Feb. 2017, nanos.co/wp-content/uploads/2017/07/2017-984-signal-january-populated-report-new-with-tabs-r.pdf. Accessed 12 Apr. 2022.

Naumetz, Tim. "Liberal Government Starts Funding Against Gangs, Guns, as Election Nears." *iPolitics*, 13 Mar. 2019, ipolitics.ca/news/liberal-government-starts-funding-against-gangs-guns-as-election-nears. Accessed 12 Apr. 2022.

Pelletier, Gérald. "Le Code Criminel Canadien, 1892-1939: Le Contrôle des Armes à Feu." *Crime, History and Societies*, vol. 6, no. 2, 2002, pp. 51-79.

Perreault, Samuel. "Canadians' Perceptions of Personal Safety and

Security, 2014." *Statistics Canada*, 2014, www150.statcan.gc.ca/n1/pub/85-002-x/2017001/article/54889-eng.htm. Accessed 12 Apr. 2022.

Pinker, Steven. *The Better Angels of Our Nature: Why Violence Has Declined*. Viking Penguin, 2011.

Pinker, Steven. "The Media Exaggerates Negative News. This Distortion Has Consequences." *The Guardian*, 17 Feb. 2018, www.theguardian.com/commentisfree/2018/feb/17/steven-pinker-media-negative-news.

"Protection Is the Key Reason Toronto Youth Turn to Guns, a New Report Finds." *CBC*, 20 Jul. 2018, www.cbc.ca/news/canada/toronto/protection-is-the-key-reason-toronto-youth-turn-to-guns-a-new-report-finds-1.4755931. Accessed 12 Apr. 2022.

Putnam, Robert D. "Bowling Alone: America's Declining Social Capital." *Journal of Democracy*, vol. 6, no. 1, 1995, pp. 166-74.

Quinn, Greg. "Canada's Gun-Related Homicide Rate Hits Its Highest Level in 25 Years." *Time*, 18 Nov. 2018, time.com/5461950/canada-homicide-rate-2017-climbs/. Accessed 12 Apr. 2022.

Rankin, Micah B. "Access to Justice and the Institutional Limits of Independent Courts." *Windsor Yearbook of Access to Justice*, vol. 30, no. 1, 2012, pp. 101-38.

Resnik, Judith, and Dennis Curtis. *Representing Justice: Invention, Controversy, and Rights in City-States and Democratic Courtrooms*. Yale University Press, 2011.

Scotti, Monique. "Canadians Still Wildly Overestimating the Level of Violent Crime." *Global News*, 3 Aug. 2017, globalnews.ca/news/3645766/canadians-still-wildly-overestimating-the-level-of-violent-crime/. Accessed 12 Apr. 2022.

Seto, Megan. "Killing Ourselves: Depression as an Institutional, Workplace and Professionalism Problem." *WJ Legal Stud.*, vol. 2, no. 2, 2012, pp. 9-11.

Sommerlad, Hilary. "Some Reflections on the Relationship Between Citizenship, Access to Justice and the Reform of Legal Aid." *Journal of Law and Society*, vol. 31, no. 3, 2004, pp. 345-368.

Stanbury W. T., and Allan Smithies. "Brief History of Canada's Gun Laws." *National Firearms Association*, nfa.ca/wp-content/

uploads/2018/04/Brief-history-of-Canadas-gun-laws-Part-II.pdf. Accessed 12 Apr. 2022.

Trottier, Daniel. "Digital Vigilantism as Weaponisation of Visibility." *Philosophy & Technology*, vol. 30, no. 1, 2017, pp. 55-72.

Standing Senate Committee on Legal and Constitutional Affairs. "Delaying Justice is Denying Justice: An Urgent Need to Address Lengthy Court Delays in Canada (Final Report)." *Senate of Canada*, 2017, sencanada.ca/content/sen/committee/421/LCJC/reports/Court_Delays_Final_Report_e.pdf. Accessed 12 Apr. 2022.

Statistics Canada. "Chart 1: Police-Reported Crime Statistics, 2017." *Statistics Canada*. 23 July 2018, www150.statcan.gc.ca/nl/pub/85-002-x/2018001/article/54974-eng.htm. Accessed 12 Apr. 2022.

Statistics Canada. "Chart 2: Police-Reported Crime Rates, 1962–2017." Statistics Canada, 23 July 2018, www150.statcan.gc.ca/nl/daily-quotidien/180723/cg-b002-eng.htm. Accessed 12 Apr. 2022.

Wallace, M., et al, "Measuring Crime in Canada: Introducing the Crime Severity Index and Improvements to Uniform Crime Reporting Survey." *Statistics Canada*, www150.statcan.gc.ca/nl/en/catalogue/85-004-X. Accessed 12 Apr. 2022.

World Justice Project. "WJP Rule of Law Index 2017–2018 Report." World Justice Project, 2019, worldjusticeproject.org/our-work/publications/rule-law-index-reports/wjp-rule-law-index-2017-2018-report. Accessed 12 Apr. 2022.

Chapter 7

Figures of the 2014 Parliament Hill Attacker: A Critical Discourse Analysis of News Media Configurations of Michel Zehaf-Bibeau

Rebecca Jaremko Bromwich

On the morning of October 22, 2014, a man opened fire with a 30-30 Winchester rifle at the National War Memorial in Ottawa, Ontario. The shooter killed reservist Corporal Nathan Cirillo, who stood on ceremonial guard duty there, then commandeered a vehicle, and stormed Parliament Hill. It was the first time shots were ever fired inside Canada's Parliament. The shooter was stopped and killed, just steps away from a government caucus meeting, only a few feet from then Prime Minister Stephen Harper.[1]

This shooting was an event that profoundly shook Canadians generally and the community of Ottawa, Ontario, specifically. This chapter undertakes a critical discourse analysis of media articles produced in the thirty days following the attack. In this chapter, I discuss the public conversations that ensued in mainstream media sites days following the incident and address how discursive figurations of Michel Zehaf-Bibeau were deployed as technologies of government, specifically to advance the federal government's political agenda in the form of Bill C-51.

My personal engagement with this situation, which was through the lens of mainstream media texts, led me to this analysis. I wanted to test whether my observations of the coverage were supported by a more systematic examination of how the case was constructed in the media and to analyze what was gained and lost by the picture of Zehaf-Bibeau that emerged. I live in Ottawa with my partner and our four young children; however, on the morning of October 22, 2014, I was not in the city, having left at 6:00 a.m. on a commuter train to attend a conference in Montreal. I watched the events unfold in the media, desperate to find out if my children were safe. My experience of this event—although it was affecting my hometown and potentially threatening the safety of my children—was mediated through the mainstream media, so I was acutely drawn to the coverage. In the moment, concerned for my home and family, I viewed it from my specific perspective as a mother. It is from this personal perspective, as well as an intellectual interest in how the media portrayed the event, that this project grew. After the event was resolved, I undertook an academic exploration of the ways in which the attacker was understood in various texts and cross-referenced my personal, anecdotal experience with the results of a critical discourse analysis, as discussed below.

The Shootings

October 22, 2014, was a crisp, cloudy autumn Wednesday. At around 9:00 in the morning, as commuters were arriving at work in downtown Ottawa, a webcam captured footage of a man opening fire at the National War Memorial across the street from Parliament Hill. There, the shooter, later identified as Michael Zehaf-Bibeau, shot Corporal Nathan Cirillo, a Canadian reservist soldier posted as a sentry on ceremonial duty. Because Cirillo was present in a ceremonial role, his weapon was not loaded, and he was not able to defend himself. Passersby rushed to give first aid to Cirillo but to no avail. He died on the scene. While this was happening, Zehaf-Bibeau drove rapidly to the adjacent Parliament buildings, where he entered the Centre Block building. In Centre Block, members of the Parliament of Canada, including the prime minister, were attending caucuses. After wrestling with a security staffer at the entrance, Zehaf-Bibeau ran inside, firing shots. Following a shootout with Parliament security personnel, Zehaf-Bibeau was killed. He had been shot thirty-one times by six officers.

Sergeant-at-Arms Kevin Vickers went to the nearby room where parliamentarians had been meeting and told the then-governing Conservative caucus: "I have engaged the assailant. He is deceased." (Palmer and Schnurr)

During the shootings, the City of Ottawa was shut down. All schools in the municipal area were placed on lockdown, as was the entire downtown core of Ottawa. It was several hours before police finished searching for additional possible threats. Surreal and nightmarish email and text alerts started popping up on my laptop from the University of Ottawa, where, but for my trip, I would otherwise have been teaching that day. These communications reported the campus was on lockdown. My heart sank when I received messages from the school board saying our children were in lockdown at their schools. In the midst of this, I wandered around the rainy streets of downtown Montreal feeling like a ghost in a nightmare. All of the TV sets I walked past turned to news coverage of the "events in Ottawa."

My personal connection with the incident as a resident of Ottawa who, at the time, worked in the area where the shootings took place and where my children went to school gave me a particular lens on the incident. I had never before experienced anything at such an emotionally unsettling level as it was to watch or listen to the news of that event.

The Analysis

This chapter reports on an analysis of news reports contemporaneous with the events of October 22, 2014, and up until November 22, 2014. The information was obtained through a search of the Dow Jones news database Factiva using search terms that include "Zehaf-Bibeau" " shooting" and "Ottawa" with dates limited to the day of the shootings and the thirty days following it. The search yielded 4,024 unique documents, all of them news stories written about the shooter. Each article was coded for its dominant portrayal of the shooting: terrorism (T), gun violence (G), mental illness (M), or something else (E).

The method of critical discourse analysis (CDA) was employed. CDA is a methodological framework for understanding how discourses function as instruments of power and control. CDA looks at social structures and processes involved in text production. It is an analytical way to make visible relationships of causality that are otherwise opaque and to see links between texts and broader social and cultural power relations and discursive processes (Fairclough). This type of analysis explores what social researcher Lauren Berlant calls the "caseness" of Zehaf-Bibeau (Berlant). The analysis involved asking how Zehaf-Bibeau is constructed as a "case." More specifically, is he portrayed as an example of a terrorist, of a mental patient, or of something else?

I worked with the concept of "figuration" (de Laurentis), which is the process by which a representation is given a particular form in discursive texts. A figuration is also described as "a specific configuration of knowledges, practices and power" (28). Accordingly, the analysis determined what figurations of Michel Zehaf-Bibeau emerged in these cultural domains. The analysis focused on how Zehaf-Bibeau was represented as a "figure" in a variety of texts from sites of discursive production in news media texts. Claudia Casteneda explains that "A figure is the simultaneously material and semiotic product of certain [discursive] processes" (3-4). The analysis captured how figures of Zehaf-Bibeau emerged in the texts, what public narratives and politics those figures supported, and to what extent each configuration of Zehaf-Bibeau was consistent or inconsistent with a philosophical orientation of maternal thinking.

The term "maternal thinking" (Ruddick), as used in this chapter, refers to a particular strain of feminist theory developed in large by philosopher Sara Ruddick and more recently expanded and clarified by leading Canadian motherhood scholar Andrea O'Reilly. Ruddick sees maternal thinking as a discipline analogous to the discourses of religion or science, with particular dimensions as a practice. Although traditionally understood as women's work, maternal thinking is not essentially female. It is a philosophical orientation that cognitively and performatively involves caregiving and emotional labour that is engaged with and involves "protection, nurturance and training ... care and respect" (Ruddick 62). Ruddick identifies this maternal standpoint as a way of looking at all children and other people as human. Ruddick thinks of mothering as a set of tasks as well as a genre of work or labour, not an identity, and focuses on the performativity of maternal thinking and not on essential biological traits, thereby disaggregating maternalism from any particular embodied subject. She focuses not on static personal attributes but on themes characteristic of maternal thinking, such as compassion and altruism (Ruddick). Similarly, O'Reilly draws together Judith Butler's notions about the performativity of gender with Ruddick's maternal thinking to further advance a nonessentialist understanding of maternal activism. She writes that far from being essentially feminine, "motherhood is similarly performed by maternalist activists" (16). Maternal thinking, therefore, is performed rather than biologically inhabited.

Findings

This analysis reveals that whereas the dominant narratives about the October 22, 2014, incident focused on security rhetoric and terrorism, mainstream news media texts provided a richer and more nuanced set of configurations of Zehaf-Bibeau. Although he was often initially portrayed simply as a terrorist monster, media narratives became more complex over time. The "terrorist" construction emerged into dominance, but as time went on, a perspective emerged consistent with Ruddick's conception of maternal thinking and maternal standpoint in advocacy for better mental health services and gun control. Most significant among these voices was Zehaf-Bibeau's mother Susan Bibeau herself, who characterized him as a desperate person with mental illness. Also significant were statements made by the leader of the official opposition, NDP leader Tom Mulcair, who explicitly refused to characterize Zehaf-Bibeau as a terrorist, preferring instead the term "criminal" ("Mulcair"). These alternative configurations, more consistent with Ruddick's maternal thinking, were invoked to support different narratives about the events and in turn different strategies for social action and divergent visions of what is needed for Canada. Maternal thinking and maternal activism have productive potential for improvements in the support for mental health endeavours and the regulation of guns, as evidenced by this case.

An abundance of media texts was generated about the shootings. Most (2,873) of the 4,204 articles obtained on this Factiva search were produced in national Canadian mainstream media sites, and a large number of others (1,730) were produced in sites local to Ottawa, where the shootings had taken place. The most common keywords across all of the articles were "political motive" and "massive investigation." Taken together, these mainstream news media articles largely—but not without exception—construct a configuration of Zehaf-Bibeau as a terrorist and of the attacks as an international political incident. The majority of the Factiva articles articulated a configuration of Zehaf-Bibeau as a politically-motivated terrorist; this configuration became more dominant as time passed (e.g., Duffy). The configuration of Zehaf-Bibeau as a terrorist certainly became the widely accepted construction of him in governmental discourses and supported the passage of Bill C-51, which became the Anti-Terrorism Act, 2015, S.C. 2015, c. 20

Prime Minister Stephen Harper, while in office, characterized the shootings as an international terrorist act, drawing opportunistically upon this characterization to support the passage of the hotly controversial Anti-Terrorism Act 2015, which, with support of the Liberals, then sitting in opposition, passed in June of 2015. Of the Act, Harper said the following:

> This will lead us to strengthen our resolve and redouble our efforts and those of our national security agencies to take all necessary steps to identify counter threats and keep Canada safe here at home, just as it will lead us to strengthen our resolve and redouble our efforts to work with our allies around the world and fight against the terrorist organizations who brutalize those in other countries with a hope of attacking Canada. (Wherry)

The implication of this statement is that the prime minister sought to leverage the attack to support his international policy agenda and militaristic approach.

I was surprised to discover that media configurations of Zehaf-Bibeau were quite varied and diverse. This was particularly the case in relation to articles produced in Canada. It is evident from this critical discourse analysis that several configurations of Zehaf-Bibeau fought for dominance in the timeframe immediately following the attack. There was not a single unified portrayal of him in media reports. Zehaf-Bibeau was constructed in the vast majority of media texts as a terrorist—termed, most colourfully, as "Canada's jihadi killer" (Bates). However, he was also constructed as "a gunman" (Palmer and Schnurr), as "mentally ill" (Fingas), as a "drug user," as a "homeless person," and as a "petty criminal" (Spargo) in a smaller number of texts framing out counternarratives.

These different configurations of Zehaf-Bibeau fought for supremacy in some instances in the same text. Even where the same author and editors were involved in producing the text, there was not a consistent portrayal of the shooter. In some instances, the contradictions and complexities in Zehaf-Bibeau's circumstances were the focus of the story. Where different configurations of Zehaf-Bibeau were presented in a text, this often ended with a resolution that made the terrorist configuration win out, but in other instances, they did not. The portrayal of the shooter was muddled and inconsistent in many instances. The mental health counternarrative was driven in part by his mother's accounts of what went wrong. The petty criminal counter-narrative was propelled by investigative reporting that had uncovered a history of minor crime on his part. In these counternarratives, there is space for readers to see Zehaf-Bibeau more tragically and compassionately, or through a more maternal lens, because they are more inclined towards his humanity and belonging within Canadian society.

Mainstream news media texts revealed much about Zehaf-Bibeau that helped build a variety of narratives about him. From mainstream news media, Canadians learned he had an upper-middle-class Canadian upbringing, divorced parents, a long criminal record for minor charges, and a history of working in Western Canada. He had been treated by psychiatrists and had disclosed his addiction to crack cocaine to police. He was homeless at the time of the incident. He was a self-professed adherent of Islam who had been kicked out of his local mosque and who abused drugs, counter to the Qur'an. Taken together, news media texts about the shootings present Zehaf-Bibeau as complex and contradictory. Because Zehaf-Bibeau was killed in the shooting, there are no trial transcripts of his own account of what happened and why—other than in his brief videotaped statement made as "selfies" moments before the event took place. The discursive configurations of Zehaf-Bibeau as a terrorist, mental patient, homeless person, and criminal are selected and incomplete. They perform certain sorts of governmental and discursive tasks. Each configuration is problematic and partial, in part because that is the nature of discourse—to both conceal and reveal (Butler)—and because Zehaf-Bibeau died at the time of the shootings, leaving many unanswered questions. Most significantly, configurations of Zehaf-Bibeau as a terrorist fit public narratives about security and the need for increased surveillance and police control, espoused by conservative politicians seeking to drive antiterrorist surveillance measures through Parliament and into law. Public narratives framing the attack as a political act served to unify Ottawa's citizens with a sense of common purpose in defense of one another and supported narratives of heroism on the part of parliamentary security and politicians. In particular, the terrorist configuration of Zehaf-Bibeau supported understandings of Corporal Cirillo as a heroic victim, and Canada's sergeant-at-arms, who was one of the officials with whom Zehaf-Bibeau engaged in a firefight, as a heroic rescuer.

Certainly, these narratives are based on important truths. Without question, Lieutenant Cirillo does deserve to be mourned and lauded. Absolutely, Sergeant-at-Arms Kevin Vickers deserves to be praised. Even so, the narratives about what happened that day were mobilized to support certain positions and political agendas while silencing others. More specifically, they were deliberately deployed by the Harper government to support its stance on international issues. Less intentionally, they played into wider discourses of xenophobia and anti-Islamic racism. The narrative that a serious political attack on an international scale had been levied against the Harper government bolstered its highly militaristic rhetoric and reaffirmed that its concerns about security and public safety, which resulted in radical changes to the Criminal Code and to Bill C-51, were valid. It supports a securitized response on a grand scale by considering this incident in the context of other attacks. In short, one-dimensional configuration of Zehaf-Bibeau as a terrorist was a discursive tool that advanced the agenda of the Harper government.

Conversely, while each discursive configuration of Zehaf-Bibeau draws readers in to more clearly understand aspects of the incident, it also obscures others. Significantly, the construction of Zehaf-Bibeau as a terrorist shifts the readers' gaze away from questions about how routine policing is conducted in Canada and how issues relating to addictions and drugs are affecting communities. It also does not support Ruddick's type of maternal thinking about Zehaf-Bibeau in relation to the incident. The dominance of the terrorist configuration led to the production of public narratives about the shootings that do not contain an analysis of how this crime might be linked to other gun crimes in the city or patterns and gaps in policing. This silence is particularly problematic when considered in the context of another Ottawa shooting that took place less than a year later. When Basil Borutski shot three women in September 2015 links were not drawn between his possession of weapons and the possession of an illegal weapon by Zehaf-Bibeau, and the incidents were not considered together. In general, texts produced about the Zehaf-Bibeau shootings, with notable but very few exceptions (Dyer), did not make reference to the illegal possession or use of the gun. This is especially significant because Zehaf-Bibeau obtained his weapon illegally. There was certainly a story that could have been told about how he procured it, but that was not the story that the dominant media portrayals or political narratives selected to relate.

When the figure of Zehaf-Bibeau was constructed by media and politicians as an archetype of the Islamic terrorist, important dimensions of his case, such as mental health, that possibly complicated and nuanced the situation, were lost. It was not refuted by anyone that he made a brief cell phone video expressing a political motive for his actions moments before he shot Cirillo. Indeed, that act of self-expression could take on a more complex meaning when it is considered in the context of his ongoing personal problems, homelessness, drug addiction, criminal record, and mental health concerns. The social problems that the shooting highlighted, when seen in these multiple dimensions, include not only the growth of Islamic radicalism but also addiction, mental illness, and the availability of weapons. In many cases, social marginality is also what makes young Canadians vulnerable to the inflammatory rhetoric of Islamic State of Iraq and the Levant (ISIL) propaganda or any sort of radicalization.

Conclusion

This chapter has discussed discursive configurations of Michel Zehaf-Bibeau in mainstream news media sites in the context of his shootings on Parliament Hill. The CDA undertaken in this case finds Canadian media articles presented more complex characterizations of him than are often assumed in retrospect. In fact, Canadian media were resistant to characterizing Zehaf-Bibeau's acts as international terrorism. Contrary to popular stereotypes about media oversimplifying complex events, Canadian mainstream media presented a more nuanced and complex picture of Zehaf-Bibeau than did the governmental rhetoric invoked in relation to the shooting. Although the majority of references to him were as a terrorist, and the narrative of the incident supported by this configuration was one about international political tensions, there existed a wide range of news articles produced in the thirty days following the incident that put forward complex and different configurations of him. In turn, these various alternative configurations of Zehaf-Bibeau support different narratives about mental health, crime, and the availability of guns in Canada.

Although the dominant configuration of Zehaf-Bibeau in the mainstream media was as a terrorist, this configuration was complicated in media texts by references made to contradictions in the available facts of the case. This terrorist configuration was much more readily adopted in the official language of the government of Canada in place at that time. Zehaf-Bibeau as a terrorist figure is a governmental construction that supports antiterrorist security agendas, specifically far-reaching curtailments of civil liberties and increases in government surveillance of Canadians affected by Bill C-51.

In contrast to political rhetoric put forward by the Harper government about the incident, media texts allowed for the possibility of alternative plausible constructions of Zehaf-Bibeau, including as a petty criminal, homeless person, or mental patient. All of these configurations are partial and necessarily limited. However, if recuperated, alternative configurations of Zehaf-Bibeau to the dominant understanding that he was a terrorist could serve to support different sorts of social action. Alternative possible narratives included a more maternal perspective on the situation (Ruddick)—one that opens a space for the possibility of empathy, or at least dispassionate analysis of the specific and individual motivations that Zehaf-Bibeau might have had for his actions.

The discursive configuration of Zehaf-Bibeau as a terrorist, and the attack as a terror attack, remained the dominant public narratives about the event. They were supported by the official legal narrative about the events, as the RCMP classified the attack as a terrorist attack under the Criminal Code. The counternarrative that Zehaf-Bibeau was motivated by mental illness had little take-up. In turn, these narratives bolstered public support for an increased presence of security, surveillance, and police use of more firepower. Little was said about Zehaf-Bibeau's use of a gun as a weapon. Two visible outcomes of the shooting—the placement of armed police at the War Memorial and the introduction of submachine guns into routine usage by the RCMP—served to increase the presence of guns in Canada's capital and normalize their presence there.

After October 22, 2014, life continued in Ottawa, and it slowly got back to what felt like normal. Some changes were made to the security protocols for Parliament Hill and the War Memorial. Some security was increased: Police were stationed at the War Memorial to guard the ceremonial guards, and better coordination was put in place between parliamentary security and Ottawa police. Almost exactly a year after the shootings, in October of 2015, Prime Minister Stephen Harper was defeated by Liberal leader Justin Trudeau in a federal election. However, the current Liberal government, although it self-identifies as progressive, did not oppose and has not amended the changes made by C-51. In consequence, the increased surveillance and curtailment of civil liberties in C-51 that the October 22, 2014, attacks were referenced to support remain in place. The measures brought into being by C-51 have, in fact, become normalized. To ameliorate the situation and remedy the excesses of C-51, the current Liberal government introduced Bill C-59, an Act Respecting National Security Matters on June 20, 2017. Bill C-59 received royal assent on June 21, 2019. This legislation ameliorates some, though not all, of the excesses of Bill C-51.

As such, the attacks of October 22, 2014, exist today not just as a past event; they have justified a particular type of political governance—one that results in ever-increasing surveillance and security-based curtailments of civil liberties. It therefore remains relevant and useful to reexamine the stories told about Zehaf-Bibeau's actions and the deployment of figures of Zehaf-Bibeau as technologies of government, especially because C-51 remains unaltered, and in force.

Works Cited

Bates, D., and N. Fagge. "Canada's Jihadi Killer Went from Catholic Private Schoolboy to Criminal Drug Addict Just Two Years after Mother's Adultery Sparked Parents' Divorce." *MailOnline*, 24 Oct. 2014, www.dailymail.co.uk/news/article-2806954/Canada-s-jihadi-killer-went-Catholic-private-schoolboy-criminal-drug-addict-just-two-years-parents-split-sparked-mother-s-adultery.

html. Accessed 12 Apr. 2022.

Berlant, Lauren. "On the Case." *Critical Inquiry*, vol. 33, no. 4, 2007, pp. 663-72.

Castaneda, Claudia. *Figurations: Child, Bodies, Worlds*. Duke University Press, 2002.

De Laurentis, Teresa. *Figures of Resistance: Essays in Feminist Theory*. Teresa de Laurentis, 2007.

Duffy, Andrew. "Day of Chaos in the Capital Leaves Soldier and Terrorist Dead." *Ottawa Citizen*, 23 Oct. 2014, ottawacitizen.com/news/local-news/soldier-shot-at-war-memorial-in-ottawa. Accessed 12 Apr. 2022.

Dyer, Evan. "Ottawa Shooting: Where did Michael Zehaf-Bibeau Get His Gun?" *CBC News*, 24 Oct. 2014, www.cbc.ca/news/politics/ottawa-shooting-where-did-michael-zehaf-bibeau-get-his-gun-1.2811249. Accessed 12 Apr. 2022.

Fairclough, Norman. *Critical Discourse Analysis: The Critical Study of Language*. Longman, 1995.

Fingas, Greg, "When Justice and Mental Health Issues Meet." *Postmedia Breaking News*, 30 Oct. 2014www.pressreader.com/canada/regina-leader-post/20141030/281663958280697. Accessed 12 Apr. 2022.

Johnson, Rebecca. *Taxing Choices: The Intersection of Class, Gender, Parenthood and the Law*. University of British Columbia Press, 2002.

"Mulcair Deems Ottawa Shooter Michael Zehaf-Bibeau a Criminal, but Not a Terrorist." *National Post*, 29. Oct. 2014, nationalpost.com/news/politics/mulcair-deems-ottawa-shooter-michael-zehaf-bibeau-a-criminal-but-not-a-terrorist. Accessed 12 Apr. 2022.

O'Reilly, Andrea. *The Twenty-First Century Motherhood Movement*. Demeter Press, 2011.

Palmer, Randall, and Leah Schnurr. "Cheers, Tributes for Canadian Guard Credited with Killing Gunman." *Reuters*, 23 Oct. 2014, www.reuters.com/article/us-canada-attacks-sergeant-idUSKCN0IC22G20141023. Accessed 12 Apr. 2022.

Ruddick, Sara. *Maternal Thinking: Toward a Politics of Peace*. Beacon Press, 1995.

Spargo, Chris. "'I Want to Be in Jail so I Can Overcome My Crack Addiction': Why 2011 Testimony from Canadian Gunman Throws into Doubt Terror Theory As It Is Revealed There Is 'No Evidence' of Jihadist Links." *MailOnline*, 24 Oct. 2014, www.dailymail.co.uk/news/ article-2805871/I-want-jail-overcome-crack-addiction-2011-psych-assessment-Canadian-gunman-throws-doubt-terror-theory-revealed-no-evidence-jihadist-links.html. Accessed 12 Apr. 2022.

Wherry, Aaron. "Stephen Harper: 'Canada Will Never Be Intimidated'." *Maclean's*, 22 Oct. 2014, www.macleans.ca/politics/parliament-hill-shooting-stephen-harpers-address-to-the-nation/. Accessed 12 Apr. 2022.

Chapter 8

Gun Ownership and Mental Health

Alisha Chohan

Criminal law and psychiatry have shown that many perpetrators of gun violence often suffer from mental illnesses or recently reported behavioural changes (Swanson). According to Statistics Canada between 2013 and 2017, sixteen major Canadian metropolitan areas saw an increase in their rate of firearm-related violence, which contributed to a 43 per cent national increase (Statistics Canada). Although gun violence accounts for only three per cent of crimes, incidents in 2017 involved 7,700 victims (Clermont). Furthermore, gun availability has been shown to be an important determinant of a suicide attempt (Shenassa, Catlin, and Buka), and since the year 2000, an average of 583 suicides by firearms have taken place yearly across Canada (Clermont). Hence, gun accessibility is a key issue. A deterrence lens should be explored if the individual demonstrates deviant behaviour patterns and mental health issues, which was seen in the *R. v. Day* reasoning. In Canada, gun law is supposed to be managed federally, not provincially. The purpose of this chapter is to specifically focus on assessing the case law related to gun violence and questioning why provinces depict such disparity in how they handle gun violations, when instead there should be a unified federal approach to gun misuse and management. An overall background about gun use in Canada will be provided, before proceeding onto the case analysis of *R. v. Day* and future steps for Canada.

Gun Regulations and Statistics in Canada

Gun license and registration in Canada are managed federally by the Royal Canadian Mounted Police's (RCMP) Canadian Firearms Program (CFP). A formal application is due, which involves a background check that is conducted by the RCMP. This background check can incorporate various measures, such as in-depth interviews, health and mental health assessment, alongside reference interviews. In addition, licenses are valid for a specific time period, usually five years, and need to be renewed regularly (Royal Canadian Mounted Police).

From a procedural standpoint, it seems that federally, Canada is adhering to a strict policy in gun management and control. Regardless, statistically, the outcomes are not as promising. A study conducted by the Institute for Clinical and Evaluative Sciences (ICES) and the Hospital for Sick Children (SickKids) demonstrated that between 2008 and 2012, there were an average of 355 firearm injuries yearly among children and youth (under twenty-four years). Furthermore, the rate of gun-related crime since 2013 has increased an astounding 42 per cent largely within the Greater Toronto Area (CBC Canada). In addition, RCMP has had a difficult time in tracking and accounting for the source of the guns used in the violence, as no such comprehensive data exist (Fletcher). This makes the issue slightly complicated, as there is no clear understanding whether the firearms used are registered, nonregistered, or even used by individuals who have an expired license.

The Canadian Firearms Advisory Committee meeting in May 2017 made important distinctions between privacy rights and public safety for gun owners. The meeting stressed the importance of doctors, therapists, and social workers having the discretion to report to police if any of their patients should commit self-harm or perpetuate public harm with their firearm (Bronskill). In Quebec, the law takes this a step further and also requires childcare facilities, schools, and shooting clubs to report deviant behaviours and to identify those who should not be eligible to hold a firearm license.

In response to the need for increasing discretion from the meeting, in September 2018, Bill C-71, an Act to Amend Certain Acts and Regulations Related to Firearms, was passed. Bill C-71 was implemented with a focus on public safety and firearm owners. This legislation focuses on enhancing the background checks conducted by the RCMP. Through this change, violent behaviour would be assessed longitudinally, throughout the entire lifespan of the person, rather than just the preceding five years. The Liberals have stated that Bill C-71 is representative of the way the US federally handles and records gun sales through licensed dealers; it would allow Canada to be in line with the American implementation technique (Tasker).

Although the prospects of Bill C-71 may seem promising in terms of the transfer and sale of firearms and gun control, there is a need for further consideration about mental health and gun ownership. Statistics show that in 2016, out of the 2,223 firearm licenses that were revoked, mental health concerns were the subject of 424 of the revocations (Bronskill). As almost 20 per cent of weapons were revoked due to mental health reasons, these numbers are concerning and point directly to the fact that more focus on mental health and gun use in Canada is required. The procedures are superficially in place, yet they need to be enhanced. Primarily, a unionized procedural approach needs to be developed that focuses on an absolute test that can be utilized in courtrooms when dealing with gun ownership and mental health. Furthermore, the focus should also be on granting greater authority to federal power rather than allowing each province to use their own interpretation and precedents when dealing with cases that involve gun mismanagement and mental illnesses. Lastly, when dealing with those who are mentally ill, weapon seizure is not the direct solution. Instead, a community hub of resources needs to be bolstered to ensure that the individual is not in danger of self-harm or public harm later on, if they are allowed access to firearms again.

Legal Definitions

R. v. Day focuses on firearms and other weapons and analyzes Section 117.04 and 117.05 of The Criminal Code, alongside issues of witness credibility and jurisdiction. The Criminal Code is a federal law that outlines the procedures all jurisdictions must follow regarding criminal law issues. Section 117.04 is the application for a warrant to search and seize done by a peace officer. The search and seize protocol can occur with or without a warrant. The warrant is issued by a justice of the peace officer. In urgent matters where a warrant cannot be obtained, a peace officer has the discretion to search and seize, if it is a matter of public safety or danger.

After firearms or other items have been searched and seized by the peace officer, the relevance of Section 117.05 comes into play. This involves the application for disposition, which allows the justice to fix a date for a hearing for the person from whom the weapon(s) were seized. In the hearing process, the justice must determine at a specific threshold level that it is not desirable as per public safety for the person to possess the weapons. If that is the case, a prohibition and weapon forfeiture order is granted. This order can be appealed by the person and also the Crown.

Credibility has to do with the accuracy and reliability of a witness's testimony. Accuracy involves the witness's ability to observe, recall, and recount accurately the events related to the issue (*R v. H.C.*, 2009 ONCA 56 [CanLII]). Another important legal subject discussed in *R. v. Day* was the issue of jurisdiction, which is the legal boundary granted to a court to limit the types of cases and physical area over which it has authority.

Facts of R. v. Day

As per the police report, Robin Day was found in a parking lot in Guelph, displaying unusual behavior. Mr. Day's vehicle contained a shotgun (with accessible ammunition), an eight-inch hunting knife, several telescopic scopes, license plates of various vehicles, and photographs of young girls. Mr. Day had a poor appearance with a torn shirt and messy clothing. He seemed agitated speaking to the police officers and mentioned that he believed he was being stalked and spoke about conspiracy theories. Constable Gemin seemed concerned with Mr. Day's demeanour and suggested for him to go to a hospital—which Mr. Day declined. Mr. Day mentioned that his shotgun was always with him because he was concerned about wild animals in Alberta. He did have a firearms licence and certification for the shotgun.

The officer contacted one of Mr. Day's brothers, Daniel, who mentioned to him that Mr. Day has been suffering from schizophrenia and that his condition was getting worse. Daniel Day was concerned about his brother's accessibility to firearms. Mr. Day had displayed schizophrenic-like behaviours in the past, such as paranoia. Mr. Day's condition has been significantly deteriorating, and he has not been assessed medically for the last thirty years.

Daniel Day mentioned that his brother was not violent, but he was concerned about what Mr. Day might do in the future. The issue was the unpredictability of the situation and the safety of Mr. Day and others. He mentioned that Mr. Day's conversations were quite frightening and that he had also been receiving rant emails from Mr. Day. There was no evidence that Mr. Day was on medication or had sought clinical help.

Furthermore, Jennifer, Mr. Day's sister, also believed that he was an undiagnosed schizophrenic. She mentioned that Mr. Day thought their father was an imposter. Jennifer and brother Patrick had both aided Mr. Day in acquiring the firearms acquisition certificate. They both regretted doing so. Although there was no reported history of violent behaviour, his brother Patrick was concerned about Mr. Day's unpredictability and irrational life choices. Patrick also did not feel comfortable knowing that Mr. Day possessed firearms. Mr. Day mentioned that his lifestyle in Alberta required him to have access to his firearms and that on his drive from Alberta to Guelph, he brought along his full camping gear and firearms (*R. v. Day*, 2006 CanLII 26587 (ON SC).

Issues on Appeal

The case *R v. Day* is an interesting and relevant case study that complements the issue of mental health and gun ownership. The lower court decision was in favour of Mr. Day and the Crown did not believe it to be satisfactory as a ruling. The lower court's Justice hastily held that neither the weapon destruction order nor the lack of access to firearms was necessary as long as Mr. Day kept his guns out of the Town of Guelph. *R v. Day* was heard again in appeal court after the Crown was dissatisfied with the lower court's decision at the initial trial. The Crown appealed and objected to the decision that allowed Mr. Day to keep his weapons. The Crown was firm in their objection to Mr. Day having access to any type of firearms for five years and also sought a destruction of weapons order for his firearms. The respondent, Mr. Day, submitted to the appeal courts that no order should have been made. Mr. Day mentioned that the order made for keeping the weapons out of Guelph was also illegal. Hence, Mr. Day was instead seeking to affirm that he should have had full access to his weapons anywhere in Canada.

The issues presented in this case are interesting, as they directly showcase the purpose of this chapter's argument—that there is a lack of uniformity in legislation for mental health and gun ownership, to the extent that even courtrooms are not apt on how to handle it. The lower court implicitly understood the negative repercussions of having someone like Mr. Day have access to weapons in the Town of Guelph and as a safety standard held that he is barred from having them within the area's proximity. Yet they never considered the public safety of others, including Mr. Day's, if the weapons were potentially used outside of the Town of Guelph. Instead, a quick bandage solution was provided by the lower court. This depicts how quickly even courtrooms decide to overlook potentially negative repercussions in these situations. Luckily, in this scenario, the Crown was able to appeal at the higher court and win. But one must wonder what may become of similar cases dealing with gun ownership and mental health without uniform legislation.

At appeal court, this case was heard a second time. Justice Durno granted the appeal; hence the Crown, as the appellant, won. Justice Durno also held that the order that prohibited firearms from being brought into Guelph be quashed. With this outcome of the appeal, Justice Durno strongly emphasized the mistake of the lower court. Hence, conclusively, at the retrial, the mistake of the lower court was fixed, and the proximity issue of the weapon usage was corrected. This is of key importance because the appellate court indirectly reaffirmed the point that gun use in Canada is not just provincial or city specific, and that when mental health is contemplated alongside gun ownership, decisions to preserve law and order in this regard should go beyond jurisdiction.

Analysis of *R. v. Day*

Mental Health Assessment and Gun Ownership

The concern of the lower court was only the firearms—not the possibility that Mr. Day may have a mental health issue. In Mr. Day's situation, the recent siblings' reports and a physician analysis done thirty years prior could not confirm that Mr. Day had a mental illness.

The lack of concrete diagnosis led the Justice of the Peace at the lower court to conclude that Mr. Day did not presently have schizophrenia, therefore should be allowed to keep his weapons. No further analysis of the concerns raised by the siblings of Mr. Day was done, and a quick and easy solution was provided to the issue.

At higher court, Mr. Day's behaviour was deemed concerning enough that it explicitly warranted the judge to have a mental health assessment check done. Justice Durno discussed the error of the lower court in using Section 117.05; hence, this was the reason the appeal was allowed. Section 117.05's purpose and real subject matter is to determine if an individual should possess a weapon when it is a matter of public and personal safety. Justice Durno was blunt in stating that the Justice of the Peace was attempting to craft a practical solution to the case facts. The Counsel and Justice Durno argued that the Justice of the Peace's decision to permit Mr. Day's weapons outside of Guelph was a clear error.

The issue of mental health definitely complicates the analysis, as judges are not trained or equipped in such knowledge. In a different case, Waren Zimmer, a Nova Scotia provincial judge who led the inquiry for Lionel Desmond's murder-suicide through firearms, overtly asked if it was possible that regular checks be conducted on holders of firearm licenses who have a history of mental illness. Lionel Desmond had been diagnosed with posttraumatic stress disorder, after serving in Afghanistan. A doctor in 2016 deemed him "stable and non-suicidal" and his firearm license was reinstated, and firearms returned. Psychiatric reports in 2017 noted that Desmond was receding mentally yet not much was done to deal with his weapon accessibility. Mr. Desmond tragically committed a murder-suicide, killing himself and also three family members in 2017 using a gun (MacDonald).

The risks presented by cases such as Lionel Desmond demonstrate that the issue of gun violence and mental illness is not as sporadic as new events make it out to be. It is in no way appropriate to assume that everyone with mental illness will likely harm themselves or others. Rather, the point I emphasize is that careful standards should be considered when mental health is in question in decisions about gun ownership.

Mr. Day's situation builds upon prior precedential holdings similarly concerned with the issue of mental health and gun ownership. The application of Section 117.05 of The Criminal Code in courts and case law demonstrates how difficult it is to utilize, as there is no adequate consensus on the type of legal test that should be used to challenge a person's capability as a gun owner. In *Canada (Attorney General) v. Pattison* (1981 ABCA 98 [CanLII]), it was noted that the true test must be the real subject matter of the legislation. The type of test to determine weapon forfeiture demonstrates levels of analyses that deviate from being strict to lax. The test utilized in Justice Durno's analysis for Mr. Day safely falls as the middle ground. Is this an appropriate choice as a test? Once again there is no leading direction to confirm it.

A lax approach was shown in *R. v. Morgan* (1995 CanLII 18 [ON CJ], in which no proof was needed, and it was enough that there was a legitimate concern that the respondent lacked the discipline and responsibility of a gun user as per law. A more restrictive approach was demonstrated in *R v. Urchuk* (2004 BCPC 129 [CanLII]), in which a substantial possibility and evidence were required from the Crown to prove that the respondent's weapons were a public and personal safety concern.

The balance of probabilities test from *R. v. Bishop* (1995 CanLII 2449 [ON CJ]) was shown to determine if a person could be regarded as a danger to himself or others. Justice Durno discusses the possibility of the other tests but concludes that the most appropriate methodology to use in this circumstance is the balance of probabilities approach, the legitimate concerns test. Legitimate concerns test is an assessment to determine if the person lacks the responsibility and the discipline required of gun owners. Weapon forfeiture and prohibition orders will be given based on a balance of probabilities analysis that would need to demonstrate that in Mr. Day's case, his behavior shows a legitimate concern, and he lacks the responsibility and discipline of a gun owner, as per law.

Regardless, in consideration of all the negative social repercussions that can potentially take place from gun violence, even a lax to strict approach is not appropriate. The primary questions are as follows: Should only one test be utilized when assessing an individual's capacity as a gun owner? Why do courtrooms have leeway to decide and approach a clear public safety concern by picking and choosing whatever legal precedent and test they deem appropriate? The issue with precedents is that as soon as something is held to be good law, a courtroom, without overanalysis, would deem it appropriate and try to pigeonhole similar cases to mesh with what other judges in their jurisdiction are doing to protect the major consensus and order. This would not be appropriate. More needs to be done when dealing with mental health and gun ownership, and a legal test needs to be built federally that is formulated to be used across all jurisdictions. Otherwise, this would take away from the entire meaning of Canada having federal control over firearm management, leaving provinces and even towns to construct their own interpretations on decisions dealing with gun users and mental health issues.

The penalty associated with weapon misuse should be unified as well as the issue of regular mental health assessments of all gun owners. Matters come into courtrooms when a mistake has been made, and if courts are not clarifying such mistakes correctly, we are opening a floodgate to arguments that set faulty precedents for the future. If Justice Durno had not fixed the lower court's decision in Mr. Day's case, in other trials, the ruling would essentially be solidified as precedential law.

Mental Health and the Responsibility of Gun Ownership

In the analysis, Justice Durno did not emphasize the siblings' report about Mr. Day's deteriorating mental state towards progressive schizophrenia. Their views were brushed off as lay persons' reports and not used as evidence in the legitimate concerns test. Furthermore, despite the unusual lifestyle habits of Mr. Day, Justice Durno notes that there has been no prior violent history. In addition, the weapon storage, during seizure, had conflicting evidence from the officers. So, it was not easy to conclude if the weapons in Mr. Day's car were stored properly or not. Finally, Mr. Day's behaviour was analyzed, and Justice Durno mentioned that it was not concerning enough to him to validate that Mr. Day lacked gun owner responsibility. After this analysis, Justice Durno surprisingly concluded that the appeal was allowed; hence, the Crown won the case.

Interestingly, there is no explicit analysis on why Mr. Day did not win at higher court. Rather, this case analysis is confusing because the reasons summarized by Justice Durno point to the Crown losing the appeal, yet the opposite occurred. As someone looking upon Mr. Day's case from a deterrence lens, of course, I highly respect the decision of the appeal court. But as a precedent to be used in courtrooms, this decision does not clearly draw the line as to what is appropriate behaviour for gun owner responsibility. It can be assumed that using the legitimate concerns test, Justice Durno must have decided that Mr. Day lacks the responsibility and discipline required of gun owners. Responsibility of gun users includes tasks as simple as storing the firearm properly to more serious considerations for preventing harm and death of others with a gun. One can assume that since there was a lack of evidence given on how well Mr. Day's guns were stored, it may have contributed to his "lack of responsibility" in Justice Durno's analysis. Furthermore, because of the absence of reasoning provided by Justice Durno, it seems that the results are subjective and maybe based on public policy reasoning, or simply to set a precedent.

Even though presumptive, not allowing an individual with undiagnosed schizophrenia to possess and keep weapons is morally and preventatively the right thing to do. It could be that Durno was emphasizing that when it comes to public safety; a cautious decision regarding mental health issues and responsible gun ownership does warrant conclusive evidence. Cases set precedent for future rulings and policy. Public Safety Canada focuses on maintaining safe communities free from risks of violent crimes, including gun violence. The Crown winning the appeal in the *R v. Day* decision gives power to the federal government and its procedures for community and public safety. Allowing Mr. Day to keep his weapons may have compromised federal mandate on personal and public safety of Canadians simply because such a decision can set the tone for future legal assessment of gun ownership responsibility.

A reformulated approach towards responsibility for gun ownership and mental health concerns is needed, as there are several risk outcomes at play. The most ideal and authoritative way to handle serious and confounding risks would be to ensure that regulations for obtaining and maintaining a gun license incorporate the mental health of the user. Furthermore, the responsibility of gun ownership should be assessed with periodic mental health checks as well as criminal history checks. This is suggested with the understanding that often there are subjectivities to mental health and wellness and determining levels of risks across individuals may be challenging. Levels of risks should be assessed alongside accountability to gun ownership to strengthen relationships with the law. Moreover, decisions about responsibility and gun ownership should be accompanied with, but not trumped by, discussions of gun ownership rights. This is important in gun control efforts intended to avoid mass shootings and other gun misuse catastrophes.

The Complication of Mental Health and Gun Ownership

There are two decisions from 2015—from the Queen's Bench for Saskatchewan and the Ontario Court of Justice—that use the case of *R. v. Day* as a precedent in their analysis. *R. v. Peters* (2015 SKQB 151 [CanLII]) is a Saskatchewan case that held that Mr. Peters was not to be allowed to possess any weapons for two years, and all the firearms seized by police were to be forfeited to the Crown. Mr. Peters had been prescribed antidepressants for his behaviours, and witness reports mentioned that he often ranted and swore at family members. Mr. Peters also made a threat to a 911 dispatcher. He mentioned to the dispatcher that the RCMP officer should "cool it," and if he doesn't, he will "tune him up." Mr. Peters also had a record of prior weapon seizures. The judge was concerned with Mr. Peters' mental state. This case is pivotal because it emphasizes that there are conflicting issues in jurisdictions about what the appropriate test for Section 117.05 is. The importance of *R. v. Day*'s case is emphasized as well as Justice Durno's decision on using the legitimate concerns test for assessing the preventative approach of Section 117.05. Hence, it was ruled that according to the test applied from *R.* v. *Day*, Mr. Peters did not show diligence on his part as a gun owner, and his appeal was dismissed.

Furthermore, the Ontario ruling of *R. v. El Masry* (2015 ONCJ 510 [CanLII]) similarly tackles the mental capacity of an individual to own a weapon. It relies on the precedential ruling of *R. v. Day* to calculate the standard of proof required for Mr. El Masry to keep his weapons. Once again, the legitimate concerns test is used from *R v. Day* to determine if Mr. El Masry has the responsibility and discipline required of gun owners. In Mr. El Masry's situation, his mental health was different from Mr. Day's and Mr. Peters'. Mr. El Masry had a short-lived depressive state. In the evidence, there were also two reports submitted from mental health professionals that mentioned that his mental health was not of any significant concern. Hence, Mr. El Masry was allowed to keep his firearms.

Within *R. v. Day, R. v. Peters* and *R. v. El Masry,* individuals were assessed according to the balance of probabilities, and legitimate concerns test to determine if they were responsible enough to keep their firearms. *R. v. Day* serves as a precedential ruling of only two cases thus far, there are actually numerous cases federally dealing with weapon forfeiture. But despite its use in these cases, there is still a lack of coherence in courtrooms as to what the appropriate measure should be to determine gun ownership when mental health is in question. In addition, case law depicts how provinces are using alternative tests ranging from less restrictive to more restrictive, which impacts the degree of proof the Crown is required to submit for demonstrating that the gun owner presents a public and personal safety concern. Hence, the lack of standardization presented by courtrooms for the evidence requirement is a major concern.

It is important to note that using mental health cases as precedents for future or current courtroom decisions can potentially lead to further misconstruction of the law. Mental illness exists on a spectrum. There may be a difference between gun ownership for someone with a short-lived depressive episode and someone who has undiagnosed schizophrenia. Making decisions between cases like these requires relevant evidence. Judges are not trained to understand the medical history and complexities of the varying mental health concerns and disorders. Then why are judges allowed to make decisions on an individual's mental health capacity, without a clinician or expert present? This issue is leading to vastly different outcomes for cases. The heterogeneity in mental capacities requires that all cases are handled uniquely. However, a federal standard of assessment can help judges better understand the scope and nuances of the mental health assessment required for these cases while regarding the evidence placed before them.

It is not easy to say what sort of test should be implemented federally to deal with the mental health assessment of a gun owner. Overall, to the best degree possible, a uniform approach in courtrooms needs to be undertaken across all jurisdictions. Judges are using a subjective approach and various methods to balance the evidence. It is critical that their decisions are informed by expert knowledge when determining a gun owner's mental capacity to responsibly own a gun. A clinical analysis should be mandatory in such hearings to get current and relevant expertise on gun ownership decisions. Regarding actual analysis, court proceedings follow approaches that are common practices used in their province or jurisdiction. But gun licensing is under federal, RCMP control. Therefore, judges should also look at relevant case procedures in jurisdictions outside of their home province to inform decisions. Some jurisdictions, such as British Columbia, are using a restrictive approach, in which the Crown is expected to show substantial possibility that it is a public and personal safety concern for the individual (*R. v. Peters*). Quebec is completely different and uses civil law in the assessment. Hence, this demonstrates that it is not easy to say what the ideal test is. Therefore, more work is needed for a fulsome understanding of this topic.

A comprehensive approach needs to be taken to dictate what approach a court should use in decisions about gun ownership and mental health. Otherwise, case-by-case scenarios may be subjected to the biased reasoning of each Justice, without well-informed and comprehensive guidelines that can be applied, especially in more complex multijurisdictional firearm issues. It is important to note that mental illness and violence have a fluctuating behavioural pattern, and it is not likely that an individual is always behaving according to their static diagnosis state (Rozel and Mulvey). Therefore, a mental health professional assessment will allow for more objective outcomes in gun owner responsibility. A clear-cut methodological test, codified as formal law, will provide courtrooms and judges confidence in their decision making.

Future Steps Through an Obama-Era Procedure

Across the border, our American counterparts have been grappling with gun control issues for several years. What is even increasingly difficult is that certain procedures that were put into place for preventative measures, dealing with the mental health and accessibility to guns, were overturned by the Trump Administration. However, the Obama Administration's procedures and methodologies can provide some insights to this matter.

The Obama Administration attempted to tackle the issue through proposing and aiming to strengthen the existing laws related to gun use. The major focus of the administration was the expansion of the National Instant Criminal Background Check System (NICS) (Bates).

Commercial gun sellers were required to perform a background check through the NICS system (Bates). In order for the recommendations to work, the administration aimed to broaden the definition for the "mentally defective" for the NICS background system. This would allow opportunities to tackle presumptive cases as well. Moreover, social security beneficiaries who have a psychiatric disability would be put on the FBI's background check database as ineligible to purchase firearms (Swanson). This social security administration (SSA) rule was predicted to affect up to seventy-five thousand people yearly who suffer from mental health issues (Vitali).

Unfortunately, Trump signed a bill revoking this Obama-era gun check that would have made it more difficult for individuals with a mental illness to obtain firearms. As a result, Obama's well-crafted and thought-out regulation was never implemented in practice. From a Canadian perspective, we can only assess this policy from textual reports. Yet even this overturned bill is pivotal in shedding light on a key issue that needs to be addressed—the mental health of gun users.

Despite all the reporting and success as a nation in comparison to the US, Canadians still do not have adequate federal measures in place for gun ownership with mental health. If such a policy had been incorporated, Mr. Day would have not even classified under the requirement to become a gun owner. Case transcripts show that Mr. Day obtained his firearm through the help of his siblings, and they themselves were concerned about his mental deficiencies. Hence, a broader definition for mental health can also potentially incorporate family reports on behavioural concerns. Lay person diagnosis on mental health is omitted in case hearings as unsatisfactory. This further emphasizes the importance of having a mandatory clinical diagnosis for mental health, which would allow for a more current assessment of the individual, to determine how they act in a home setting with people they know. Thus, better and adequate judgments can be made when applying the legitimate concerns test.

Conclusion

Overall, the Canadian scope of gun management demonstrates a dire need for uniformity. It seems that courts are reinforcing precedent based on subjective approaches rather than a concrete reason. *R. v. Day* shed light on the issue of assessing the mental capacity of a gun owner and how there has not been an appropriate test in practice to use in courtrooms. Furthermore, there were also many unanswered questions in the case law analysis. The evidence of the photos of car license plates and young girls were ignored; what was Mr. Day's reasoning to have such peculiar things? In addition, Mr. Day's siblings mentioned that they had helped him obtain his firearms license. With the strict federal RCMP procedures in practice how was this legally possible? Moreover, Justice Durno explains and elaborates on his reason for choosing the legitimate concerns balance of probability test to assess Section 117.05. But that is Durno's subjective choice. If this case were heard in a different jurisdiction or province, is it possible that results would have been different? There is no adequate formulated test in courtrooms to deal with mental capacity assessments in regard to gun ownership. The lower court erred and allowed Mr. Day to keep his weapons, even if they were outside Guelph. A judge's bias can skew a case; the decision made in *R. v. Day* may not necessarily be a success in all courts.

Cases like *R. v. Day* demonstrate that this is just the start of procedural change that needs to take place at different levels, but especially in legislation. Courtrooms need to be better equipped. Uniformity is direly needed, and a legal test needs to be federal because gun licensing is federal. Moreover, if judges are unable to deduce from witness testimony and lay person reports about an individual's mental state, expert medical analysis should be used. The focus on mental health also demonstrates that judgments should also recommend seeking clinical support. From a public health aspect, more needs to be done for individuals who are deemed not fit to be gun owners. If someone is deemed unfit, it means that they are at risk of harming the public and/or themselves. So how can an individual, after weapon forfeiture, be let out without a judge recommending or offering them appropriate medical interventions and social support? A time restricted prohibition on weapons is also not a proper solution because an individual's mental state could worsen later. How does it make sense that after the time restriction, an individual may legally be allowed to have access to their weapons again? This was the case in Desmond, and it led to a murder-suicide occurring with a gun.

In conclusion, as a nation, we have the opportunity to move towards better gun control. This can be done through the government demanding more public safety mandates and having stricter background checks, specifically with a mental health lens. A proper formulation of policies and procedures in legislation will allow courtrooms to formulate an ideal test for assessing those on trial as gun owners, which is pivotal because a courtroom is a direct factor in maintaining law and order. Providing courts and judges with the legal tools they need will allow them to treat firearm abusers uniformly and directly, as much as possible.

In April 2020, Gabriel Wortman committed a mass shooting that killed twenty-two people, before police fatally shot him. A former neighbour of Wortman stated that she had actually reported to police in 2013 about Wortman's domestic abuse and illegal firearms (Tutton). Hence, cases such as Gabriel Wortman and Lionel Desmond demonstrate that if more was done to strictly address public reporting of peculiar behaviours observed among gun owners, the mass murders committed by them may have been prevented. Following Wortman's mass shooting, the Trudeau government announced a ban on fifteen hundred types of assault style firearms (Tasker). Solidifying gun ownership procedures that incorporate mental health assessments are more important than ever before. We need to be vigilant, prepared, and prevent future gun violence catastrophes by focusing specifically on their root causes at the firearm accessibility level. By improving gun ownership procedures with regular mental health assessments, it is possible to prevent a domino of negative repercussions.

Works Cited

Bates, Adam. "A Round-Up of President Obama's Gun Control Proposals." *Cato Institute*, 7 January 2016, www.cato.org/blog/round-president-obamas-gun-control-proposals. Accessed 12 Apr. 2022.

Bronskill, Jim. "Feds Eye Tougher Screening of Gun Owners for Mental Health, Violence Concerns." *The Canadian Press*, 7 March 2018, www.cp24.com/news/feds-eye-tougher-screening-of-gun-owners-for-mental-health-violence-concerns-1.3832148. Accessed 12 Apr. 2022.

Canada (Attorney General) v. Pattison (1981 ABCA 98 [CanLII])

CBC Canada. "Gun Violence, by the Numbers." *CBC Docs POV*, 2019, www.cbc.ca/cbcdocspov/features/gun-violence-by-the-numbers. Accessed 12 Apr. 2022.

Clermont, Yvan. "Firearm-related crime in Canada." *Canadian Centre for Justice Statistics, Statistics Canada,* 18 Feb 2019, sencanada.ca/content/sen/committee/421/SECD/Briefs/Stats_Can_Presentation_ppt_e.pdf. Accessed 12 Apr. 2022.

Criminal Code, RSC 1985, c C-46,117.04, https://canlii.ca/t/55c9q. Accessed 12 Apr. 2022.

Criminal Code, RSC 1985, c C-46,117.05, https://canlii.ca/t/55c9q. Accessed 12 Apr. 2022.

Fletcher, Robson. "Canada Gun Facts: Here Are the Latest Stats on Firearm Deaths, Injuries and Crime." *CBC News,* 30 Aug. 2018, www.cbc.ca/news/canada/calgary/canada-gun-facts-crime-accidental-shootings-suicides-1.4803378. Accessed 12 Apr. 2022.

MacDonald, Michael. "Judge Overseeing Nova Scotia Fatality Inquiry Asks About Mental Health Check". *CTV Atlantic News,* 2 Mar 2020, atlantic.ctvnews.ca/mobile/judge-overseeing-nova-scotia-fatality-inquiry-asks-about-mental-health-checks-1.4834789?cache=ityrlpnlmderht. Accessed 12 Apr. 2022.

R. v. Bishop (1995 CanLII 2449 [ON CJ]).

R. v. Day (2006 CanLII 26587 [ON SC]).

R. v. El Masry (2015 ONCJ 510 [CanLII]).

R v. H.C. (2009 ONCA 56 [CanLII]).

R. v. Morgan (1995 CanLII 18 [ON CJ].

R. v. Peters (2015 SKQB 151 [CanLII]).

R v. Urchuk (2004 BCPC 129 [CanLII]).

Royal Canadian Mounted Police. "Firearms Licensing." *Firearms Licensing—Royal Canadian Mounted Police,* 27 Feb. 2018, www.rcmp-grc.gc.ca/en/history-firearms-canada. Accessed 12 Feb. 2022.

Rozel, John S., and Edward P. Mulvey. "The Link between Mental Illness and Firearm Violence: Implications for Social Policy and Clinical Practice." *Annual Review of Clinical Psychology,* vol.13, 2017, pp. 445-69,

Shenassa, E., S. Catlin, and S. Buka. "Gun Availability, Psychopathology, and Risk of Death from Suicide Attempt by Gun." *Annals of Epidemiology,* vol 10, no. 7, 2000, p. 482.

Statistics Canada. "Firearm-Related Violent Crime, 2009 To 2017", *Statistics Canada—Government of Canada,* 27 Aug. 2018, www150.statcan.gc.ca/n1/pub/89-28-0001/2018001/article/00004-eng.htm. Accessed 12 Apr. 2022.

Swanson, Jeffrey. "The Ban on Mentally Ill People Buying Guns Wasn't Ever Based on Evidence." *The Washington Post,* 10 Feb. 2017, www.washingtonpost.com/posteverything/wp/2017/02/10/the-gop-is-making-it-easier-for-mentally-ill-people-to-buy-guns-they-have-a-point/. Accessed 12 Apr. 2022.

Tasker, John Paul. "Trudeau Announces Ban On 1,500 Types Of 'Assault-Style' Firearms—Effective Immediately." *CBC News,* 4 May 2020, www.cbc.ca/news/politics/trudeau-gun-control-measures-ban-1.5552131. Accessed 12 Apr. 2022.

Tasker, John Paul. "What Gun Owners Need to Know about Ottawa's New Firearms Bill." *CBC News,* 22 Sept. 2018, www.cbc.ca/news/politics/tasker-gun-bill-c71-explainer-1.4833034. Accessed 12 Apr. 2022.

Tutton, Michael. "Neighbour Reported N.S. Mass Shooter's Domestic Violence, Weapons To Police." *CBC News,* 13 May 2020, www.cbc.ca/news/canada/nova-scotia/mass-shooting-nova-scotia-firearms-gun-violence-1.5567330. Accessed 12 Apr. 2022.

Vitali, Ali. "Trump Signs Bill Revoking Obama-Era Gun Checks for Mental Illness." *NBC News,* 28 Feb. 2017, www.nbcnews.com/news/us-news/trump-signs-bill-revoking-obama-era-gun-checks-people-mental-n727221. Accessed 12 Apr. 2022.

Chapter 9

Dog Whistles, Coded Language, and the Gun-Range Debate

Lynn M. Eckert and JoAnne Myers

In a small upstate New York city, a prominent physician sought to transform the building that once housed his midtown orthopaedic practice into a five-lane shooting range. The location of the proposed gun range sat between art galleries and coffee shops that dotted a slowly gentrifying yet disproportionately poor and minority area of the city. The range, if authorized by the city's planning board, would sit roughly five hundred feet from the YMCA and approximately one thousand feet from the local high school. The proposal also sought authorization for gun sales at the site. The planning process quickly became a political one, when the city realized that a previous law prevented any discharge of a gun within city limits. Although the law seemingly violated the Supreme Court's current understanding of the Second Amendment in the US Constitution, the proposal also required the city's Common Council to implement new zoning guidelines.[1] The debates that followed not only involved the state of gun violence and gun control in US society and the meaning of the Second Amendment to the US Constitution but also concerned politics intricately rooted in identity, gentrification, class, property rights, race, and gender.

This chapter begins to unpack and analyze the proposition that one's position on gun rights is a proxy for broader and larger symbolic political commitments and identities in the US.

The Proposal

On October 13, 2015, a prominent physician and property owner in Kingston, NY proposed an indoor shooting range, Safeshoot, to be located in the midtown section of the city. The owner of the property hired an architect to design the five-lane, fifteen-yard indoor shooting range, retail shop, and educational facility. Kingston's city code required the planning board to consider laws currently on the books that could potentially affect a land development deal and to consider whether the proposal complied with local, state and federal guidelines.[2] Specifically, in the case of Safeshoot, the planning board had to consider any laws within the city that addressed the issue of firearms as well as whether the indoor shooting range development plans comported the city's comprehensive zoning plan.

The planning board scheduled an initial, low key, uneventful meeting about the indoor shooting range on October 13 (Zanglia). The following meeting on November 10 brought out vocal opponents of the gun range. During the public comment portion, several citizens challenged the board's initial decision and requested a public hearing on the range.[3] A local public interest group, Kingston Citizens, became involved in mobilizing opposition to the range uploading a "What to Expect" blog post urging citizens to attend and speak at the hearing. Forty-one speakers attended that hearing, but one speaker in particular upended the possibility that the range issue would be decided within the confines of the planning board meeting. In testimony during the public hearing portion of the meeting, an Ulster County legislator and urban planner cited the 1984 law passed by the Common Council prohibiting the discharge of firearms within Kingston city limits. Although the planning director, a full-time city employee, had flagged the prohibitive administrative law earlier in the application process, neither the chief of police nor the corporation counsel interpreted the law to apply to Safeshoot, the proposed gun range. When the legislator testified, the political landscape had shifted with the election of a new mayor and new policy priorities.

The 1984 prohibition suddenly became relevant to the gun range debate.

The Problematic Law

The local law, administrative law 223-3, violated the current legal understanding of the Second Amendment to the US Constitution and would have to be repealed or amended by the Common Council (Kirby).[4] At an April meeting of the Common Council's Laws & Rules Committee, two alderwomen offered language to repeal the discharge law while allowing for the gun range. The meeting began with public comment, where approximately forty-two speakers conveyed their views on the shooting range. The speakers were roughly divided in half with slightly more against the range than for it. At the end of public comment, the Ward 7 alderwoman moved to amend the current prohibitive law using language proposed by the Ward 9 alderwoman. The language proposed is below:

> No person, other than in self-defense or in the discharge of official duties, shall willfully fire, any species of firearms within the City limits of the City of Kingston, NY except in an indoor facility designed and constructed as a shooting range, pursuant to a site plan approved by the City of Kingston Planning Board and operated in compliance with the laws and regulations of the New York State Department of Environmental Conservation and the Division of Safety and Health of the New York department of Labor.

To be clear, most political players involved in the controversy agreed: The law would have to be amended, but the dispositive question was about how to amend. As a result, the Common Council was left with one of two options: They could vote in favour of the Ward 9 alderwoman's amendment, which would permit Safeshoot, or table the resolution and consider other options.[5] Eventually, at the next meeting, the Common Council moved to adopt a zoning model limiting gun ranges based upon the city of Rochester, NY. The model adopted by Rochester if applied to Kingston would have made the location of the gun range unviable.

After a long process, both the amendment proposed by the alderwoman and the Rochester model amendment would be voted on. At the July meeting, the Rochester model amendment won passage by a vote of six to two. On July 29, 2016, the mayor signed local law #3 (the

Rochester model) into law. Opponents of the range's location won. The new law consisted of eleven additional pages of code where it explicitly defined a firearm, handgun, automatic weapon, shooting range, and negligent discharge.[6] The new law sought to remedy the ambiguity of the past code providing clear and rigorous guidelines for obtaining a special permit and licensing.[7] The remainder of the chapter will explore the arguments offered by proponents and opponents and analyze the ways in which those arguments were about far more than gun ownership.

The Public Speaks

On April 19, 2016, the Laws and Rules Committee on Kingston's Common Council held extended public gatherings to amend the proposed firearm law. As noted above, two prorange members of the Council sought to remove language prohibiting the discharge of firearms within the city of Kingston. The amendment language cited above sought to make an explicit exemption for the ban with respect to firing ranges.

Forty-two speakers offered comments with nineteen in favour of the amendment allowing the gun range and twenty-three against changes. Thirty-six of the speakers identified themselves as living in Kingston or having a business located there. Of the speakers twenty were women: six spoke in favor of the range, whereas fourteen spoke against the range. Fourteen men spoke in favour of the range, whereas eight spoke against the range. All but two of the speakers identified as white; one self-identified Latino and one self-identified Black woman spoke in each instance against the location of the range. All of the speakers in favour of the range identified themselves as white. Of those speaking against the location of the range, eighteen out of twenty-three lived outside of the city before becoming residents.

Those in favor of the range set forth several arguments. Under US constitutional law, the Second Amendment allows for both the individual ownership of guns and the right to access training in places like gun ranges. Therefore, to prohibit gun ranges in a locale is effectively to violate the Second Amendment. Several speakers emphasized that the law protects their right not just to gun ownership but to train for purposes of safety and acumen. Others stressed that the doctor's gun range would bring potential customers to the city. After time at the gun range, they argued, many would seek to have lunch, dinner or observe a local art show. They also stressed the trustworthiness of the individual building the range, the local doctor. They believed that the doctor had led an exemplary life committed to the community and its economic and moral development. They rejected the notion that the doctor would engage in any endeavour that would harm the community either through improper disposal of lead or a lack of security. The progun range defense of the doctor's trustworthiness became particularly prominent when the opposition raised concerns about noise and lead pollution. None of the proponents of the range considered that advocating to change the law on the basis of the doctor's good character constituted spot zoning, an action prohibited by law. Legitimate zoning law provides generally applicable guidelines to all individuals rather than special rules for special individuals.

Throughout the process the doctor advanced the idea that the police would utilize the shooting range for training and instruction purposes. Several speakers also provided the police training rationale as a reason to move forwards with the construction of the range. Yet throughout the process, the City of Kingston Police Department and the Ulster County Sheriff's office explained that the range was too short for their purposes of target practice and training. Nonetheless, supporters repeatedly asserted that law enforcement officials needed nearby indoor ranges to train as a crucial reason to build Safeshoot in midtown.

These constructive talking points were often followed by more critical comments directed at those opposed to the range. Several speakers argued that the attempt to amend the laws in ways that made locating a gun range within the city difficult was just a pretext for pure antigun sympathies. Others argued that the suggestion by opponents to table the progun range amendment and better vet alternatives in the Laws & Rules Committee was nothing more than a stalling tactic. Many felt that the opposition had mischaracterized gun owners when, in fact, those carrying licensed guns were law-abiding, upstanding lawyers, teachers, physicians, and college professors. The call to prohibit the gun range in midtown, they suggested, was based upon ignorance and fear. Veterans argued with particular indignation that without an amendment to the current law, they would not be able to fire symbolic (blank) shots at military funerals nor fire muskets in the annual reenactment of the burning of Kingston celebration.[8] Before making this point, one veteran insisted on taking a moment outside of public comment to lead the entire meeting in the pledge of allegiance to highlight the patriotism of gun owners and the disconnected cosmopolitanism of range opponents (Stroud).[9]

Several speakers made veiled statements about the disproportionate violence in midtown and obscurely referenced a certain type of individuals populating the area, which many understood as a racially coded message. Some of the more intriguing arguments advanced by proponents of the gun range concerned fears around the need to protect against drug dealers, theft, violence, and sexual assault. Again, to many opponents of the gun range, these comments appeared racially tinged. Among the women speaking in favour of the range, at least two, noted that having a gun and having access to training would allow them to protect themselves in the face of danger. One woman argued that the violence in midtown, including gunshots, led to a sense that residents were unsafe. One speaker suggested that the gun range would protect the neighbourhood from an unsavory crowd of young people hanging out in the area, specifically in the parking lot of the YMCA. The speaker perceived that this young group of individuals was selling drugs or engaging in illegal activity. In a disproportionately minority neighbourhood, and in the racial context of the US, the unspoken understanding in the room was that these youths were young Black men. In the eyes of Safeshoot proponents, owning a gun would allow for a levelling of the playing field between law-abiding citizens and criminals, particularly for women (Stroud; Carlson). Another noted that gun ranges, especially outdoor ranges, are dominated by men and are an unwelcoming place for women to train. The doctor's wife as well as at least one other proponent argued that the proposed gun range would not only welcome women but would encourage a chapter of the Pink Guns, a gay and lesbian shooting organization. These comments sought to upend the typical assumptions about the identity of gun owners as largely white, heterosexual, and conservative men.

The doctor and his wife took the opportunity to speak to the public at this meeting to address the opposition's concerns. They noted their long residence in the city as well as the fact that they have three sons attending the local high school. As a physician, the doctor asserted that he would never act in a way that harmed the health of the community, explaining that Safeshoot would be built with the latest technology in an effort to reduce noise levels and filter toxic lead deposits. He maintained that the gun range located next to the schools and daycare facilities would make the area safer rather than more dangerous. He and his wife sought to include information about the location of other gun ranges in similarly densely populated areas close to schools and businesses.[10] He also took the opportunity to identify himself as a veteran of the United States military who saw gun ownership as a Second Amendment right that he had fought to defend. His wife explained that the city identified the building they hoped to renovate for the shooting range as subject to demolition. Not only did they save the building, but they also intended to repurpose it with the goal of bringing new jobs. The number of jobs and the nature of the pay varied and decreased over time with each successive meeting.

Finally, the doctor argued that gun owners had a vested interest in locating the indoor range nearby due to state laws requiring training that often took them far afield of Kingston. Instructors saw an opportunity to hold classes nearby. The doctor, too, saw the development of the range as a business transaction that would provide a profit for an activity that he happened to enjoy. It was clear that the proponents of the range spent time attempting to coordinate their messages. The Ulster County past president of the Sportsman Foundation spoke in favour of the range location as did several members of a local gun club, paid gun safety trainers, veterans, and former police officers and firefighters. In some instances, the reliance on messaging focused on the fear of crime and protecting women, gays, and lesbians, which echoed NRA talking points.

The progun range speakers were met in the legislative chambers with two antigun range organizations who filled the room with opponents and protesters. One such group, Citizens Action, a nonprofit organization with eight local affiliate chapters across New York State, understood the gun range as an issue that affected racial justice. They believed that the proposed location of the gun range in a disproportionately poor and minority-populated neighbourhood was no accident but instead an instance of environmental racism.[11] In their view, not only would the gun range add noise and lead pollution to the challenges in midtown but would affect public safety in an area already threatened by violence.[12]

Citizens Action drew upon the work of scholars and activists who have defined environmental racism as instances when municipalities locate noxious industries in poorer areas or minority communities.[13] No one wants noxious land use in their neighbourhood, despite desiring the benefits from economic development. Frequently, the rejection of problematic and toxic land-use development is both needed yet rejected by communities with greater resources. Whereas wealthier communities with greater social capital, such as uptown Kingston, can make successful NIMBY ("not in my backyard") arguments, those with less social, economic, and racial privileges often fail (Hirt). Organizers against the proposed gun range were determined to prevent yet another underdeveloped minority community faced with a toxic land use because no other wealthier area wanted the project.

At the meeting, members of Citizens Action held up signs opposed to gun ownership, the sale of guns (the proposal included a gun and ammo sales showroom), and the location of the gun range. They were more likely to resort to challenging the rightness of the Second Amendment while arguing that gun ownership was a public health threat.

Members from Kingston Citizens also attended the committee meeting with talking points meant to steer clear of the Second Amendment issue while stressing the need to properly vet and follow procedure when amending the law. The founder of Kingston Citizens epitomized the opponents' characterization of the "New Kingston." Founded in 2006 by a transplanted musician and producer, it was founded to understand the complex processes of local government by creating a platform for citizen engagement.Kingston Citizens advised opponents to avoid Second Amendment arguments and to stay within the language and the concepts of zoning law, which allowed for ample justifications to prohibit the midtown location.

Without the organized opposition of these two groups, legislators opposed to the range would have little cover. Both sides intensely held their views, although the collective action problem seemed more severe for opponents of the range than proponents (Lacombe).[14] For proponents, the building of the range was not a public good but rather a private good from which they would disproportionately benefit. On the contrary, opponents of the range had more difficulty mobilizing individuals. They argued that if the range was not built, people would benefit whether or not they participated. The role of public interest groups like Citizens Action and Kingston Citizens was crucial to preventing a range in midtown. They helped to overcome a collective action problem and countered the intense and often angry views of proponents with equally and passionately delivered views.

One other actor became relevant to the gun range discussion—the Kingston City School Board. The school board as well as the Ulster County Human Rights Commission (UCHRC) were designing and adopting a restorative justice model in an effort to break the school-to-prison pipeline. Both the school board and the UCHRC felt the location and the justifications in favour of the range violated their core respective missions. Specifically, in the view of the UCHRC, the arguments for a private gun range raised concerns inconsistent with fostering respect for all citizens. Those concerns entailed locating the range in a predominately low income area where the residents and business owners were trying to improve their quality of life in response to concerns about high lead and noise pollution levels. Importantly, the UCHRC highlighted some of the proponents' language in defending the need for a gun range. Those proponents argued that the gun range would provide needed protection against the residents of midtown themselves. The commission was concerned that property rights might trump the political voice of the neighbourhood residents, and they raised the prospect that veiled racism may be at play.

Those opposing the location of the range presented several arguments. They asserted that the proximity of the proposed range to local schools and daycare centres violated the Gun-Free School Zones Act (1990) as amended in 1997. School board representatives and the doctor debated whether the range fell within the one thousand foot prohibited zone of the school. In the end, after some contentiousness, the doctor conceded that the range did fall within it. The opposition raised concerns about placing the range in a densely populated area where noise and lead pollution would have a greater effect. They worried that a gun range would halt further economic development rather than increase it. Although everyone wanted greater economic development, they deeply disagreed about the sorts of businesses that would add or detract from greater growth. Art exhibitions, theater productions, coffee houses, antique furniture stores, and quaint cafes mix poorly with the activity and noise from a shooting range. Some held that those seeking to amend the current code either in ways that enabled the Planning Board to grant or deny permission to Safeshoot needed further vetting. The push to amend the administrative code so quickly without sufficient discussion of implications and alternatives reflected irresponsible decision making on the part of the Common Council.

The closest the opposition came to directly confronting the Second Amendment occurred when several speakers raised public safety and public health concerns. Whereas opponents discussed gun violence as a public health or public safety concern, proponents understood those arguments as a pretext. To proponents of the range, public safety or public health concerns were coded language for opponents who simply do not like guns and oppose the Second Amendment.

They believed that opponents wrongly conflated the spate of gun violence with lawful gun ownership that sought to protect rather than contribute to such wanton violence.

Analysis

What does the battle over a gun range location in a small upstate New York city tell us about the state of gun culture and politics? How did opponents of the gun range manage to win when national advocates of gun control consistently lose at the federal level? How did the political dynamics at the local level square with what we know about the national gun control debate? What does the local victory tell us about the possibility of moving beyond the identity politics of gun control?

Much of what we know about national gun control politics was confirmed in the debate about the gun range in Kingston. For example, more women than men opposed the location of the gun range (Goss). Proponents of the gun range, mostly men and all white, emphasized the significance of training as a corollary to the Second Amendment right to gun ownership. In speaking at public comment, they noted the significance of protecting oneself and one's family from violence and crime (Carlson, "Citizen-Protectors"; Carlson, "Mourning Mayberry"; Stroud). Often the perpetrator of the crimes they imagined were implicitly racialized (Carlson, "Citizen-Protectors"; Carlson, "Mourning Mayberry"; Johnson; Winkler). They emphasized self-reliance, individual autonomy, and respect for tradition while conveying that gun ownership was a significant component of their social lives

(Lacombe, "The Political Weaponization"; Lacombe, "Gun Ownership"). Moreover, the stated commitment to gun rights correlated with their position on later contentious, conservative issues, such as sanctuary city policies and support for Donald Trump. The relationship between these positions suggests a positive correlation between gun rights and conservative politics more generally (Joslyn). Some of the comments indicated that gun owners felt oppressed and victimized by characterizations of them made by opponents of the range. It is this sense of oppression, victimization, or unfairness that creates and encourages divisive identity politics of the sort that led one prorange veteran to say that he resented his military sacrifice if it meant defending antigun citizens.

On a broader level, the degree of anger and emotion surrounding the debate on the gun range was a clear indication that the issue touched upon more than simply location. In fact, after the passage of the new Rochester-model zoning code, the doctor moved the project to an adjoining town where there was ample space in an industrial area with a readily available empty building. The range was certainly more profitable and faced no opposition in the next town. The debate about the range, in effect, was a proxy for a wide range of identity issues. Old Kingston felt displaced by the gentrification of New York City. They saw the range as an attack on their values, their political power, and their way of life.

Donald Braman and Dan M. Kahan's research confirms the view that gun politics is about identity politics. They write that understanding the gun debate and crafting winning public policy strategies depend on recognizing that the arguments are driven by the differing cultural values and worldviews of each side. We must, they argue, "investigate deeper than the statistics and address the competing American social attitudes on guns themselves: guns symbolizing honor, human mastery over nature, and individual self-sufficiency on the one hand, and guns creating the perpetuation of illicit social hierarchies, the elevation of force over reason, and the expression of collective indifference to the well-being of strangers on the other" (Braman and Kahan 570). These views underlined the debate in Kingston: The background context of the debate included concerns about gentrification, loss of employment, declining social status, and a sense of nostalgia for the social hierarchies of the past. These are the same background issues that occurred in the debate about whether Kingston should adopt sanctuary city status.

The coalition of antirange proponents had a political identity and worldview as well. Their coalition consisted of liberal-leaning New York City transplants, local artists and craftsmen, professors from local colleges and universities, writers, and organizations, such as Citizens Action, who represented the minority community's interests. They raised public health concerns about gun violence and introduced data about the correlation between ranges and gun accidents (Galeo; Galeo and Abdalla). They highlighted the close proximity of after-school programs at the YMCA and the high school. They invoked the spectre of environmental racism, noting that all gun ranges, even those with state-of-the-art noise and lead filters, produce pollutants. Shooting ranges release residual lead either into the air, soil, or water with poisonous results. Although only two self-identified persons of colour spoke during public comment, they also opposed the range, questioning whether minority members of the community would be welcome as members or guests at the range.

Members of Citizens Action best articulated the specific concerns of minority residents, arguing that the location of the shooting range raised questions about racial justice and the public safety of persons of colour in a neighbourhood already struggling with drugs and poverty-born violence (Braman). The alderwoman from Ward 4, who represented the area of the proposed location of the shooting range, and a person of colour asserted that some of the comments from proponents of the range negatively referenced and made false assumptions about the people who live in midtown. She found those comments imbricated with racism. Members of the Ulster County Human Rights Commission, in a letter to the Common Council, also expressed concerns about the potential racial justice implications of locating the gun range in a disproportionately poor and minority neighbourhood. School board members from the local high school understood the location of the range in both public health and safety terms as well as a social justice matter in recognizing the role of guns in the school-to-prison pipeline they sought to sever.

The coalition of those opposed to the range location drew upon the very ideological underpinnings that Braman and Kahan articulate. They had a different sense of public safety—one founded in a more communitarian worldview that seeks to break down traditions or practices that reinforce hierarchies, including racial hierarchy, or that emphasize force over reason and the rule of law. Given the racial history of the United States, whites have often sought to limit gun ownership to avoid allowing African-Americans to be armed (Johnson). Early advocates of gun control include such organizations as the Ku Klux Klan (Winkler). Gun control politics are suffused with the racist history of the US.

In many respects, both sides of the debate engaged in a kind of "dog whistling" and/or coded language. The classic definition of dog whistle politics is that speakers' comments have one benign meaning to the larger public but a special, specific, and typically more racist and or classist meaning to an in-group. Racist comments are rarely explicit; they must be interpreted within a context of power, history, and the material reality of the community. Interpretation is not fact; it is about assigning meaning wherein there is always room for plausible deniability. Many of those who spoke in favour of the range would simply deny that they spoke with a racist intent. To push the point further, they may have had no consciousness of racist motivations—a kind of implicit bias—yet comments are subjected to interpretation and held against the standards of public meaning. In an institutionalized racist society, facially neutral comments can take on invidious meaning despite the speaker's conscious intent. Many speakers simply reinforced the core narrative: Ranges provided crucial safety training; those lawfully using guns increased rather than decreased community safety, checking lawlessness; guns protect the most vulnerable among us; and those against the range had an irrational prejudice against guns. Yet some spoke more vehemently about guns as a means to protect their safety and about the role that guns play in their lives as part of their upbringing and culture. At those moments, everyone heard the same language but interpreted the meaning and implications differently.

Another rhetorical device deployed by proponents of the range was the assertion about the doctor's commitment to the welfare of the community. Whereas proponents left the assertion of the doctor's community mindedness undefined, opponents left it unchallenged. Yet not only is the concept and substance of community mindedness contested, but no debate followed about whether a gun range is an appropriate marker of such a commitment to community welfare, especially from someone financially benefiting from such a divisive and contentious project.

Similarly, opponents of the range never directly challenged the Second Amendment. Under US constitutional law, the Second Amendment guarantees the right of individuals to own guns. Among scholars, a debate rages about whether the Second Amendment is properly understood to protect an individual or collective (state militias) right to gun ownership (Cornell). Those opposed to the range used zoning law and public health studies to evade any arguments that guns are morally wrong. Yet if philosopher Hillary Putnam is correct in that we have no fact/value distinctions in how we come to know, then one's underlying negative views about guns would drive what one sees as a relevant analytical fact. In this sense, public health studies indicating an epidemic of gun violence will be variously understood by different sides of the gun debate based upon their underlying values and beliefs about the usefulness and meaning of guns. For proponents of gun rights, these facts demonstrate the need for more guns to protect individuals, not less. For opponents of gun rights, these studies align with an understanding that guns have no place in a civilized society committed to regulating violence through the rule of law.

Sandro Galea and Salma M. Abdalla argue that any debate about guns must also include an understanding of the social meaning of guns in our culture: "The social meaning of guns is a construction that shapes values and expectations, informs and reflects the public conversation, and sets the bounds within which any conversation around gun safety reform can take place" (2). The debate over the gun range location in Kingston reflects Galea and Abdalla's insights. Both sides took positions defined within the cramped space of zoning law, property rights, environmental regulations, and the Second Amendment. Yet underlying comments confined by narrowly rigid legal boundaries were more capacious arguments about political identity, values, and ideologies.

Opponents of the gun range won a limited victory. Given the myopic legal boundaries of the debate within the context of the Second Amendment, the adoption of the Rochester model did not ban ranges within the City of Kingston but limited where they may locate according to population and housing density. For those who advocate for gun control, this zoning battle is a circumscribed victory at best.

For those in favour of the gun range, the City Council's adoption of the Rochester model law effectively, as a de facto matter, barred gun ranges within city limits due to lack of available sites. The fissure lines concerning the gun range carried over into other battles within the city, including deeply divisive disagreements about sanctuary city status and low-income housing. The gun range location debate rendered the divisions over political identity visible and they remain. Without a recognition that gun rights are about more than guns and without a recognition that our values influence our interpretation of facts, the debate about guns will remain ossified, contentious, and intractable.

Conclusion

The story of this debate about an upstate gun range is a microcosm—an ethnographic exploration—of the larger polarization around gun ownership in the US and elsewhere. It provides us with a close lens analysis of the political, legal, and philosophical boundaries of the gun debate in a small community struggling with economic development, gentrification, as well as race, class, and gender divisions. The debate in Kingston was as much about identity and partisanship as about the location of the range itself. It reflects the deep divisions in the US over guns and how one's views on guns link to politics, identity, and demographics. It offers insights into the local political dynamics of a small city and its policymaking landscape as well. As long as gun ownership reflects how we understand ourselves, our beliefs about the proper role of government in protecting liberty, and the best defense against a chaotic and violent society, the potential for transformative worldviews about guns remains slim. In short, one's feelings about gun ownership serve as a proxy for partisan identification and a broader world perspective about the role of government, liberty, tradition, and social status.

Although this chapter is hardly exhaustive, opting for ethnographic detail rather than statistical generalization, its findings align with those larger statistical surveys finding a correlation between beliefs on guns and partisanship.

Endnotes

1. The city was not equipped to handle such a challenge financially or otherwise and wanted to avoid a costly and lengthy legal battle.
2. In Kingston, the mayor appoints members to the planning board for set terms. The members are volunteers and hold no other elected positions. Many city governments have a similar governmental structure that attempts to separate planning from partisan politics.
3. With a critical mass of citizens requesting a public hearing, the planning board reconsidered its initial stance. Although the board is supposed to avoid partisan politics, at the same time, it cannot afford to be altogether tone deaf to public opinion. At this point, the board began to understand that the decision regarding the shooting range might require a more complex process that allowed for greater public participation. To all those attentive to the gun range issue, it became increasingly clear that the board process would be contentious.
4. Opponents of the range wrongly believed that the shooting range controversy was over. Yet at the end of March, the issue would resurface at a Public Safety/General Government Committee meeting of the Common Council. Ward 7 alderwoman requested that the committee consider amending 223-3 to allow for an indoor shooting range.
5. The resolution was ultimately sent back to the Laws & Rules Committee for further evaluation. In committee, another alderman from Ward 3 advocated the adoption of a code passed by the City of Rochester, NY. Two proposals to amend administrative code 223 would now make it to the floor of the Common Council chambers for a vote. The Rochester model had stringent criteria for the location of gun ranges within city limits. Of particular concern for the City of Rochester was the location of ranges next to schools and childcare establishments.
6. The owner of any proposed range would have to provide certified reports concerning the high quality of the ventilation and noise baffling systems; submit proof of insurance and bond coverage; follow procedures outlined for the supervision of ranges within city limits; handle ballistic security; and produce records of the addresses of all partners, among many other detailed provisions.

7. Most controversially, the new adopted law allowed for protesters meeting certain specified requirements to trigger a heightened Planning Board approval process.
8. A celebration that takes place every other year to commemorate the British Army marching through Kingston during the Revolutionary War.
9. The idea that gun ownership is connected with the desire to defend the most vulnerable among us is noble.
10. He noted the location of ranges in New York City (Manhattan) and in Green Island, adjacent to the city of Troy, New York.
11. "TAKE ACTION NOW is a progressive organization that seeks quality public education, affordable healthcare, the dismantling of racism, a more progressive tax system, and public financing on elections.
12. Environmental impact was one of the issues raised, as shooting ranges have been noted to release residual lead either into the air, soil, or water with poisonous results. Shooting ranges have an environmental impact on the areas in which they are situated. In terms of environmental justice, opponents noted that ranges release residual lead into the air, soil and/or water with toxic results. Inevitably, shooting ranges have an environmental impact in the areas in which they are located. A geological survey from the Department of Interior had noted that the average indoor shooting range could use upwards to two tons of lead shot and or bullets annually. Employees have been tested and found to have heightened levels of lead.

    Lead toxicity may lead to organ failure in adults and diminished mental capacities in children. Although some lawyers for gun ranges say that environmental issues are a red herring used by antigun activists, in this situation, claims went beyond environmental impacts to claims of environmental racism.
13. Kingston Citizens successfully initiated over one hundred local projects, including challenging a national corporation that intended to bottle the city's local water source and supply for sale. This group organized the opposition to that water project, defeating several powerful interests who would directly benefit from the sale. Following on their success, they used the same game plan:

organizing strategic sessions and informing the public about the arguments that could be used to defeat the amendment to locate the range in midtown.

14. In political science, we define a "collective action problem" as one which people are less likely to participate in the political process for change when public goods are at stake. A public good is one where the benefits are not exclusive: Everyone enjoys them whether one participates in obtaining the public good or free rides.

Works Cited

Braman, Donald, and Dan M. Kahan. "Overcoming the Fear of Guns, the Fear of Gun Control, and the Fear of Cultural Politics: Constructing a Better Gun Debate." *Emory LJ*, vol. 55, 2006, pp. 569-608.

Carlson, Jennifer. *Citizen-Protectors: The Everyday Politics of Guns in An Age of Decline*. Oxford University Press, 2015.

Carlson, Jennifer. "Mourning Mayberry." *Gender & Society*, vol. 29, no. 3, 2015, pp. 386-409.

Cornell, Saul. *A Well-Regulated Militia: The Founding Fathers and the Origins of Gun Control in America*. Oxford University Press, 2008.

Galea, Sandro. "Making The Case for a World Without Guns." *The Lancet Public Health*, vol. 4, no. 6, 2019, pp. e266-e267.

Galea, Sandro, and Salma M. Abdalla. "The Public's Health and the Social Meaning of Guns." *Palgrave Communications*, vol. 5, no. 1, 2019, pp. 1-4.

Goss, Kristin A. "The Socialization of Conflict and Its Limits: Gender and Gun Politics in America." *Social Science Quarterly*, vol. 98, no. 2, 2017, pp. 455-70.

Hirt, Sonia A. *Zones in the USA: The Origins and Implications of American Land-Use Regulation*. Cornell University Press, 2014.

Johnson, Nicholas. *Negroes and the Gun: The Black Tradition of Arms*. Prometheus Books, 2014.

Joslyn, Mark R., et al. "Emerging Political Identities? Gun Ownership and Voting in Presidential Elections." *Social Science Quarterly*, vol. 98, no. 2, 2017, pp. 382-96.

Kirby, Paul. "Kingston Mayor Says Shooting Range Would Violate 1984 Law." *Daily Freeman.*

MediaNews Group. 12 Feb. 2016, www.dailyfreeman.com/2016/03/28/kingstons-1978-no-shooting-law-could-be-reviewed-council-president-says/. Accessed 13 Apr. 2022.

Lacombe, Matthew J., Adam J. Howat, and Jacob E. Rothschild. "Gun Ownership As a Social Identity: Estimating Behavioral and Attitudinal Relationships." *Social Science Quarterly*, vol. 100, no. 6, 2019, pp. 2408-24.

Lacombe, Matthew J. "The Political Weaponization of Gun Owners: The National Rifle Association's Cultivation, Dissemination, and Use of a Group Social Identity." *The Journal of Politics*, vol. 81, no. 4, 2019, pp. 1342-56.

Putnam, Hilary. *Reason, Truth and History.* Cambridge University Press, 1981.

Stroud, Angela. *Good Guys with Guns: The Appeal and Consequences of Concealed Carry.* University of North Carolina Press, 2016.

Winkler, Adam. *Gunfight: The Battle Over the Right to Bear Arms in America.* W. W. Norton & Company, 2013.

Zangla, Arial. "Kingston Planners Decline to Hold Public Hearing on Proposed Shooting Range." *Daily Freeman*, 13 Oct. 2015, www.dailyfreeman.com/2016/04/20/kingston-lawmakers-narrowly-recommend-no-change-in-law-prohibiting-discharge-of-firearms-in-city/. Accessed 13 Apr. 2022.

Chapter 10

Legacy of Endearment: The OK Tournament and Festival

Sky Starr

Children ... are our legacy.
Our responsibility.
They are our destiny and we are theirs.
—Dirk Benedict

The incandescent hues of the August sun paint a lasting insignia. Flurries of busyness subside as slackening feet are encouraged by simmered yet upbeat music. Community patrons assist in dismantling tents and loading containers to waiting vehicles. It is the end of the fourth annual OK tournament, and it has left an irrefutable air of accomplishment. Communal synergy has solidified two mothers' desire to have their sons' names reverberate in the minds and spirits of a grieving yet solaced community.

Mothers often regard their children as their legacy and, as such, envision children outliving them. But when a mother has to face the unimagined, undeniable circumstance of her child's death to gun violence, she is compelled to redefine her meaning of "legacy." A meaning that for some mothers becomes laden with a deeper level of evocative significance. Death by homicide is often deemed as senseless, with no apparent meaning. Mass pandemonium with intense stupefaction and disorientation are among the emotions felt by mothers, which often linger long after the funeral, accompanied by clouded thoughts. Elusive equilibrium becomes a daily companion for many suffering mothers. However, some mothers are able to achieve meaning making—a process of making sense of their loss, learned from a cognitive system of appraisal, which is central to legacy building (Bailey et al.). The mantra "I don't want my child's death to be in vain" carries new connotation for surviving mothers and becomes foundational to legacy building amid the torrent of tumultuous traumatic pain.

Upon learning of their child's death to gun violence, mothers wrestle to understand the senseless, inhumane acts and hopelessness that shroud their thoughts. Meaning making is a major theme in these mothers' healing and wellness journey. Despite the lingering pain, loss, and trauma, meaning making plays a key role in building mothers' capacity to heal, endure, and gradually attain resilience. Robert Neimeyer and Diana Sands have discussed that in the aftermath of a life-altering loss, a search for meaning occurs at levels that range from the practical (How did my loved one die?), through the relational (Who am I now?), and to the spiritual or existential (Why did God allow this to happen?). How and whether mothers engage these questions and resolve them shape how they accommodate the loss itself and who they become in light of it. Psychotherapist Gordon Allport penned the famous words: "To live is to suffer; to survive is to find meaning in the suffering—if there is a purpose in life at all, there must be a purpose in suffering and dying—but no-one can tell another what that purpose is" (qtd. in Frankl 9).

This chapter serves the dual purpose of depicting the intricacies of traumatic grief in the context of gun violence and highlighting the perseverance of two mothers who lost their children to gun violence as they create a communal legacy on their journey of healing.

Maternal Grief and Gun Violence Loss

Grief-related trauma research, especially connected to gun violence survivors, is infused with concepts of healing, restoration, and resilience. It is well documented that survivors of gun homicide loss experience complicated grief (CG). Symptoms of CG are associated with and predictive of substantial morbidity (e.g., depression and suicidal ideation), including adverse health behaviours, which warrants immediate and prolonged care (American Psychiatric Association).

Mothers who lose children to gun violence are often left in a state of perpetual disarray and with a lingering sense of dis-ease and feelings of incompetence, as death from gun violence presents a number of complex issues for them. A tragic death to gun violence shatters a mother's sense of direction, invokes immediate disorder, and thrusts her into a world where unfamiliarity and normalcy interchange. Maternal grief is an incredibly profound and persistent grief, with an intensity that surprises mothers themselves (Davidson and Stahls). Their grief is compounded by multifaceted reactions of grief-related posttraumatic stress disorder (PTSD), intensified by the suddenness of the loss, and can also be delayed. One mother who participated in Out Of Bounds trauma-informed training recounts the following: "I was too numb to cry. I didn't believe that it was my son, although I bathed and dressed his dead body myself...On his first death anniversary, the tears started to flow like a flood" (Mother from Trauma-Focused Training). With little or no opportunity to prepare for the loss, say good-bye, manage unfinished business, or prepare for bereavement, mothers are suddenly forced into a life of torment without their children.

Such instantaneous trauma generates a severity of grief reactions for mothers, including shock, confusion, disorientation, numbness, anger, guilt, deep depression, despair, and hopelessness with coinciding physical symptoms of palpitations, intense headaches, blurred vision, and memory loss, to name but a few. Even the investigative process undertaken by law enforcement immediately after the death of their children contributes to mothers' state of shock and grief.[1] Mothers often do not see the bodies of their children until they are released by the coroner and sent to a funeral home, which can be two to three weeks and in severe cases up to one month. This delay creates excessive traumatic wonderings and yearnings.

Along with the primary loss of a child, mothers also experience concurrent crises and multiple secondary losses: lost income, loss of home, loss of social status, loss of friends, and particularly loss of equilibrium (Hannays-King et al.). Fear becomes a constant companion not only for their personal safety but also for their remaining children. Many recounted the duality of desperately needing to protect their remaining children and the contrasting actions of overprotective mothering. During a group session, Stephanie shared how her hypervigilance and overprotectiveness formed a densely fortified opposition like "the wall of Gibraltar" between her sixteen-year-old and her twelve-year-old sons. "I needed to know where they were within fifteen minutes if they weren't in school. They were not allowed to be outside if I couldn't actually see them; I insisted on driving them to and from school; they were not permitted to visit their friends' house, but their friends could visit at any time."

Additional compounding issues in studies support the conclusion that the impact of mothers' trauma is not only cumulative. The more times a traumatic event is experienced the impact is not only greater but also additive and summative—that is, exposure to additional different types of trauma is correlated with greater impact (Finkelhor et al.; Turner and Lloyd). Traumatic impact is never conceived or experienced in silos or in isolation. Like the proverbial pebble in a pond, the sudden, traumatic death of a loved one from gun violence ushers in vast, multiple ripple effects, which expand beyond time, space, and imaginings. These deaths erode the family system's equilibrium and create insurmountable challenges for the functionality of each family unit. In cases where the lost member contributed to the family's emotional, social, spiritual, and financial functioning, family disintegration is inevitable (Bailey and Starr). Rapid healing trauma techniques highlight ways of quickly and permanently helping people to overcome the negative effects of trauma.[2] The many mothers and families who experienced gun violence trauma refute this claim of permanently overcoming the traumatic effects of gun violence. Mothers in their twenty-third year of traumatic loss affirm that they enjoy periods of respite, when they feel less anxious, but a disarming flashback can bring them back to intense grief pangs that often last for hours or even days, depending on the time of year.

Because gun violence survivorship is shaped by social depravities, families in marginalized communities experience more severe grief and PTSD symptoms, as compared to those in better socioeconomic situations (Bailey et al.; McDevitt-Murphy et al.). In such communities—such as Jane and Finch, a marginalized community in Toronto already vulnerable to regularity of gun violence deaths—retraumatization is an inevitable relapse into subsequent triggers of traumatic events (West). The necessity to create supportive environments that are conducive to mothers' healing and empowerment, especially in communities riddled by gun violence trauma, is paramount.

Out of Bounds Grief Support

Out Of Bounds (OOB) is a charitable organization that responds to crises and provides violence prevention/intervention education and postcare to victims and survivor youth, families, and communities. With a mandate to empower and strengthen the resilience of grievers, OOB specializes in providing culturally responsive, compassionate, and nondenominational mutual peer support for youth, individuals, families, and communities.

Recovery from gun violence trauma and distress requires meaningful support to meet the unique traumatic grief needs of survivors. This is seen as morally imperative and a fundamental human right (Buchanan). However, what has become clear is that assisting survivors to heal through their experiences with grief, loss, and trauma requires fresh perspectives, practical and cutting-edge strategies, customized care, and collective obligations. Under the mandate to empower, promote healing, and strengthen the resilience of bereaved families, particularly mothers who have lost a child to gun violence, OOB understands and appreciates that strategies to promote meaning making are among the most compelling healing approaches. OOB's work with survivors over eighteen years shows that the grief process related to gun violence loss is distinct from an expected or anticipated death.

Although gun violence trauma sparks interest broadly, there is a lack of traction in sustainable support for mothers, families, and affected communities. In the Jane and Finch community, where gun violence and gun-related deaths are prevalent, OOB works closely with mothers and families to provide reliable, sensitive, and customized grief and trauma care that is necessary for their healing process. With consistent as well as pragmatic grief and trauma support and education to bereaved mothers, OOB supports these mothers to rebuild their lives and create legacies for their loved ones. OOB garners a unique approach in working with mothers, specifically targeting grief-related trauma, while documenting and customizing care. Mothers who grieve due to violent, traumatic deaths do not experience normal grief patterns but rather pathological grief. OOB's model of care, specific to gun violence trauma, will be portrayed throughout this chapter, focusing on mothers' participation in and commitment to a process of legacy building and meaning making. The OK tournament described below is one such legacy-building initiative, initiated on the basis of two mothers' perseverance to keep their sons' memory alive after they were shot to death in the community. Their real names and their experiences are used with the mothers' permission. The recounting of events of this legacy-building initiative and the participation of communities in this communal healing process is also factual.

The OK Tournament: Creation and Implementation

An immortal legacy...
None is immortal all destined to die;
The humble mason or the wisest king
Be it those winged creatures that soar humming,
One day all will perish under the sky.
Yet... there may be much more than meets the eye
Whispering melodies resurge to sing
Trail of shadows persistent lingering
Enshrined in sobs interlaced with that sigh.
Does one truly transcend to high heaven,
Or merely swap a realm for another
Yesteryear's [sons] now live in the [present]
To reweave reveries torn asunder —
As kindred souls club to get forged as one
Life immortalised through gracious venture.

—Sushma A. Singh

Sixteen-year-old O'She Doyles Whyte and his friend, fifteen-year-old Kwame Duodo, were quiet, soft-spoken youth who loved sports, music, and bonded in a close-knit friendship. They went to programs together, walked each other home, and were enjoying the summer of 2013. On August 23, they were both shot at Kwame's doorstep by two youths on bikes. Their mothers were beyond devastated. Their worlds had crumbled with no conceivable signs of reparation.

No strangers to gun violence death, the Jane and Finch community displayed a strong eruption of moral panic (Elson and Ferguson), anger, and frustration amid a comradery that was never seen before. The code of silence that generally followed a shooting was broken and many residents spoke openly to law officials. The mothers received overwhelming communal support because these youth, as model residents, were loved, admired and valued. Both mothers attended OOB's G-Social group. The G-Social group is a psychosocial group for mothers and others who have experienced a traumatic loss. Both also participated in OOB's research project "Getting A Grip On Grief." On December 17, 2013, as they celebrated O'She's birthday, his mom, Stephanie, and Kwame's mom, Comfort, requested OOB's support to organize an annual event to keep both their names alive in memory, with an overarching purpose to remind residents of the importance of communal safety and security. They both emphatically expressed the mantra that mothers before them had chanted: "We don't want our children's death to be in vain." This was OOB's first encounter with a double gun homicide.

During OOB's group sessions, mothers with similar losses were often paired in a peer mutual support "buddy system" developed through an OOB model of care, specifically designed for gun violence survivors. Without realizing it, these two mothers were rubbing shoulders, demonstrating an affinity from having experienced an identical loss, which fused a natural bond. Though at different points on their journey of fresh, intensely raw grief, they shared the ultimate bond of sadness (Lang).

"The OK tournament" was suggested as the name for the annual event by Stephanie, with Comfort's agreement. The OK tournament ("O" = O'She and "K" = Kwame) would create a legacy to keep these young men alive and vibrant in hearts, minds, and community awareness. The death date was chosen as a fixed time to host the event, since it carried profound intrinsic implications. Although they had no idea what it would look like, they were resolved in their intent to move forwards despite the financial costs or time demands. The final piece was clarifying these mothers' purpose, with specific objectives for this free event.

Through guided discussions, the group had three specific goals:

1. To build a lasting legacy in O'She's and Kwame's names
2. To raise awareness to the devastation of gun violence death in communities
3. To promote/sustain safety and security and encourage restorative justice.

A trust fund would be established to assist the mothers in accomplishing their legacy-building goal. This fund would be generated from the OK tournament activities, where teams compete and participate in a day-long festival, pickup basketball, and t-shirt sales. Donations from outside sources in conjunction with fees collected from participating teams, would accumulate towards an annual scholarship, that would be given to two deserving youth, in O'She's and Kwame's names. The funds will assist with postsecondary education, while youth between ages fourteen to eighteen would be treated to an annual excursion trip, to expand their horizons.

Youth would follow an application process with specific criteria for the scholarship, such as academic excellence with consistent school attendance, respectful character traits, good moral attitude, and healthy sportsmanship with consistent community engagement. The OK tournament is open to young people and residents from all ethnicities in the Greater Toronto Areas to commemorate these two fallen youth. This legacy for O'She and Kwame not only encourages and promotes the mothers' healing but also assists youth in their educational aspirations and personal growth. Moreover, it fosters community togetherness, collaboration, and comradery.

This huge undertaking at such an early stage on the grief journey was a first occurrence for this therapist and for OOB. But we also recognize resilience as strength and model the Ottawa Charter, which fosters supportive environments for bereaved mothers to heal as well, by providing access to information, services, and encouragement for their innate capacity to gain personal empowerment (WHO, *The Ottawa Charter*). By busying themselves to plan the OK tournament, these mothers engaged in their own survival and took ownership of their own health and destiny through personal empowerment.

Despite their differing cultural backgrounds, there was no hint of "culturalizing" the trauma they each were enduring or "pathologizing" the uniqueness of their journey (Pashang and Gruner). Coping with and overcoming society's pervasive influence and biases are a huge deterrence for gun violence survivors' resilience building. Yet these mothers embraced the challenge (Bailey et al.; Bailey et al.), as they were both fuelled by an innate desire to attain empowerment within the holistic emblem of spirituality, cultural fortitude, and communal support as they worked towards their envisioned legacy building.

Preparation

The mothers nominated me, therapist and OOB's executive director, as lead organizer for the OK tournament, with OOB acting as the lead organization. Community agencies where O'She and Kwame volunteered and worked partnered with OOB members to form the OK team, which was commissioned to plan the yearly OK tournament. After five months of groundwork and bi-weekly planning, the first OK tournament was launched on Saturday, August 23rd, 2014. The launch date was exactly the same as the date O'She and Kwame died. The community supported the event with in-kind, financial, and volunteer donations, which were beyond our expectation. Attendance exceeded our approximation of three to six hundred. The first OK tournament was extremely difficult and emotionally taxing for the mothers. However, with the support of trained facilitators, they survived the moment of silence and tributes to their fallen sons.

Progressive Implementation

August 2019 marked our sixth annual OK tournament. The original partners have cemented their commitment and efforts in this event. Community participation continued to increase. Stephanie and Comfort, though still on the healing trail, have made gradual shifts in their healing. They were showing fresh buds on their marked trauma tree. They both participated in planning, decision making, and activities for the event, albeit to different degrees. Grief is an individual journey, and both mothers were unique in their coping, processing, and healing. Whereas one mother relied heavily on spirituality, the other clung to cultural and traditional remedies. However private, individual, or culturally diverse their grief might have been at times, they remained constant and resolute in their decision to sustain the OK tournament. These mothers' ongoing involvement in this communal event promoted their personal, holistic, and incremental healing, with wider gaps of relapses and emotional distress. This growth is an embodiment of OOB's empowerment model, which highlights spiritual and cultural fortitude among the chief elements of meaning making. This also works in tandem with other strategies OOB uses to assist mothers in finding their way through the maze of fresh grief (Bailey and Starr).

The mothers wept openly during the moment of silence, grieving simultaneously for themselves and for their slain sons, which signified that the bond with their children did not differentiate between life and death (Bennett). In a spirit of comradery, they were joined by residents, family, and participating community agencies in supportive encirclement, which was a truly soul-stirring and poignant moment. It was solemn and respectful, with a deafening silence. O'She's and Kwane's legacies are etched in people's hearts and the community. Acquisition of collaborative comradery was cemented in a splendidly responsive tribute to these mothers' tenacity. Although Stephanie and Comfort pursued legacy building and meaning making, they concurrently wished their sons were present and that there was no need for legacies.

I conducted the ritual of commemoration and observation of silence each year as participants of all ages—including volunteers, community staff members, police officers, firefighters, families, mothers, and the media—crowded the basketball court. The poem "We Haven't Forgotten" was adapted from various poems and personalized to express what the mothers and those present needed to say. Poetry and artwork play a significant role in expressing and representing grief (Bailey and Starr), particularly when the heart is overlaid with emotions. The 2017 OK tournament's poem conveyed a message that burned brightly on Stephanie's and Comfort's hearts.

We Haven't Forgotten

A little tribute small and tender, Just to say we still remember.
There is a link death cannot sever,
Love and remembrance last forever.
A garden of beautiful memories Sprayed with a million tears.
Tenderly we treasure the past With memories that will last.
Silent memories true and tender, Just to show we still remember,
Your memories are as dear today As in the hour you passed away.
Memories are like threads of gold, They never tarnish or grow old.
It's just a little but means a lot To say dear O'She / Kwame —
we haven't forgotten.
YOU left us early, it's difficult sometimes,
But we want you to know that...we haven't forgotten.
One thing we will always cherish, No matter what life sends.
A memory of the happiness of Just having you both here...
TODAY...
A page in the book of memory, We pause to silently turn...
We remember you in silence And make no outward show.
For what it meant to lose you, both, No one will ever know.
Memory is a lovely lane, Where hearts are ever true.
A lane we'll often travel down, Because it leads to you.
So today we pause in unison to tell you both, again...
We haven't forgotten.

(Author Anonymous, Modified, Rev. Sky, 2017)

Benefits from the OK Tournament: Community

"Herein lies an important distinction: ... communal grief ... insist[s] upon intimate, concrete, particular details, images, and narratives. Grief must have a human face; consolation must have a human voice" (Espada). Isolated suffering is among the chief detriments that follow grief, especially gun violence-related trauma. An intricate part of grief and traumatic support for gun homicide survivors is ongoing trauma-informed strategies that are tailored to address their unique grieving needs (Bailey and Velasco). Many aspects of gun violence trauma relate to mental health. OOB concurs with the Mental Health Charter, which states that in order to promote healing and recovery among mental health sufferers, equitable access to appropriate and effective treatment programs and services are needed. Martin Espada praises and emphasizes the need and courage to mourn publicly. Communal grieving promotes comradery and creates a larger marginal shift for mothers who receive the distinct message that they are not alone in their suffering but that the entire community stands with them.

As residents witnessed the inclusivity of diverse stakeholders, including police officers, many expressed their gratitude and commended the approach. Such cascading effects enhance accommodation, sensitivity, restoration, and healing as positive byproducts for both mothers and the community. The participants at the OK tournament consisted mainly of children and youth, many of whom knew and interacted with the slain youth. Yet these youth stood in unanimity to remember their fallen friends and to support their mothers. They are reminded of the important role they play in procuring safety and security for themselves, their families, and their community. Each year they listen with rapt attention, in community presence, as Rev. Sky admonishes them on the risk factors for youth violence, predictable and preventable factors in youth violence, and their role in promoting personal and community safety. Youth violence has severe consequences. Some are visible and harmful to communities, whereas others are hidden and drain economies (WHO, "Preventing Youth Violence").

The tournament climaxed with the presentation of scholarships in O'She's and Kwame's names to two youth who vied for and received the awards. Their bios are read, including the postsecondary college or university they will be attending. This brief ceremony encourages youth not only to be vigilant but also to make intelligent, positive choices that will promote their personal safety and that of the community. The consequences of gun violence are more pervasive and affect entire communities, families, youth, and children (Finkelhor et al.). Promoting safety and security for youth is of paramount importance, since traumatic events happen to all people at all ages, across all socioeconomic strata of our society (The Trauma-Informed Toolkit).

Benefits from the OK Tournament: Mothers

Social support is among the most frequently mentioned needs of bereaved persons, including traumatized mothers (Coor, Nabe, and Coor). In the context of bereaved mothers' frequent lack of social support (Hannays-King, Bailey, and Akhtar), this annual community gathering serves several purposes. Stephanie and Comfort were recipients of a communal "cradling," as the community gathered to remember the slain youth and support them by reassuring their presence. They were further encouraged by the poems of communal grief, which serve the purpose of connecting the mothers with an empathetic community. Encircled by neighbours, friends, and well wishers whose faces mirror their own, these mothers were grounded in essential empathy, without which none of us truly survives (Espada).

Additionally, the project's longevity propels them towards their quest to prevent other mothers from experiencing the agonizing turmoil they endure. Maternal grief is diverse, inconsistent, and changes over a lifetime. Healing from the death of a child is also a lifelong process, as grief changes rather than ends (Davidson). In conjunction with the healing and psychological shift in their grieving process, they also attained empowerment and resilience. Several studies suggest that outcomes of resilience and empowerment in grief support are achieved when survivors can engage in meaning making to find a purpose in their lives (Armour; Johnson). Most significant, however, is the attendance of other mothers who have lost a child to gun violence and other traumatic deaths. Healing synergies generated through the OK tournament benefit other mothers and reverberates to several homes and communities. These mothers' efforts to memorialize their sons are surging into an authentic movement.

Discussion

Whereas some mothers can shift towards meaning making and legacy building in the early stages of fresh trauma, this is not a normative reaction. Traumatic effects are individual, and mothers in the throes of such publicly exposed trauma are profoundly impacted. The period directly after a funeral is intricately precarious to mothers (Bailey et al.).

Grief-related trauma has crippling effects on mothers' capacity to function, especially within the early months and first year subsequent to the death. The stigma attached to gun violence homicide in relation to criminality drives mothers to suffer in silence and isolation, with limited social support (Bailey et al.). Communal initiatives, such as the OK tournament, bring community members and stakeholders together in unity against a social issue that affects us all.

The neurobiological and psychological effects of trauma make parenting, emotional functioning, and ADL (activities of daily living) virtually impossible for mothers. Mothers suffering from gun violence trauma need wraparound, long-term, culturally responsive, and trauma-informed care, where such initiatives as trauma-specific psychological support, peer-support initiatives, social inclusion, and nondiscriminatory approaches overlap (Buchanan).

The scarcity of trauma-informed care for gun violence survivors remains a heartbreaking reality, despite the prevalence of gun violence deaths in this and similar communities. OOB's customized care for these mothers focuses on their psychological pain and validates their innate ability to find empowerment and resilience with adequate support. The OK tournament demonstrates a good example of mothers' empowerment, and their will to thrive in the face of limited attention and resources for gun violence survivorship.

With the regularity of shootings in Canadian and United States urban communities, it is clear that gun violence has accelerated far beyond the endemic stage. A multifaceted approach—where all levels of governments combine collaborative efforts with researchers and stakeholders to develop and/or strengthen normative frameworks and policies—is a necessity. In the meantime, creative approaches, such as the OK tournament, can complement policy developments and survivor-sensitive gun laws. Combating gun violence necessitates a holistic, integrated approach as well as input from community members, survivors, and stakeholders. The societal factors that perpetuate poverty, trauma, stigma, scrutiny, and dehumanization must also be considered alongside preventative measures and gun control efforts (Bailey et al.).

In one mother's words: "There always seems to be something threatening my emotional and spiritual equilibrium, but I will keep travelling on for my son." Gun violence continues to plague our communities with devastating effects. With limited social support, mothers' traumatic grief threatens their very existence. But while distressingly bereft, empty, and wearied, many mothers remain tenacious and hopeful. Community events, such as the OK tournament, give mothers the lift they need to attain progressive empowerment.

Endnotes

1. Under Ontario's bylaws, certain types of deaths must be reported to a coroner and investigated (i.e., deaths that occur suddenly and unexpectedly) (Government of Ontario, "Coroners Act, 1990").
2. Rapid healing is a technique suitable for anyone who "desires to heal, remove old hurts, fears, traumas, frustrations, anger, pain and fear of pain." This theory is relatively new and was developed and introduced by Dr. Jon Connelly, with a fast and relatively painless approach.

Works Cited

American Psychiatric Association. *Diagnostic and Statistical Manual of Mental Disorders (DSM-5®)*. American Psychiatric Pub., 2013.

Anonymous. "We Haven't Forgot." *Roadhouse & Rose Funeral Homes*. No. 28, August, 2017.

Armour, Marilyn. "Meaning Making in the Aftermath of Homicide." *Death Studies*, vol. 27, no. 6, 2003, pp. 519-40.

Bailey, Annette, et al. "Intersecting Individual, Social and Cultural Factors in Black Mothers' Resilience Building Following Loss to Gun Violence in Canada." *Women's Mental Health: Resistance and Resilience in Community and Society*, edited by Nazilla Khanlou and Beryl Pilkington, Springer International Publishing, 2015, pp. 311-25.

Bailey, Annette, and Divine Velasco. "Canada." *Gun Violence, Disability and Recovery: Surviving Gun Violence Project*, edited by Cate Buchanan, Xlibris Corporation, 2014, pp. 207-21.

Bailey, Annette, and Sky Starr. "Empowering Mothers of Murdered Children: A Community-Based Traumatic Grief Model." *Canadian Community as Partner: Theory & Multidisciplinary Practice*. 5th ed., edited by Ardene Vollman and Suzanne Jackson. Lippincott Williams & Wilkins, 2020.

Benedict, Dirk. "Quotes." *Brainy Quote*, www.brainyquote.com/lists/authors/top-10-dirk-benedict-quotes. Accessed 7 Apr. 2022.

Bennett, Deb. "" I Am Still a Mother": A Hermeneutic Inquiry into BereavedMotherhood." *Journal of the Motherhood Initiative for Research and Community Involvement*, vol. 1, no. 2, 2010, p. 54.

Buchanan, Cate. *Gun Violence, Disability and Recovery*. Xlibris Corporation, 2014.

Cattell, Vicky. "Community Resilience." *Poverty, Community and Health: Cooperation and the Good Society*, edited by Vickey Cattell, Palgrave Macmillan, 2012, pp. 53-71.

Collins, Julie, and Emily Swoveland. "The Impact of Gun Violence on Children, Families, & Communities." *The Child Welfare League of America*, 2013, www.cwla.org/the-impact-of-gun-violence-on-children-families-communities/. Accessed 7 Apr. 2022.

Corr, Charles A., Clyde Nabe, and Donna M. Corr. *Death and Dying, Life and Living*. Borrks/Cole, 1997.

Davidson, Deborah. "Grief, Loss of Child." *Encyclopedia of Motherhood*, edited by Andrea O'Reilly and Geoffrey J. Gordon, Sage, 2010, pp. 466-69.

Davidson, Deborah, and Helena Stahls. "Maternal Grief: Creating an Environment for Dialogue." *Journal of the Motherhood Initiative for Research and Community Involvement*, vol. 1, no. 2, 2010, pp. 16-25.

Elson, Malte, and Christopher J. Ferguson. "Gun Violence and Media Effects: Challenges for Science and Public Policy." *The British Journal of Psychiatry*, vol. 203, no. 5, 2013, pp. 322-24.

Espada, Martin. "Can Poetry Console a Grieving Public?" *Poetry Foundation*, www.poetryfoundation.org/articles/68670/can-poetry-console-a-grieving-public-56d24846cd077 N.pub. 12 Sept 2006. Web. 9 May 2010. Accessed 7 Apr. 2022.

Falconer, Julian, and Peter Pliszka. *Annotated Ontario Coroners Act, 2008/2009 Edition*. LexisNexis Canada, 2008.

Finkelhor, David, et al. "Children's Exposure to Violence: A Comprehensive National Survey." *Juvenile Justice Bulletin*, 2009, www.ojp.gov/pdffiles1/ojjdp/227744.pdf. Accessed 7 Apr. 2022.

Frankl, Viktor E. *Man's Search for Meaning: An Introduction to Logotherapy.* Touchstone, 1984.

Garbarino, James, Catherine P. Bradshaw, and Joseph A. Vorrasi. "Mitigating the Effects of Gun Violence on Children and Youth." *The Future of Children*, vol. 12, no. 2, 2002, pp. 73-85.

Government of Ontario. Coroners Act, R.S.O. 1990, c. C.37, *Ontario*, www.ontario.ca/laws/statute/90c37. Accessed 7 Apr. 2022.

Hannays-King, Camille, Annette Bailey, and Mahlon Akhtar. "Social Support and Black Mothers' Bereavement Experience of Losing a Child to Gun Homicide." *Bereavement Care*, vol. 34, no. 1, 2015, pp. 10-16.

Johnson, Celeste M. "African-American Teen Girls Grieve the Loss of Friends to Homicide: Meaning Making and Resilience." *OMEGA: Journal of Death and Dying*, vol. 61, no. 2, 2010, pp. 121-43.

Lang, Sharon. "Life at the Cemetery." *Journal of the Motherhood Initiative for Research and Community Involvement*, vol. 1, no. 2, 2010, p. 29.

Means, James E. *Tearful Celebration: Finding God in the Midst of Loss.* Multnomah Publishers, Inc., 2006.

McDevitt-Murphy, Meghan, et al. "The Toll of Traumatic Loss in African Americans Bereaved by Homicide." *Psychological Trauma: Theory, Research, Practice, and Policy*, vol. 4, no. 3, 2012, pp. 303-11.

Mother from Trauma-Focused Training. *Out of Bounds*, 15 Aug. 2018, outofboundsjf.org/news/. Accessed 7 Apr. 2022.

Neimeyer, Robert A., and Diana C. Sands. *Meaning Reconstruction in Bereavement: From Principles to Practice.* American Psychological Association, 2011.

O'Hara, Kathleen. *A Grief Like No Other: Surviving the Violent Death of Someone You Love.* Marlowe & Company, 2006.

Pashang, Soheila, and Sheila Gruner, editors. *Roots and Routes of Displacement and Trauma: From Analysis to Advocacy and Policy to Practice.* Rock's Mills Press, 2015.

Sharkey, Patrick. "The Acute Effect of Local Homicides on Children's Cognitive Performance." *Proceedings of the National Academy of Sciences*, vol. 107, no. 26, 2010, pp. 11733-38.

Singh, Sushma A. "An Immortal Legacy." *Poetry Soup*, 28 Feb 2017, www.poetrysoup.com/poem/an_immortal_legacy_880751. Accessed 7 Apr. 2022.

The Trauma-Informed Toolkit. *Klinic Community Health Centre*. 2013, trauma-informed.ca/wp-content/uploads/2013/10/Trauma-informed_Toolkit.pdf. Accessed 7 Apr. 2022.

Turner, Heather A., David Finkelhor, and Richard Ormrod. "The Effect of Lifetime Victimization on the Mental Health of Children and Adolescents." *Social science & medicine*, vol. 62, no. 1, 2006, pp. 13-27.

Turner, R. Jay, and Donald A. Lloyd. "Lifetime Traumas and Mental Health: The Significance of Cumulative Adversity." *Journal of Health and Social Behavior*, vol. 36, no. 4, 1995, pp. 360-76.

West, Carolyn. *Violence in the Lives of Black Women: Battered, Black, and Blue*. Routledge, 2014.

World Health Organization. *Preventing Youth Violence: An Overview of the Evidence*. WHO, 2015.

World Health Organization. *The Ottawa Charter for Health Promotion*. WHO, 1986.

The Devil in the Details: Why Trudeau's Ban on Assault Weapons Might Not Be Effective to Reduce Gun Crime after Canada's Largest Mass Shooting in Nova Scotia

Thomas S. Harrison

Social worker Tim Landon isn't your typical gun owner. A self-described social justice advocate, he witnessed a violent gun crime as a young adult. He's now an unlikely opponent of the Canadian government's recent ban on fifteen hundred military style assault weapons. Yet that's exactly where he finds himself in the gun control debate, reignited by Canada's largest mass shooting on the East coast last April. Landon became a firearms advocate after moving to British Columbia two decades ago, where he perceived a more accepting attitude to ownership. He also wasn't opposed to earlier regulation, so happily complied when he later took up sport shooting.

But he says new restrictions, introduced swiftly last spring under existing legislation following a rampage that resulted in the deaths of 22 people in Nova Scotia, goes too far.

"What it means is that no gun owner in Canada can ever own a modern rifle," he says, since the restrictions will apply to weapons that have already been used for decades by hunters and sport shooters.

He also thinks that criminals will not follow the new laws, observing the recent East Coast shooter was widely reported to be in illegal possession of prohibited weapons, several of which are believed to have come from the US. "We live beside the most heavily armed nation on Earth," says Landon pointing out the easy access to a supply of firearms which can readily be brought across the Canadian border.

But those who support the new restrictions see firearms as a significant threat to community security. For them, there is a direct connection to reducing gun crime: less weapons here equals less violence involving firearms.

Others suggest that both sides oversimplify an issue that depends on context. Blake Brown, a professor of legal history at St. Mary's University in Halifax, says regulating firearms has a long history that can be traced in Canada back to the seventeenth century. Real concerns arose with "the mass production of weapons like pistols" and the misuse of handguns in the late 1800s. He notes that even then it was not uncommon for Canadian politicians to turn a wary eye to gun violence in the US. And some Canadians have always thought that, like our southern neighbours, people should have legal rights to own a gun. Even though the Supreme Court said in a 1993 decision that there is no constitutional right to bear arms, some continue to make the progun legal argument.

In May, an advocacy group called the Canadian Coalition for Firearms Rights (CCFR) started a legal proceeding before the Federal Court arguing that the direct imposition of new gun regulations last spring was unconstitutional. Their lawsuit also seeks to overturn the new federal ban on the basis that there is "no persuasive evidence" that reclassification of the guns as prohibited firearms will achieve the desired purpose of "decreasing mass shootings or otherwise increasing public safety."

Aside from the argument about "rights" the CCFR's position relies on evidence that does not draw a direct connection between crime and firearms regulation. A 2018 report from Statistics Canada shows overall crime in Canada has been on a sustained downwards trend for three decades, since peaking in the early 1990s. While there has been a small uptick in the last few years, overall more severe crime, including offences that involve guns, have also been declining, putting firearms offences near historic lows.

Whatever the actual rate, public perceptions about the relation between crime and guns also vary greatly depending on context. A

2014 Stats Can study showed most Canadians feel safe, but that this sense of security is not evenly distributed. Higher levels of concern are common, based on where people live, especially for those in large urban centres and on the prairies. Social situations also affect attitudes, with minorities and women displaying higher levels of anxiety.

Dr. Rebecca Bromwich, a former crown attorney and adjunct law professor at Carlton University, says perceptions of social context also influence how the perpetrators of gun crime are characterized. In the 2014 shooting on Parliament Hill, for example, the shooter was described as a "terrorist" of "Middle-Eastern descent," even though he was Canadian born. She says this portrayal "foreclosed public conversations about gun control" and ultimately led instead to new federal security legislation: "This is an interesting contrast to the 2020 shootings in Nova Scotia, where gun control measures were enacted swiftly. There, the shooter was not described as a terrorist and, interestingly, was white."

Bromwich notes similar characterizations may be in play in the attack on the Governor-General's home at Rideau Hall on July 2, 2020. There, an armed white male, who is reported to have engaged with right-wing conspiracy theories online, is alleged to have rammed his truck through wrought iron gates blocking a pedestrian entrance and to then evade police on the grounds of the official residence for many minutes.

Despite what one commentator later described as an attempted "assassination," initial reports focused on sympathetic details, such as those that highlighted the suspect's background as a small business owner, active volunteer in his community, and as a veteran army ranger, who just gained access to the grounds in order to talk to the prime minister.

The different contexts around gun control have influenced public policy and perceptions in Canada for decades. In the end, while the debate about regulation is often presented simply, the problem is complex, says Professor Brown. He notes, too, that the challenge is neither new nor easy. "It's a big complicated question," he says.

For now at least, it appears Canadians have settled on an answer. In the wake of last spring's new federal government ban, an Angus Reid survey showed the vast majority, four in five Canadians, support limiting access to military "assault-style" weapons, such as those that are now prohibited.

Originally published August 5, 2020, by RobsonCrim, online blog, reprinted with permission. Retrieved March 18, 2021: www.robsoncrim.com/single-post/the-devil-in-the-details-by-dr-ts-harrison

Notes on Contributors

Paul Banahene Adjei is an associate professor at the School of Social Work, Memorial University of Newfoundland, Canada. Dr. Adjei's scholarship draws on anti-Black racism theory, critical race theories, critical whiteness studies, and anticolonial theory to ask new questions as well as to identify potential answers to what WEB. Dubois (1903) describes as "colour-line problem" in Euro-American, Canadian, and African society. He also draws on African Indigeneity as rich cultural knowledge to (re)imagine a new future for social work education.

Jheanelle Anderson is a research assistant at The Centre for Research & Innovation for Black Survivors of Homicide Victims (The CRIB). In her role, she works to advance research and policy relevant to Black survivors of homicide victims and to develop culturally responsive supports and services to serve this population. Jheanelle holds a master's degree in social work from the University of Toronto with a specialization in community development. Her research interest lies in the intersections of immigration, ableism, and anti-Black racism.

Annette Bailey holds a PhD in public health science. Her research explores gun violence prevention and survivorship, with a focus on understanding grief and trauma experiences of survivors of gun homicide. Dr. Bailey has conducted research with mothers who lost children to gun violence, with youth who lost friends and siblings to gun homicide, and with key stakeholders across Canada and other countries to establish policy recommendations for supporting gun violence survivors.

Renée Bailey is a graduate of the Biomedical Sciences program at Ryerson University and a graduate of the Masters in Global Health program at McMaster University. Renee was recently accepted to medical school at the University of Toronto. Renee has partnered with academic and mentorship programs such as Pathways to Education and Inner City Outreach to support Black youth residing in marginalized communities in Toronto. Renee engages in spoken word art to translate Black communities' lived experiences with oppression and resilience.

Rebecca Jaremko Bromwich is an Ontario lawyer and legal scholar. She has worked as a crown attorney, a criminal defence lawyer, a civil litigator, and a law reform lawyer. After receiving her PhD in 2015, she accepted a fulltime faculty position at Carleton University, where she taught and researched for four years. She has authored and coauthored academic textbooks and coedited several anthologies. Dr. Bromwich is currently working with a large, international firm, tasked with advancing diversity and inclusion across their offices.

Alisha Chohan is currently completing her Ontario Lawyer Licensing Process and has an undergraduate degree in Psychology. She is passionate about utilizing the law to address and tackle issues faced by Indigenous, immigrant, and minority communities. With a strong track record of leading research and policy files, Alisha has had the privilege to work in diverse areas of health, natural resources, business, legal and Indigenous affairs. Alisha's love for academia stems from idolizing her father's role as a physician-scientist. She aims to complement her legal career by advancing academia and bridging the gaps in legislation and case law that fail to incorporate societal implications and mental health.

Lynn M. Eckert is associate professor of political science at Marist College in Poughkeepsie, NY. She earned a PhD from Syracuse University's Maxwell School of Citizenship and Public Affairs. She is the author of *Free Speech Law and the Pornography Debate: A Gender-Based Approach to Regulating Inegalitarian Pornography* (Lexington Press, 2020) as well as numerous law-related articles. Dr. Eckert served as a member of Kingston, New York's Common Council as an alderwoman representing Ward 1.

Sulaimon Giwa is an assistant professor at Memorial University, School of Social Work, with a cross-appointment to the Department of Sociology (police studies). He is the Endowed Chair in Criminology and Criminal Justice at St. Thomas University in Fredericton, New Brunswick. His research interests are in the areas of race and sexuality, critical social work pedagogy, anti-Black racism/oppression and the criminal justice system.

Thomas Harrison is a coauthor of *Negotiation and Conflict Resolution in Criminal Practice* (2018, Canadian Scholars Press). His dissertation (Queen's Law 2016) examined the independent role of judges and lawyers in Canada's justice system. After articling with the Honourable Mr. Justice Archie Campbell, he served as crown counsel with Ontario's Ministry of the Attorney General until 2013, working primarily as a policy advisor to the chief justice of the Superior Court. He currently teaches classes in animal law and critical thinking at Durham College in Whitby.

Michelle Jubin is a mental health nurse consultant at Toronto Public Health. In this role, she works with internal public health teams and programs to build capacity and develop population-level mental health interventions to enhance community wellbeing outcomes. She also provides training support and consultation on diverse mental health promotion topics and interventions. Michelle specializes in community youth mental health promotion, suicide prevention, and trauma-informed community psychosocial response interventions during critical incidents.

Akwatu Khenti is an affiliate scientist with the Institute for Mental Health Policy Research (IMHPR) at the Centre for Addiction and Mental Health (CAMH) and an assistant professor with the Dalla Lana School of Public Health. He is formerly the assistant deputy minister for Ontario's Anti-Racism Directorate. Dr. Khenti has a specialist degree in economics, a master's in political science from the University of Toronto, and a PhD in health policy and equity from York University. His doctoral research chronicled the effects of social determinants of racialized gun violence in Toronto's 140 neighborhoods from 2004 to 2014.

Delores Mullings is a Full professor at Memorial University, School of Social Work. Dr. Mullings's scholarly interests fall under the umbrella of anti-Black racism and critical race theoretical orientation through which she explores topics including decolonizing post-secondary education, Black parenting, health and social needs of older Black Caribbean Canadians, whiteness and white privilege, racialized LGBTQ people, older immigrants, settlement and integration in small urban centres, rural and remote areas, and racist human rights policy.

JoAnne Myers (Skidmore, RPI) is an associate professor of political science, Marist College. Before joining faculty, she works for the NYC mayor and Department of Sanitation. Currently, she is the vice chair of the Ulster County Human Rights Commission and works towards zero waste on the Ulster County Resource Recovery Agency. Her recently authored works include *The Good Citizen: The Markers of Privilege in America* (Routledge 2019); *"Justice" in Misogyny in American Culture* (Guglielmo, ed., ABC-CLIO, 2018); and *The Historical Dictionary of the Lesbian and Gay Liberation Movement* (Rowman and Littlefield, 2013).

Tanya L. Sharpe is an associate professor at the Factor-Inwentash Faculty of Social Work at the University of Toronto. Dr. Sharpe's research examines sociocultural factors that influence the coping strategies of Black survivors of homicide victims. Dr. Sharpe is the founder and director of the Centre for Research & Innovation for Black Survivors of Homicide Victims (The CRIB), a multidisciplinary initiative designed to advance research, policy, and practice for Black survivors of homicide victims.

Santana Stallberg has a master's degree in sociology with a focus on criminology and law from Queen's University. Her master's thesis focused on the ineffectiveness of the criminal justice system in reducing recidivism among Aboriginal offenders and the need for specific restorative justice programs to address the effects of colonization. She is an authorized court transcriptionist and an avid editor, tutor, and mentor. As such, she developed the business model for beyond transcription services through recognizing that there is a niche area for assisting clients and businesses with various tasks.

Sky Starr is the founder and executive director of Out of Bounds: Grief & Trauma Support. She is a marriage and family therapist as well as a grief/trauma specialist. Rev. Sky works with schools and organizations from a unique trans-cultural perspective, providing customized, compassionate care for those traumatized by gun violence. Her work and services include group facilitation, trauma-focused training, and restorative justice mediation. She also works closely with mothers who have lost a child/children to gun violence.

Divine Velasco is a registered nurse and holds a master's degree in nursing. She is interested in addressing social determinants of health for diverse populations in Toronto. Divine has coauthored several journal and book chapter publications focused on gun violence trauma and the survivorship experiences of Black communities in Toronto.

Kendra Van de Water has worked extensively with police to change policies and practices to improve how people in Philadelphia are policed and interact with law enforcement. Kendra cofounded Youth Empowerment for Advancement Hangout (YEAH) Inc. YEAH is a teen-led, nonprofit initiative focused on empowering teens in Philadelphia who have witnessed or engaged in violence. Kendra's area of expertise includes collaborating with law enforcement to reduce violence and improve policy and program implementation to address violence.

Deepest appreciation to
Demeter's monthly Donors

DEMETER

Daughters

Rebecca Bromwich
Summer Cunningham
Tatjana Takseva
Debbie Byrd
Fiona Green
Tanya Cassidy
Vicki Noble
Naomi McPherson
Myrel Chernick

Sisters

Amber Kinser
Nicole Willey
Christine Peets